Imperial Politics in the 21st Century
War, Torture and
The Killing Fields of Asia

IMPERIAL, POLITICS IN THE 21ST CENTURY

WAR, TOURTURE AND THE KILLING FIELDS OF ASIA

James Petras

GYAN PUBLISHING HOUSE
NEW DELHI-110002

Imperial, Politics in the 21st Century :
War, Torture and the Killing Fields of Asia

Rs. 690

ISBN : 81-212-0922-6

Published in 2007 in India by
Gyan Publishing House
5, Ansari Road, Daryaganj,
New Delhi - 110002
Phones: 23261060, 23282060
Fax: 091+23285914
e-mail : books@gyanbooks.com
website : gyanbooks.com

Laser Typesetting at : Vinayak Printers, Delhi
Printed at : Salasar Imaging System, Delhi

Contents

Introduction

To understand US-Latin American relations this year and its likely trajectory in 2007 it is obligatory to consider three dimensions: 1) the global context of US-LA relations; 2) internal dynamics of the US and 3) the real practical political-economic consequences of the 2006 elections in Latin America.

US imperial policy continues to pursue military victories in Iraq and Afghanistan, to give unconditional support to Israel's war against the elected Palestinian Government and to threaten a direct or Israeli attack on Iran. In other words, the prolonged, costly and inconclusive wars in Iraq, Afghanistan, Lebanon and Palestine during 2006 will continue in 2007. Further military escalation, includes increased US troops and spending for wars in the Middle East; an extra $800 million USD in addition to the annual $3 billion USD for Israeli war plans against Lebanon, Palestine and especially Iran. Those commentators who interpreted US policy via public opinion polls, electoral processes (the victory of the Democrats), advisory reports (Baker's Iraq Study Group) and casualty rates in Iraq, and predicted a 'gradual' withdrawal, failed to understand the logic of the White House's political strategy. For the Bush regime, the military failures are a result of the application of insufficient power; what is necessary, they argue, is greater numbers of soldiers and bigger military budgets (BBC 12/16/06).

Polarization

Both in the United States, Latin America and in the world at large, profound and deepening divisions are driving policy and provoking increasing conflicts. The lines of division in the United States on the fundamental questions of confrontation or negotiation in the Middle East and Latin America cut across the two major parties, and the liberal-conservative spectrum. On the one side the White House, backed by pro-war Democrats, Republicans, the Presidents of the Major Jewish Organizations, right-wing veteran groups and neo-conservative intellectuals and the majority of the corporate mass media. On the other side, minorities in the major parties and mass media, the majority of public opinion, sectors of the active and retired military officers, establishment intellectual and prominent political critics of the Zionist lobby and war policies like Brzezinski, James Carter, James Broker among others.

- Similar divisions appear with regard to Latin American policy. The White House, backed by the Cuban (exile) lobby, the Pentagon and a minority of right-wing ideologues and business groups favor forceful pressure and intervention against Cuba, Venezuela and Bolivia and support of illegitimate President Calderon, the Santa Cruz separatists in Bolivia and other authoritarian extremists the region. In varying degrees of opposition, stand liberal and conservative congress-members backed by agro-business exporters, tourists agencies, a majority of public opinion and sectors of the State Department headed by Undersecretary for Latin American Affairs, Shannon, who support greater emphasis on diplomacy, negotiations and a 'two-track' approach.

Within Latin America similar profound divisions emerged in 2006 which will deepen in 2007. In Mexico, the minority Calderon regime faces major opposition from the AMLO coalition, Oaxaca popular assemblies, the trade unions and social movements. As he proceeds to deepen the liberalization of the economy and he militarizes the country to implement his program, the polarization will deepen.

In Bolivia, rightwing business and agro-business elites regrouped, taking advantage of Morales conciliatory policies and incapacity to carry-out any major redistributive policies (in land and income) – and have consolidated a power base in Santa Cruz, which has forced Morales to retreat further in his reforms and aroused mass popular discontent. Similar divisions have appeared in Ecuador, between the peasants/Indians of the Andean region and the land barons and bankers of the Coast. In Colombia the divisions between the paramilitary forces allied to President Uribe and the popular civil society organizations (and the guerrilla) have deepened (Boston Globe December 14, 2006). In Venezuela the polarization between the Socialist and social-liberal Chavistas (and their allies among the 'moderate' opposition) will surface in 2007 as Chavez implements party and cabinet changes in pursuit of a socialist agenda.

These internal divisions in the US and Latin

America are played out in an international context which radicalizes the class and national confrontations.

International Context

Two world-historic processes affect US policy toward Latin America: 1) the prolonged Middle East wars and 2) the dynamic growth of the four Asian powers led by China. The Middle Eastern/South Asian wars have severely overextended US military forces, undermined domestic support for new wars and severely strained the budget. These outcomes have weakened the US military capacity for intervention in Latin America in support of a military coup, or, even less, a direct military invasion. As a result the US increasingly relies on domestic (Latin American) clients to defend its interests (Calderon, Santa Cruz land/business barons, Garcia, Uribe).

Asia's (particularly China and India) dynamic growth and demand for raw materials (iron, copper and oil), food and agricultural products (like soya) has resulted in greater competition with the US/EU for access to Latin American exporters and suppliers, and increased prices and revenues for Latin American treasuries (major trade and budget surpluses). Asia increases the diversity of markets and investors for Latin American exporters. These changes mean less dependence on external financing (especially the IMF) and US markets which in turn means Washington has less political and diplomatic leverage over Latin American regimes, even neo-liberal governments like Lula, Bachelet, Kirchner and Vazquez.

Faced with a loss of military capacity and a decline in economic leverage, Washington is moving toward a 'compromise' between the White House's hard line militarists and the State Department's market-driven 'negotiators'. The essence of the compromise is to pursue a 'two-track policy' : combining support for the subversive opposition in countries where it is strong (Bolivia) with negotiation in countries where it is weak (Venezuela). With regard to the neo-liberal regimes, which have some degree of autonomy (Brazil, Chile and Argentina), Washington will emphasize bilateral relations and try to maximize economic opportunities while discouraging any concession to the mass movements especially demands to reverse privatizations. The two-track policy will e combined in the cases of Cuba and Venezuela: with promises of dialogue and agreements conditional on major concessions in diplomacy, property and investments combined with continued financial support for agents of destabilization.

Latin America: Political Changes and US Response

The mild response of the US to the regime changes resulting from the Latin American elections of 2006 can easily be explained by the fact that they did not produce any consequential socio-economic structural changes, at least for the foreseeable future.

The clearest demonstration of the marginal effects of 'center-left' electoral victories is the case of the electoral victory of Lula who made it clear to even his own most ardent intellectual supporters (Frei Betto, Emir Sader, Joao Pedro Stedile) that he considered 'leftism an infantile disorder' (La Jornada 12/14/2006), a remark much appreciated in business circles throughout the hemisphere. No doubt Wall Street was pleased that the Brazilian 'Workers Party' voted to double

Congressional salaries from $6500 USD to $12000 USD per month (and doubling each Congress member's individual monthly budget to $75000 USD) while increasing the minimum wage by $7 USD a month from $159 to $166 USD (about 1.7% after inflation) (Financial Times December 16-17, 2006). One out of five Brazilian Congress members (many from Lula's coalition) are currently under investigation for corruption. Wall Street speculators who also were recently investigated for fraud and yet received huge year-end bonuses would feel a real identity of condition with Brazilian lawmakers who doubled their salaries, while awaiting criminal charges.

Contrary to White House expectations, but much to its liking, Evo Morales' regime pursued orthodox, austere fiscal policies aimed at budget surpluses, eschewed any redistributive policies (virtually no land, mining or energy expropriations). While Morales demobilized the social movements and focused on endless legal procedures, the oligarchy regrouped, expanded its power base in Santa Cruz and threatens to bring down the government. While Washington's oligarchic Bolivian clients advanced toward power (La Jornada December 16, 2006) Evo Morales continued his self destructive policies of symbolic radical populist rhetoric and greater concessions to elites. Washington has maintained a foot in both camps, providing over $60 million dollars in foreign aid to Morales and untold millions to the opposition in Santa Cruz organizing Massive 'separatist' demonstrations (HoyBolivia.com December 16, 2006).

Washington's 'soft-line' negotiators (Shannon) strengthened their position vis-à-vis the White House's 'hard line' policy toward Venezuela by pointing to Hugo

Chavez' electoral victory (63% of the vote) as a reason for a rapprochement (La Jornada, December 14, 2006). Shannon has advanced the argument in Washington that significant sector of the Chavez government was open to a negotiated pact with involves freezing the status quo, softening criticism of US imperial policies, consolidating oil and gas agreements and blocking any steps toward socializing the economy.

Perspective for 2007

The international position of the US during 2007 will continue to deteriorate – the coming massive military escalation in Iraq, the large-scale transfer of arms for Israel to threaten or attack Iran, Syria, Hezbollah or Hamas (or all simultaneously) – will not lessen the armed resistance in Iraq. A US-backed Israeli attack on Iran will extend warfare throughout the Gulf States including Saudi Arabia. On December 15, 2006, Bush presented the Presidential Medal of Freedom to Israeli extremist, Natan Sharansky – advocate for the genocidal 'transfer' of all Palestinians from 'Greater Israel' – symbolizing the meeting of the minds of US imperial militarism and Israeli brutal colonial expansionism. The total discarding of any new diplomatic initiative (like the recommendations of Baker's Iraq study Group), is the result of the combined strength of the powerful pro-Israel Lobby and the Bush-Cheney-Rice White House.

Washington, overextended militarily in the Middle East, will follow its 'two-track' policy in Latin America. The White House will support incumbent clients (like Uribe, Calderon and Garcia); the State, Treasury and Commence Departments will engage in trade agreements with more 'autonomous' neo-liberal regimes like Lula, Bachelet, Vazquez and Kirchner), encouraging greater distance from Cuba and Venezuela and closer diplomatic relations with the US. With regard to Bolivia, Washington will continue to pressure Morales to make further concessions to the far-right civic-oligarchic coalition based in Santa Cruz, allowing the local business elite to 'carry the ball' for US imperial interests. In Venezuela, the 'two track policy' will attempt to deepen the political divisions in the Chavista movement, in order to block new Chavez initiatives toward greater socialization and in order to promote new political configuration of 'moderate oppositionists' and liberal Chavistas.

The weakest link in Washington's projected strategy in Latin America is the re-emergence of socio-political movements, like those which burst forth in the late 1990's and first years of the new century: The MST in Brazil, the workers, peasant and Indian movements in Bolivia and Ecuador and the mass uprising in Oaxaca and electoral protests in Mexico are in the process of re-grouping, none having suffered a historic defeat. All the major popular movements retain their organizational structures and have recovered their political independence. They will soon be capable of once again engaging in major uprising and political confrontations with the oligarchies in power or with their shock troops in the streets.

The New Year does not promise 'more of the same': it will start with a major US military escalation in the Middle East but it will likely end with a greater military debacle, ensuring deepening political crises and increased economic instability both in the Middle East, the US and Latin America. The weakening of the US political regime will open a window of opportunity for a decisive break with the US Empire, providing that the re-emerging social-political movements can overcome the obstacles posed by the new political elites of ex-leftists and traditional oligarchs.

PART-I: ASIA

1

Philippines: Killing Fields of Asia

James Petras and Robin Eastman-Abaya
March 2006

Introduction

Since President Gloria Macapagal Arroyo joined the US global "War on Terrorism", the Philippines has become the site of an on-going undeclared war against peasant and union activists, progressive political dissidents and lawmakers, human rights lawyers and activists, women leaders and a wide range of print and broadcast journalists. Because of the links between the Army, the regime and the death squads, political assassinations take place in an atmosphere of absolute impunity. The vast majority of the attacks occur in the countryside and provincial towns. The reign of terror in the Philippines is of similar scope and depth as in Colombia. Unlike Colombia, the rampaging state terrorism has not drawn sufficient attention from international public opinion.

Between 2001 and 2006 hundreds of killings, disappearances, death threats and cases of torture have been documented by the independent human rights center, KARAPATAN, and the church-linked

Ecumenical Institute for Labor Education and Research. Since Macapagal Arroyo came to power in 2001 there have been 400 documented extrajudicial killings. In 2004, 63 were killed and in 2005, 179 were assassinated and another 46 disappeared and presumed dead. So far in the first 2½ months of 2006 there have been 26 documented political assassinations.

An analysis of the class and social background of the victims of this systematic state terror in 2005 demonstrates that the largest sector, about 70, have been peasants and peasant leaders involved in land and farm labor disputes. The military has invariably accused the murdered and disappeared peasants of links to or sympathy with the communist guerrillas or Muslim separatists. The victims include members of the national farmers' association, Kilusang Magbubukid ng Pilipinas (KMP), as well as Igorot, Agta and Moro indigenous minority peasant leaders involved in protecting their lands. One notorious massacre occurred in late November 2005 when 47 peasants and their legal representatives held an open, public meeting over a land dispute in Palo, Leyte in the Visayas. A large force of soldiers surrounded and attacked the meeting killing 9 peasants outright and arresting over a dozen. An additional 18 'disappeared' and are presumed dead. The 'Palo Massacre' of the members of the San Agustin Farmers Beneficiaries Cooperative and Alang-Alang Small Farmers Association was at first presented by the armed forces as a military encounter with the New Peoples Army and a few homemade weapons were planted on the victims. In this, as in all other cases, none of the perpetrators have been punished and there has been no official investigation.

Workers and labor leaders form the next largest group of victims of assassination (at least 18) not including the disappeared and presumed dead. Members of a national labour federation, Kilusan Mayo Uno (May First Movement), Nestle's Worker's Union, Central Azucareara de Tarlac, Negros Federation of Sugar Workers, a leader of the Department of Agrarian Reform Employee Association, regional college employee union leaders and various militants in both the electrical company and bus company employee unions were murdered in 2005.

Earlier in 2005, 26 unarmed Muslim detainees in a military prison in Manila were shot protesting against their prolonged and arbitrary detention, lack of a trial date and horrific prison conditions. These men were mostly vendors and displaced peasants and fishermen living with their families in Manila. They were accused, but never convicted, of membership in the 'Abu Sayaf' kidnapping gang.

Seven print and radio journalists and writers were killed in 2005 as well as seven attorneys and judges involved in human rights, labor and land dispute cases. Among the religious community, there were 3 targeted assassinations of clergy and 7 church workers, all involved in advocacy work with the poor, peasants, workers and national minorities.

This listing of killings in 2005 doesn't included attempted assassinations, illegal detention and torture and unreported disappearances. The victims were killed by death squads controlled by the military with the aim of protecting the power of the large landowners and land grabbers, timber and mining barons and company bosses with the connivance of the regime.

Another important group of victims, which overlaps with peasants and workers associations, are the 83 leaders and members of the popular left political party, Bayan Muna (The People First) and its 'party list' affiliates. Most were systematically murdered in the provinces outside of Metro Manila between 2001-2005 (67 in 2005 alone). Leaders and coordinators of allied party-list groups, such as the women's party Gabriela and the urban poor people's party, Anakpawis (Toiling Masses), have been murdered, disappeared or wounded. Elected officials from Bayan Muna, such a Tarlac City councilman, Abelardo Ladera, were shot in broad daylight, prompting defiant provincial funeral marches. His killing followed the notorious 2004 massacre of hacienda union workers in Tarlac and the subsequent systematic elimination of witnesses.

A breakdown of the 66 death squad killings of members and supporters of the progressive political parties in 2005 include 33 from militant urban poor peoples party Anakpawis and 30 from Bayan Muna. Five members of Anakpawis and 3 from Bayan Muna have 'disappeared' and are presumed dead in 2005. So far three Bayan Muna officials have been assassinated in the first 10 weeks of 2006.

Since 2003, the Philippines became the 2nd most dangerous country for journalists after Iraq because of the staggering number of reporters killed and disappeared by death squads. Most recently a radio reporter involved in exposing abuses at a local mine was kidnapped by death squads working for the mine owners in late February 2006 and is presumed dead.

State sponsored terror today is reminiscent of the worst days of martial law, under the Dictator Ferdinand Marcos (1972-1986). As under Marcos the entire countryside is virtually under military control sharply limiting the role of civilian administrators. A manual published by the Macapagal regime, entitled "Knowing the Enemy" is used by the Armed Forces throughout the country to label legal mass organizations and civil rights groups, like the Philippine Association of Protestant Lawyers, as supporters of 'terrorism'.

The combined military-death squad campaign has all the earmarks of US-sponsored 'low intensity' warfare against the civilian population. The military "proscribes" or labels individuals and groups as terrorists on the basis of what it claims to be 'secret intelligence' in order to criminalize their right to resist oppression and fight for self-determination and justify their elimination. The creation of these 'lists' is outside of the process of judicial scrutiny and limits any legal protection for the victims or their survivors. Using the black propaganda of a psychological warfare operation, the victims and their associations are invariably described as 'terrorists'.

Background

A de-facto civilian-military alliance has been ruling the Philippines, since with the declaration of Martial Law by Marcos in 1972. In the 1960's most economists considered the Philippines to be the most economically progressive nation in South East Asia. With the advent of the liberalization of the economy, it has become and remains the one of the poorest and most socially polarized country in Asia, with a per capita GDP of $950/year, about half of Thailand's. With over 50 per cent of total private assets controlled by 15 extended super-rich families it is one of most unequal societies in the world. In stark contrast to the rest of Asia, there has been no economic progress in the past two decades. The Philippines with a population of over 85 million has one of the highest unemployment rates (20 per cent) and an additional 30 per cent underemployed in the informal sector. Over 40 per cent of the households are unable secure adequate shelter and food; they are the indigent poor. The once highly regarded public educational and health systems have sharply deteriorated due to massive government cuts in social spending and privatization. The nation, whose research institutions produced the high yield 'miracle rice', is now a net importer of rice and other food staples. Malnutrition is widespread, according to the World Health Organization. Upwards of eight million Filipinos, unable to find decent work at home, are working abroad to support their families *'Better to die working in Iraq, than to stay home and watch your family starve'* was the pitiful, but common slogan of Filipino workers clamoring for exit visas to perform menial work for the US occupation army in Iraq. As many as 4,000 Filipino workers are believed to be in Iraq.

In the years following the overthrow of the Marcos dictatorship (Feb. 26, 1986) by a military and Church-backed revolt, the subsequent elected presidents have failed to stem the ongoing deterioration of the country. The new rulers like Corazon Aquino (1986-1992), and former General Fidel Ramos (1992-1998), simply favored a new set of oligarchs and set the stage for the rise to power of a corrupt populist, Joseph Estrada. His "anti-oligarch" rhetoric brought him to the presidential palace in 1998 with widespread support among the poor. Estrada became an irritant to Washington and the traditional oligarchy by welcoming Venezuelan President Hugo Chavez in 1999 and for his populist social policies, such as handing out thousands of land titles to urban squatters.

US-designed, upper class-backed, street demonstrations supported by sectors of the military elite culminated in the ouster of Estrada in January 2001. The same forces hoisted his Vice President, Gloria Macapagal Arroyo to the Presidency. Macapagal is a US educated, neo-liberal economist and favourite of the US Embassy.

This political putsch led to the expansion of US military basing rights and a new military agreement, quickly signed by Macapagal after a two year delay during Estrada's presidency. With the rise of Macapagal-Arroyo, Washington has a reliable client.

From Populism to Neo-Liberal Terror

The newly 'installed' Macapagal Arroyo quickly instituted a neo-liberal program of privatizations, drastic cuts for public education and public hospitals and onerous value-added taxes which impacted the poor and lower middle-class. By 2005, the Philippine total external and internal debt ballooned to over $100 billion dollars and yearly debt servicing exceed 30 per cent of the budget. Even 8 million overseas Filipino workers (including a significant section of the educated professionals) sending home $12.5 billion dollars of remittances in 2005 could not begin to cover debt servicing. The Philippines bears the dubious distinction of being the only country in Asia to have seen a drop in per capita GDP during and since the heady years of the 'Asian Tiger' boom.

Macapagal Arroyo's family and cronies have been implicated in the same levels of corruption as that attributed to the deposed President Estrada. Mike Arroyo, the President's husband, remains in self-imposed exile in the US to avoid facing charges of graft and fraud. Macapagal Arroyo maintains her support among the military by offering lucrative concessions to favourite generals and key officials in the military leading to deep discontent among the junior ranks of the armed forces forced to survive on low wages. As a result, several mutinies of junior officers and soldiers occurred, the largest of which was the takeover of an upscale Manila shopping and apartment complex in July 2003 by 300 soldiers from the special forces and the more recent uprising of Marines in January of this year.

Military intelligence has been implicated in a campaign of bombings both in Manila and on the southern island of Mindanao, targeting markets, buses, commuter trains, airports and mosques. The Macapagal regime blamed a Moslem kidnapping gang, Abu Sayaf, and used the bombings as a justification for greater militarization of the country. The curious timing of the bombings, for example the December 2004 bombing of a Manila shopping center, which killed 15, happened very soon after a devastating landslide burying almost 1,000 townspeople in a province near Manila, exposed the regimes incompetence in civil assistance.

Local journalist with sources in the military believe the campaign of bombings have been carried out by the regime itself to justify requests for more military 'aid' from the US.

The US Connection

In December 2002 the US announced a significant expansion of its joint US-Philippine military training exercises. The first contingent of US troops landing on the southern island of Mindanao engaged in field operations against the Muslim separatists. In early 2003 then-Assistant US Secretary of Defense, Paul Wolfowitz called the Philippines the 'Second Front in the War on Terror'. Since then tens of thousands of Muslem villagers have been forcibly displaced and hundreds have been tortured, killed or disappeared. As a result Muslim guerrilla activity has increased.

In October 2003, during a visit to the Philippines, Bush cited the Philippines as a model for the re-building of Iraq. Forgetting to mention the US invasion of the Philippines in 1898 and 13-year pacification campaign when upwards of 1 million Filipinos died, Bush described the Philippines as a "model of democracy" – a bonafide death squad democracy.

The Bush Administration's support for the Macapagal Arroyo regime has been reciprocated: A contingent of Philippine troops was sent to Iraq over the protests of hundreds of thousands of Filipinos. These troops were only withdrawn when Iraqi resistance fighters threatened to execute captured Filipino labourers in Iraq: the Philippine economy is more dependent on remittances from its workers in the Middle East than on US aid. The lucrative reconstruction contracts, which the Philippine elite had expected to be awarded for its services to the Bush Administration in Iraq, never materialized. During 2006, another contingent 5,500 US soldiers are scheduled to arrive in Mindanao and the number of joint exercises has doubled.

US troops are not confined to the separatist stronghold in the far south of the country. More and more "joint operations" occur in the central islands and Luzon where the communist New Peoples Army has been conducting a campaign against the government for 40 years over issues of land reform and oligarchic-imperialist control of the economy. With an estimated 10,000 fighters, the NPA is clearly viewed as a threat to US and local ruling class interests.

Urban Popular Protest and Emergency Decrees

In 2004, Macapagal Arroyo narrowly defeated her rival in the Presidential elections in a campaign marred by violence and fraud. An audiotape released in the spring of 2005 recorded the President discussing with a top election official the rigging of the election. Amid resignations of members of her cabinet and calls for her resignation from the general public, she narrowly escaped a vote of impeachment in November 2005.

Macapagal Arroyo's disastrous neo-liberal economic policies, the growing social and economic deterioration of the country, frantic attempts by the professionals to escape through immigration, moves by restive middle level officers and demonstrations by popular mass social movements put the Philippines back in the international news. In early February 2006, an even more devastating landslide brought on by rains and de-forestation, buried almost 2,000 townspeople on the island of Leyte. The inability of the regime to provide even the most basic aid to the victims angered the entire nation.

On February 23, 2006, the eve of the 20th anniversary of the overthrow of the Marcos dictatorship, Macapagal Arroyo declared a state of emergency banning all rallies, demonstrations and closing opposition media. She issued orders for the arrest of 59 individuals including members of the Congress, military officers and social critics, on charges of rebellion against her regime. Rallies were planned to commemorate the end of the Marcos dictatorship and to protest the electoral fraud, corruption, economic mismanagement and human rights violations of the Macapagal Arroyo regime. Some rallies defied the President's decree, went ahead and were violently repressed.

Those charged with rebellion included 6 Congress people from leftwing political parties, a human rights attorney, retired and active military officers and social activists. Most of the charges have no substance and are totally arbitrary. For example, Anakpawis (Toiling Masses) Congressman Crispin Beltran, age 73, veteran labor leader and anti-Marcos activist, was arrested shortly after the Emergency Rule declaration, at first on the basis of a 25-year-old charge made during the Marcos dictatorship. When these charges were shown to have been dropped decades earlier, he was charged with rebellion.

This is the latest of a series of attacks on the part of the Macapagal Arroyo regime aimed specifically at destroying class-based political parties and trade union activity, including Bayan Muna and its coalition partners. The campaign of assassination and disappearances of 80 members of this party alliance between 2001-2005, including mayors and provincial elected representatives has finally reached the top elected representatives in the Philippine Congress. In 2006, repression turned from the countryside to the capital, from peasant leaders to Manila-based Congress people, media, working class and left party leaders. Of the 26 political assassinations in the first 10 weeks of 2006, 3 have been Bayan Muna officials.

The arbitrary arrest of Congressional representatives sends a signal to the legal left that the regime will not tolerate dissent or challenges to its policies even from within Congress.

Who are the Perpetrators?

According to the KARAPATAN, the independent human rights organization involved in documenting and providing legal support to victims of human rights abuses, the disappearances and assassinations are committed by death squads in some of the most heavily militarized areas in the Philippines. The death squads would not be able to act with impunity without the complicity of the military. Witnesses to the killings have themselves disappeared and the Philippine judicial system has failed to prosecute the intellectual authors or perpetrators. Nor has the military made any effort to investigate and arrest identified death squad leaders. Human rights groups provide evidence that death squads operate under the protective umbrella of regional military commands, especially the US-trained Special Forces. Macapagal's promotion of the notorious Colonel Jovito Palparan, ('Butcher of Mindoro') to General, despite extensive documentation and testimony of gross human rights abuses points to the President's support for military-backed state terrorism. When Palparan was assigned to Central Luzon in September 2005, the number of political assassinations in that region alone jumped to 52 in four months. Prior to his promotion, the regions with the largest number of summary executions like Eastern Visayas and Central Luzon were under then-Colonel Palparan.

State of the Resistance

In the face the disintegration of the economy and society, and the regime's use of force to sustain its hold on power, faced with its gross incompetence in the face of several natural/ecological disasters, popular resistance has spread from the countryside to the cities. The popular mass organizations, involving peasant and indigenous minority farmers, industrial workers, teachers, journalists, civil servants, students, women, artists, human rights workers, lawyers and clergy have grown despite the campaign of state terror. On the 20th Anniversary of the 1986 overthrow of Marcos, tens of thousands defied the State of Emergency and marched in Manila and in cities throughout the country. Over 10,000 women defied police bans to march on International Women's Day. Students and teachers are mounting campaigns on the campuses around the country. Former Presidents, business executives and clergy are calling for Macapagal Arroyo's resignation and a 'smooth transition' within the elite, while the popular mass movements and their besieged political representatives are demanding justice for the victims of state terror, an end to US military presence, a repeal of the value added taxes, an increase in the minimum wage, land reform, a moratorium of debt payments, re-nationalization of key economic sectors and consequential peace negotiations between the state and the NPA and Muslim separatists. That Macapagal Arroyo will eventually be forced to resign is, according to officials, a likely outcome. The question is when and by whom?

2

Jenin: Auschwitz or the Warsaw Ghetto?

April 29, 2002
James Petras

While I agree with Saramago's general characterization of the Israeli attack on the Palestinians, I think the most appropriate analogy is the Warsaw ghetto uprising against the Nazis and not Auschwitz. Of course, both the Israelis and the Nazis were intent on destroying the social fabric of the oppressed people and expelling them from the conquered land. In the case of the Nazis via the ovens and gas chambers; in the Occupied territories by systemic terror and destruction of the basic structures of society: housing, hospitals, schools, roads, electricity, water, stores, food, trade, agriculture and industry. In both cases there was systematic roundup of young men aged 15 to 60 years old and their detention in concentration camps.

However, the Palestinian resistance in Jenin and the other cities and refugee camps is similar to the violent uprising of the Jews in Warsaw against the Nazis and unlike the passive submission of the Jews who were shipped to Auschwitz. Irony of history the Israeli Jews were destroying Jenin on the same date (April 19) on which Jews commemorate the Warsaw uprising. The Israeli military borrowed explicitly from the Nazis their tactics of urban warfare - engaging in massive destruction using tanks and armored personnel carriers after encountering tough resistence in house to house warfare. The Jewish High Command ordered that tanks shell buildings, with all their inhabitants inside, and then bulldozed the buildings burying the victims under the rubble. The Nazi Storm Troopers practiced the same "scorched earth" policy. The result is that Jenin and the Jewish ghetto in Warsaw have exactly the same desolate landscape, the same foul smell of rotting corpses buried under the rubble.

The responses of the two governments to their crimes against humanity are similar: the Palestinian and Jewish resistance fighters are "terrorists". To their people the story is different: the Jewish street fighters of Warsaw and the Palestinian militia are viewed as national heroes.

The propaganda machines of the Jewish and Nazi states spew out the same mendacious propaganda: the invasion of the ghettos and destruction of the resistence are portrayed as "defensive policies", the destruction of the social fabric of society is described as destroying the terrorist infrastructure. Sharon, like Goebbels, speaks of seeking "peace"...through genocide.

Both Hitler and the Israeli state refused to allow the Red Cross to enter the ghettos to tend the wounded, sick or the mentally ill. The same paranoid vision that drove Hitler's war machine to kill women and children, drives the Israelis to defy and denounce all Human Rights groups, United Nations, European Union and other humanitarian agencies which are appalled by the slaughter. While Hitler's paranoia drove him to denounce all democratic critics as "Aryan haters", Sharon and his fanatical accomplices inside and outside of Israel scream "anti-Semitism" against the UN, the Red Cross and other humanitarian organization in perpetual outbursts of psychotic behavior.

The profound irrationality which afflicts Israeli leaders is best illustrated by an incident involving the Palestinian mental hospital in Ramallah. After an Israeli tank had blown apart a wall in the asylum, one mental patient asked his doctor "Can I have your mobile phone, I want to call CNN and tell Ariel Sharon he can come here and be treated free." The response of the supporters of the Israeli and Nazi state to Warsaw and Jenin were similar: victory celebrations and pledges of additional support. An estimated 100,000 mostly Jews marched on Washington pledging unconditional support for Sharon and his genocidal campaign. Respectable doctors, dentists, business people, mass media celebrities raised millions of dollars to fund the Israeli war machine. As Israeli Jewish professionals and progressives flee from insecurity or disgust, U.S. and Israeli Jewish leaders visit Argentina, to recruit impoverished middle class Jews, offering them free tickets, homes, subsidies, jobs and gardens - stolen from the Palestinians. Just as the Nazis displaced Jews and seized their property handing it over to loyal followers.

Warsaw and Jenin, Jews as victims, Jews as oppressors. The descendants of the heros of the Warsaw ghettos practicing the tactics and strategy of their grandfathers' murderers. Obviously there were and are opponents to Nazi and the Israeli war machine among Germans and Jews. Millions of German Socialists, Communists, trade unionists and democrats opposed who the Nazi regime were killed, jailed and repressed. Today a minority of courageous Israelis speak out against Sharon and his accomplices. Progressive German exiles condemned the Nazi slaughter of Jews in Warsaw and some even expressed solidarity with the resistence. Likewise, in the U.S. and Europe, groups of Jewish critics condemn Sharon's military machine. But the mass media do not report their criticism. They are silenced critics. In the U.S. only the voice and images of the Israeli State is heard: powerful trade unions officials continue to buy Israeli bonds with their members' pension funds. Israel bond sales are booming.

Hollywood is an accomplice: What is different is that unlike Nazi Germany, no Hollywood producer has emerged to produce a "Triumph of the Will". Leni Reisenthal glorification of Hitler's rallies.

Consider Jenin and Warsaw. In both cases, the world, Western democratic countries stood by and watched the slaughter. Horrified but unwilling to act. But today, in Jenin, unlike during the Nazi slaughter of the Jews in Warsaw, no one can say they didn't know.

Jenin: genocide in our lifetime. The destruction of the Warsaw ghetto was not a unique act by a unique evil power. Jews are not the only people to suffer a holocaust. Jenin is our holocaust. The Palestinian uprising is led by our resistance fighters. On April 19, in a ceremony in Buenos Aires commemorating the anniversary of the Warsaw uprising, Osvaldo Bayer reminded his predominantly Jewish audience of the Palestinian resistance in Jenin. Some of the audience applauded. Most were silent.

Some critics may object. Israel is a democracy, Germany was a totalitarian state. Israel is a democracy for Jews and a violent oppressor of Palestinians in the colonized territories. In the territories Israeli acts like Nazis - seizing Palestinian land, water, imprisoning thousands and destroying the homes of the "inferior people". Other critics might argue that Palestinians engage in terrorism against the settlers and in Israel against ordinary civilians, unlike the Warsaw resisters, who fought the Nazi army. The difference is only marginal: the Warsaw fighters also killed German civilian functionaries, Polish and even Jewish collaborators. The main difference was distance and geography: then the German civilians were too far away. After the war, the entire German civilian population was severely punished for their government's crimes. James Petras Like all analogies the Warsaw/Jenin analogy has its limits in time and place. But on the basic points there is a shocking convergence: in both cases a heroic people stood up and fought back against the military machines of genocidal states.

3

The Meaning of War: A Heterodox Perspective

James Petras
January 2005

Introduction

This paper will discuss the social, political, economic, psychological and ideological causes and impacts of war in contemporary history. Obviously we cannot explore all of these dimensions in detail; instead we will focus on what we consider the most important dimensions of these general categories.

The first question that requires clarification is "what wars?" There are at least four kinds of war which have global significance. First and most significant in terms of the present and future configuration of inter-state relations are imperialist wars – such as the US invasion of Yugoslavia, Afghanistan and Iraq, leading to the forced imposition of direct or indirect colonial rule, military bases and appropriation of strategic resources and/or water or overland routes.

The second type of war is "separatist-ethnic conflicts" such as the Albanian seizure of Yugoslav

Kosovo, or the Kurdish seizure of Northern Iraq. While separatist conflicts are played out within the larger Imperial strategic framework, the local participants bring their own "historical claims" to justify their war on the existing central government.

The third type of war is the "colonial-territorial" wars, best exemplified by the Israel expulsion of Palestinians, the arbitrary appropriation of land and resources, their denial of self-government and the settlement of Jews on Palestinian land seized through armed force.

The fourth type of war is "regional wars", found mainly in Africa and Asia, where aggressive regimes invade neighbouring countries especially adjoining territory – usually containing precious metals. This is the issue in Southern Africa, where Rwanda has occupied a significant swathe of Eastern Zaire.

While each of these wars has its specificities – the question arises as to whether these wars are linked to the empire building projects of the US, European Union (EU) or other emerging imperial powers? The answer is complex and contingent on the level of analysis at which the problem is posed. Many of these conflicts predate current empire building efforts by the US; in many cases, local elites visualize war as a source of class, personal or national enrichment. We can speculate that conflicts of this sort will continue at some (distant) future in a "post-imperial" period, as local satraps attempt to seize 'fragments' of a declining world empire.

Nevertheless whatever the 'historical claims' and local interests involved, all these contemporary wars are linked in specific ways with the ongoing empire building of the US and the EU. The US has consistently supported separatist ethnic-based movements, like the Kosova Liberation Army or the Chechen terrorists to weaken national-states (Yugoslavia, Russia) which Washington targeted. As a consequence Washington secures a new client regime, major military bases and strategic geopolitical advantages while undermining an enemy to its uni-polar pretensions. The US provides arms and financial aid to Israeli colonial expansion and war against Palestinians and Arab countries. This has both weakened the Arab states opposed to US empire building and provoked greater mass popular resistance. The ideological influence and political and financial power of the pro-Israeli organizations and individuals inside and outside the government have reinforced the most bellicose and militarist wing of the US empire builders, especially in the Middle East, often times at the expense of US multi-national corporations seeking to enter in agreements with local regimes.

US imperialism has a contradictory relationship with the separatists and colonial states: on the one hand they undermine anti-imperialist nationalists and on the other hand, their territorial claims threaten to undermine imperial ties with client regimes (as in the case of Iraqi Kurdistan and the Republic of Turkey). Moreover the imperial strategy of supporting Islamic nationalists against secular leftists (as in the case of Afghanistan and Yugoslavia) has led to new violent confrontations between the empire and former Islamic 'allies' as Washington attempted to use and discard them for more docile neo-liberal puppet regimes.

Under conditions in which US and European empire building is driven by a doctrine of permanent wars, there are few if any regional, local or separatist wars which are purely local – in their causes or consequences.

II Driving Force of War: Inter-Imperial Collaboration and Competition

The key to the accelerated pace of empire building over the past decade is the "open spaces" resulting from the demise of the collectivist states (USSR, Eastern Europe and Asia) and their overseas dependencies and allies in Africa and elsewhere. Both the US and the EU successfully incorporated these 'ex-collectivist' countries into their sphere of domination - militarily, economically and culturally. Europe gained control of strategic resources, cheap skilled labor and major industries, incorporating these countries as subordinates within the European Union. The US secured similar economic advantages but also established military bases and recruited mercenary military forces for its imperial invasions (in Yugoslavia, Afghanistan and Iraq) and political supporters in the United Nations. Washington backed the illegal seizure of power by Yeltsin and then provided backing for his corrupt, destructive, oligarchic regime that literally destroyed the Russian economy and society. In the course of supporting Yeltsin, the US financial system received hundreds of billions of dollars in illegal transfers by US backed oligarchs. Europe and the US joined in partnership with the oligarchs to plunder Russia's oil and gas resources. The US secured world military supremacy and proceeded to construct an "arc of encirclement" around the weakened Russian state via its new client states incorporated into NATO. From the Baltic States through Central-Eastern Europe to the Balkans and across the Caucuses to Central and Southern Asia, Washington has established local armies and military bases under US command.

Europe, concentrating on economic dominance, penetrated these same regions, relying on aid and financing of their multi-nationals and the corruption of the new capitalist politicians.

The 'co-operative' joint conquest by the US and the EU of Eastern Europe, Balkans and Baltic countries was based on "shared decisions and shared division of the spoils of conquest". This re-division of the world between the US and the EU however came to an end with the most recent wave of imperial wars, beginning with the US invasions of Afghanistan and Iraq. Washington decided to act unilaterally in order to monopolize decision-making and the colonial occupation of these countries, relegating Europe to a subordinate role under US command and with few claims on the spoils of conquest. The two leading EU powers, France and Germany, conceded US supremacy in Afghanistan but balked over the US monopoly of Iraqi oil wealth. The US-EU conflict over Iraq illustrates inter-imperialist competition in the re-division of the world's wealth and neo-colonies. The EU imperial states, relying mostly on their economic instruments – banks, multi-national corporations, state-sponsored trade and investment agreements – was challenging US attempts to establish regional and world supremacy and subordination of Europe via a monopoly of energy resources.

In Iran, Iraq, Libya, Russia, the Caucasus and Latin America, EU multi-national oil and gas companies have secured long-term energy supplies via direct investments or state-to-state agreements. The architects of US global power decided to undercut stiff economic competition from the EU by relying on Washington's "comparative advantage" in military power – to unilaterally launch the Iraq invasion, to monopolize Iraq's oil wealth and to prepare for future oil wars in the Middle East (Iran and others) and elsewhere (Venezuela).

Washington's permanent war doctrine was in strategic opposition to the EU's doctrine of 'economic imperialism' and selective and limited military intervention. Despite the significant differences in the Middle East, both the EU and the US still find room to co-operate in imposing spheres of joint influence in several countries and regions, namely in Afghanistan, Haiti and in Africa. Co-operation and conflict between the great imperial powers in re-dividing the world into spheres of colonization, domination and influence are the key to understanding the meaning of war in the late 20th century and into the new millennium.

Erosion and "Reversal of Historical Memory

The re-emergence of colonial wars and colonial rule in the 21st century and the growth of national liberation movements and anti-colonial resistance reflects the erosion of historical memory in the imperial countries, among Western intellectuals as well as sectors of the masses (especially in the US) and the elites.

The "erosion of historical memory" was evident in Europe between the two world wars, as Germany re-armed and prepared to conquer and colonize Europe. Germany's pacifist, and even revolutionary, anti-military consciousness immediately following World War I lasted at most 15 years, after which the Nazis were able to launch Germany into a new frenzy of re-armament and territorial conquest. In the post-WWII period, US mass anti-war sentiment reflecting the horrors of death and disability have been of short duration: A brief 5-year period after World War II (1945-49) before launching war on the Korean peninsula (1950-53); followed by mass "anti-war" sentiment from 1953-1963; the US invasion of Indo-China and the 12-year war (1963-1975) led to the re-emergence of very extensive mass anti-war sentiment which continued for 15 years till the First Gulf War. During the 1990's, US anti-war sentiment temporarily re-emerged just prior to the Second Gulf War (January-February 2003) and then virtually disappeared, at least from the streets. "Mass historical memory", history teaches us, can be a temporarily powerful sentiment in imposing restraint on the militarist side of imperialist expansion, but history also demonstrates that "memory" can be eroded and overcome over time (shorter or longer) by determined imperial decision-makers and propagandists.

"Historical memory" plays a positive role in limiting imperial wars under certain conditions and within a limited time frame. Memory of large scale deaths and casualties among imperial soldiers, deep economic crises resulting from military spending and loss of commercial markets, profound internal political conflicts and instability, demoralization and discontent among soldiers impose serious, but time-bound, constraints on imperial war-making capacity. The mass anti-war syndrome is anathema to imperialist ideologues, policymakers and international corporations. As a consequence, a conscious deliberate process of erosion is set in place. "Historical Memory" is modified by a cumulative set of events, ambiguous ideological pronouncements and small-scale military actions which over time lead to the resurgence of pro-war mass sentiment and the eclipse of historical memory.

"Historical memory" is strongest among those who most closely experienced and lived through the devastating consequences of a 'losing imperialist war'. The high point of "memory" is the moment immediately following a destructive, costly, imperial war.

Subsequently, the memory erodes over time, as a new generation emerges and ideology overcomes experiences and beliefs transmitted between generations.

The US experience following the imperial defeat in the Indo-Chinese war is illustrative of the mechanisms of "memory erosion".

The first steps toward erosion took place right after the end of the Vietnam War during the presidency of James Carter (1976-80). Carter developed the doctrine of human rights intervention – selectively applying "humanitarian" rhetoric to attempt to re-legitimate US 'intervention' at a time in which mass consciousness was deeply opposed to new imperialist wars but responsive to appeals for human rights. Secondly Carter financed and backed a series of surrogate terrorist movements and regimes in Central America (Nicaragua, Southern Africa and Afghanistan) which allowed Washington to continue its quest for empire building. Thirdly Carter provoked a major confrontation with Iran by providing asylum to the deposed and despised Shah – leading to the seizure of the US Embassy. Carter used the incident to reverse the decline in military spending. Fourthly, the Carter Administration, with financial backing from Saudi Arabia and logistical support from Pakistan, recruited and armed tens of thousands of Islamic fundamentalists to join forces with indigenous Afghan landlords, warlords and mullahs in an attack on the secular, reform-minded pro-Soviet Afghan regime. The Carter regime's purpose was to provoke large-scale Soviet military assistance to the beleaguered Afghan regime, as a pretext for re-launching a "Second Cold War" – and accelerate the re-militarization of the US Empire. Through propaganda moves and indirect military engagement, Carter began the gradual process of gaining adherents for imperial wars and foremost eroding the powerful 'historical memory' of opposition to war.

President Reagan extended and deepened this process by accelerating the arms build-up, engaging in a mercenary war against Nicaragua, and deepening the surrogate wars in Afghanistan and Southern Africa. Under Reagan and subsequently Bush (father) the US launched imperial wars against Grenada and Panama – weak, small countries – which Washington succeeded in conquering with a minimum of casualties. Given the 'low costs' in US lives lost and the rapid and successful outcomes, mass historical consciousness was 'modified'— to accept or acquiesce once more in the use of war to establish US power, in specific circumstances. Yet historical memory was still a majoritarian sentiment in the lead up to the first Gulf War: most of the US public was opposed to the Gulf War in 1990 until it began. Once again the overwhelming military triumph and the minimum loss of US lives led to a dramatic shift toward mass support for the war.

President Clinton continued the aerial war against Iraq and the military occupation of Northern Iraq. Historical memory was eroding. Clinton faced no opposition to the aerial war but when he sent US troops to Somalia and nearly two-dozen US soldiers were killed, "memories" re-emerged and Clinton quickly withdrew forces.

One of the greatest blows to 'historical memory' and an event which cleared the way for the subsequent imperial wars against Afghanistan and Iraq, was Clinton's war against Yugoslavia. Clinton, aided by a massive falsification propaganda campaign, declared that the Yugoslav government was practicing genocide against the Bosnian Moslems and the Kosovo Albanians. Hence the imperialist war was transformed into a "humanitarian war". Cities, hospitals, factories, radio stations and civilian population centers were bombed and the US/NATO alliance broke up Yugoslavia into client mini-states. Once again there was mass public support, as "humanitarian" imperialism, the small number of US casualties and an early quick victory eroded the last traces of historical memory. The ideological and political basis for mass-backed imperialist policies were in place – but lacked a "trigger event".

The events of September 11, 2001 provided the Second Bush Administration, composed of extremists civilian militarists and Zionist fanatics, the pretext to launch the first in a series of wars in Afghanistan and Iraq, and to enunciate the totalitarian doctrines of permanent wars, preventive wars and the extraterritoriality of US imperial laws. The best evidence available suggests that the Bush Administration was deeply complicit in the 9/11 events leading up to the final destruction of historical memory.

However unlike other recent imperialist wars, the Iraq War is a prolonged peoples war (there are no quick and easy victories) resulting in large-scale death and casualties of US soldiers and out of control spending with no end in sight. A new "historical memory" may be in the making based on the new realities in Iraq.

IV War: Political Institutions and Social Movements

Historical consciousness is embodied by activists sustained by political organizations. Based on historical experience, we can say that social movements have great capacity to 'create' the memory in the course of dynamic mobilizations and memorable mass meeting, but it is political institutions which will sustain or erode that historical memory.

The principle political institutions (particularly in the United States), including the mass media, have consistently worked to dissolve historical consciousness of the death and destruction caused by imperialist wars. While they claim to "honour the dead soldiers" they do so only in so far as they served the empire, their "heroism" is praised in sacrificing their lives to further the global reach of imperial institutions. The electoral process is not used to advance an anti-militarist agenda but to eliminate independent mass mobilizations which act directly against the instruments of imperial wars.

As anti-war activity moves toward electoral politics, it is absorbed by the established electoral parties and politicians, who opportunistically tip their hat to anti-war sentiment in exchange for diluting anti-war consciousness. The electoral process involves anti-war social movements making deep compromises with the pro-war financiers of campaigns, with politicians articulating ambiguous and inconsistent positions and with political parties having long-time, large-scale allegiances to imperial policies and interests. Such is the experience in the US and elsewhere: Established political institutions bend sufficiently to question an unpopular war in order to attract the mass opposition, and once capturing their allegiance, return to re-building the military capacity for imperial wars. The moment in which the movements dissolve into established political parties, competing in electoral campaigns through "dissident" politicians, "historical consciousness" is severely eroded.

The original impetus for organizing mass anti-war movements came precisely through the recognition that existing political parties and 'normal political processes' are deeply immersed and corrupted by their structural ties to imperial interests. By returning to these institutions, with new personalities and slogans, mass consciousness lost sight of its historical insights into the nature of imperial power.

In contrast "historical consciousness" emerged with great power when masses of people moved into direct collective action, taking local initiatives and linking the economic and political institutions directing imperial wars. Action and knowledge grew into collective anti-militarist consciousness which over time evolved from awareness of everyday present-day destruction ("empirical consciousness") into "historical consciousness", understanding of the systemic pillage by imperialism over time and space.

Direct action movements bypass the distorting influence of the "political guardians" (conventional politicians, accepted ideologues and media pundits) and directly articulate the anti-war ideas and anti-militarist interests of the mass of the people. Movements acted directly against the militarist policies which negatively impacted on the populations - conscription, forced and extended war duties - and against the policy-makers who sent hundreds of thousands to death and disability.

In this conflict between the anti-war movements and pro-war political institutions, the pre-eminance of the former was most evident in time of imperial defeat, soldier discontent, and political leaders in disgrace for lies and broken promises. These are crucial moments, but they are short-lived. Pro-war political institutions, that outlive and/or overcome the crisis of imperial war, re-group, absorb the 'best' of their adversaries in the anti-war opposition and return to pursue the policy of imperial war – until the next crisis — ultimately asserting a dominant position. Historical consciousness becomes a "footnote" to conventional history of "Great Wars".

"Historical consciousness" of anti-imperialist wars retains continuity when it leads to a large-scale, long-term transformation of the political institutions. The continued process of struggle links generations, and the transmission of anti-militarist ideas. This continual renewal of historical consciousness depends on, in part, the active role of anti-imperialist intellectuals.

War and Intellectuals

Left intellectuals have been fervent critics of war in general, until they face the reality of their country engaging in war – and then opposition gives way to evasive statements, ambiguous moral temporizing and, among the most "courageous", a condemnation of the violence of the aggressor and as well as the victim. Even worst, many left and progressive intellectuals have argued for, defended and propagated the doctrine of "humanitarian intervention (imperialism)". This moral betrayal was evident during the US invasion and destruction of Yugoslavia, and support for the terrorist Kosovo Liberation (sic) Army and the "ethnic cleansing" of hundreds of thousands of Serbs from Kosovo, Croatia and elsewhere. US progressive intellectuals were conspicuously silent. The "progressive intellectuals" repeated their performance: providing tendentious political justifications for the invasion of Afghanistan and Iraq — though in the latter case, up until the start of the war, a minority of intellectuals condemned the war and the victimized regime. Even those progressive intellectuals, who criticized the imperialist wars, refused to support the anti-colonial resistance and many opposed the immediate withdrawal of the colonial armies.

The question of war and peace is a momentous issue. In the events leading up to an imperialist war, all the propaganda machinery is set in motion, the mass media dramatize the righteousness of the imperial cause and the evil of the country which is to be invaded. Repressive legislation ("security measures") is enacted by large congressional majorities. Publicists, religious notables, demagogues, statesmen, and respectable leaders of civil society find lofty moral purposes to laud "this war". The latent chauvinist "instincts" of the masses are aroused. The progressive intellectuals become fearful; the repressive legislation may ruin a career and undermine everyday routines – their classes, seminars and completion of their latest article or book. Their professional colleagues eye them with suspicion unless they openly pledge allegiance – "beyond any criticism in other times, in time of our survival, we must join forces" – with the military invaders. It is not merely fear of material losses or disruption of everyday routines which causes our progressive intellectuals to embrace the war or remain silent or (in the case of the most courageous minority) to condemn both sides, but the sense of being left out of national history, of being shunned by neighbors and colleagues, of having to accept the consequences of living in a savage imperial civilization that thrives on war, especially a successful war. The progressive intellectuals respond far more often to the pressures of their milieu than to the suffering of the colonized people.

The commitment of the progressive intellectual is not fixed in stone – they change with the conditions of their milieu and the strength and fortunes of the imperial government. With the colonial occupation, and the graphic visuals of death and destruction of the colonized countries, the progressive intellectuals argue for a humanitarian mission, to correct the excesses of the war. They even raise their voices a few decibels before the abuse and torture of certain prisoners in certain prisons. But rarely do progressive intellectuals dare to transgress the colonial frontiers to publicly support the anti-colonial resistance. They claim that to commit to the resistance would call into question their "moral credentials" with the moderate imperial institutional power wielders.

Since the end of the Vietnam War, Western intellectuals have not expressed solidarity with the popular resistance to any of the imperialist invasions. Grenada, Panama, Somalia, Yugoslavia, Afghanistan, Iraq, Palestine and Lebanon, the imperial wars are numerous, but the list of committed intellectuals is short.

The principle reason that many of the intellectuals oppose prolonged imperialist wars is because of the casualties to US soldiers and the cost to the US treasury. There is a kind of political narcissism in the slogan "Bring our boys home" in which the center of attention is on the invading troops not on the anti-colonial resistance. Even in "opposition" the Western intellectuals derive their politics from an ethno-centric view of the world.

At a deeper level this political narcissism is also a way of making concessions to the chauvinist fever which grips much of their countrymen: "We too share you concern, for our imperialist country – but lets not spend "our boys" lives on this". Of course if and when the imperial rulers recruit mercenaries, client regimes and local collaborators to murder resistance fighters – nothing will be said of any consequence because "our boys" will be home safe...

The historical shift of intellectuals from opposition to pro-war politics and support of imperial candidates is not simply a "pragmatic choice" of the lesser evil against the greater evil. The transformation is the result of fear, fear of those in power — even as they face no real threat to their lives, careers or living standards. But intellectuals imagine a threat, and they concoct wild scenarios of "fascist" repression to hide their moral cowardice. This imagined fear is magnified by the possible threat to personal safety, security, and property if the imperial force is defeated and the rulers "take their revenge" against internal critics. Supporting the war or "opposing both sides" as the moral hypocrites prefer it, is insurance for the future. In the black fantasy world of intellectuals, when the imagined state investigation takes place, they can always present as evidence in their favor, their articles and speeches condemning the "moral barbarians" who attacked "our boys".

But if there is one universal truth about our progressive intellectuals it is that they do no "stand in one place" – they move with the times – they gauge the changing winds of political fortune.

When those suffering the war, the "average people" turn against the war, when the imperial regime is split with elite conflicts, when the soldiers question their orders, their officers, the war, the president and the generals, then our moral intellectuals concoct a new set of moral imperatives, adding their voices to the multitudes who question the war. Once it is safe, once the ravages of a losing imperial war have torn asunder the tissues of official lies, out bold progressive intellectuals step up, seize the center stage and proclaim their opposition to war. Intellectuals never sell-out, they are rented to the strongest party, the rising new political configuration. As opposition to the imperial war grows our progressive intellectuals become bolder.

In the war of words, the ideological warfare in the cultural sphere, our progressive intellectuals take on the neo-conservatives, they expose the lies of the mass media, they become the self-promoted "face of the opposition" to the outside world, even if their claims have little merit.

Even as the intellectuals diagnose the sources of wars, they overlook the specific and concrete configurations of power in favor of focusing on easy targets, ones which offer no threats to their professional careers and intellectual acceptance.

War and Oil

Let us turn to a specific imperialist war, the US invasion and colonial occupation of Iraq to illustrate how the progressive intellectual opposition to the war is profoundly influenced by a unique set of political allegiances.

Conventional wisdom among progressive intellectuals argues that the US invasion of Iraq is driven by US multinational oil companies seeking to control that country's oil resources. A more sophisticated version of this hypothesis argues that the war is directed by a strategic policy to monopolize oil as a weapon and hence dominate its imperial rivals in Europe and Asia. In both cases, the economic and strategic hypothesis, fail to take account of the political loyalties of the specific policymakers who designed the war, propagandized in favor of the war and became its most fanatical and influential executioners. Few if any of the progressive intellectuals examined the political loyalties of the key militarist policymakers.

The hypothesis that "oil" and the US petroleum multinationals were the main force behind the Iraq war fails every empirical test. If we examine the policy statements of the major oil companies and their public spokespeople in the five years leading up to the war we find no systematic political and propaganda campaign in favor of war. One looks in vain through all the major financial and specialized petroleum journals for evidence of organized pro-war politics. The reason is that the major oil companies were doing quite well with the status quo: profits and prices were reasonably high, investments were relatively secure, anti-imperialist sentiment was extensive but not intense and, most of all, opportunities for important new investments were opening in Saudi Arabia, Iran, Libya and possibly (via third parties) in Iraq.

The US war in Iraq and Afghanistan reversed the picture creating a very hostile environment, increasing dangers of destructive attacks, insecurity of Western personnel, and augmenting the power of OPEC against the major private US companies. Only a very few oil-related companies can be said to have benefited from the war – Haliburton, for example –most of which had direct ties to Vice President Cheney. They are the exception that proves the rule. The oil industry as an investor, producer and seller have not really benefited from the war. Even after the colonial occupation of Iraq, (and even after the illegal privatization of Iraq's state oil companies) the predominant sentiment among oil companies is at best ambivalent: while future opportunities may have increased so have the present threats to supply and transport.

The war has created greater volatility, favoring speculators over long-term oil investors. Moreover, rising prices prejudice the overall performance of the imperialist economies, adding costs, increasing trade imbalances and making the oil companies conspicuous targets of public ire. Moreover the unconditional support for Israel within the Bush Administration in the context of the Iraq war, has created a difficult climate for high level negotiations between the petroleum CEO's and the oil-rich Arab leaders.

In summary, there is no empirical evidence that the major oil companies drove US war policy either before or after the colonial occupation.

The second hypothesis argues that the war was part of a strategic policy to monopolize oil supply toward establishing the US as the undisputed world power, and subordinating Europe and Asia to its command. A corollary to this argument is that in the recent past US political and military triumphs, had been accompanied by a policy of sharing the spoils of imperial victories with their European and Japanese allies. The new US military doctrine of unilateral offensive wars (euphemistically referred to as "preventive wars") was designed to seize strategic advantage and claim exclusive control over the spoils of war: petroleum, military bases and trade routes. Imperialist strategic planners miscalculated, presuming an easy military victory over "the Arabs" and a rapid seizure and privatization of public enterprises and unhindered exploitation of oil wealth.

This hypothesis has a lot of merit in explaining some of the motivations – especially by focusing on the importance of the political decision-makers within the imperial state apparatus. However there are several important weaknesses in this hypothesis. For one, there was and is sharp differences between different power centers in the imperial state apparatus and even within each "center". For example, many of the top professional military commanders were opposed to the war, as were members of the State Department. CIA analysts did not share the assumptions that the colonized people would welcome the imperial armies. Numerous former high military, CIA officials, and United Nations weapons inspectors challenged the pretext put forth by the pro-war sectors of the US imperial state, that Iraq possessed weapons of mass destruction and posed a threat to the United States.

If the imperial state itself was divided and some sectors were not convinced of the need to go to war, which group was able to overcome that resistance, by-pass established intelligence channels (and create its own circuit), fabricate its own "intelligence and successfully lead the US to war? If war was not promoted by and in the interests of the US oil companies, and contrary to military doctrine of fighting two wars simultaneously, in whose geo-political interests was the war?

The War and the Israel-Zionist Hypothesis

The hypothesis which most fits the data is the Israel hypothesis – specifically that the principal architects and theoreticians of US world supremacy and the principal promoters of sequential wars, particularly in the Middle East, were influential Zionists in the top echelons of the Pentagon, National Security Council and in well-connected research centers "advising" the government while acting on behalf of the expansionist interests of the State of Israel.

The key author of the strategic doctrine of undisputed US world power was Wolfowitz, back in the first Bush Administration (1991). He joined with other influential Zionists like Richard Perle, Douglas Feith and a host of pro-Israel extremists to prepare a strategy paper for the Israeli state (1996) in which the Palestinians were to be physically driven from all of Palestine and Israel would become the regional power in the Middle East. Both Feith and Wolfowitz, early in their public careers were accused and chastised for turning US government documents over to the Israeli government. For at least twenty years they have been actively collaborating over Israeli policy and, in and out of government, they have worked intimately with Israeli officials in the United States and Israel.

The Zionist influentials, even before securing high positions in the Pentagon and State Department, were strong proponents of US military attacks against Israel's Middle East adversaries, which included Lebanon, Syria, Iran, Saudi Arabia and, of course, Iraq. Their militarist advocacy was independent of how such wars would affect US oil interests, regional stability, relations with Europe, the Muslim countries or the rest of the world.

The Pentagon Zionists were among the first to link Iraq with the events of 9/11 in an attempt to manipulate US public anger against the secular Iraqi state. They were responsible for fabricating the story that Iraq was importing uranium from Niger for the purposes of developing nuclear weapons. Wolfowitz admitted that he promoted the false pretext that Iraq possessed weapons of mass destruction to create a "consensus" to go to war – and every major Zionist writer and 'expert' pushed the same line.

The principal pro-Israeli lobby in the US, AIPEC, worked intensely and closely with the State of Israel, and the key Zionists in the Pentagon and their advisory groups in pushing for the US invasion of Iraq. Major Jewish organizations and influential propagandists in the mass media promoted the war, demonizing Iraq and fabricating stories of imminent threats.

The only major beneficiary of the US war in Iraq is the State of Israel: The war destroyed a major supporter of the Palestinian Intifada and Israel got a free hand in its terror and territorial colonization Palestinian land.

The US, isolated from almost all the major European powers and Islamic countries, because of its pro-Israel agenda, took on the pariah status of the Israeli clerical colonial regime. All the predictions and assumptions of the pro-war, anti-Arab Zionists were proven false. The Iraqi Arabs did not submit to the US occupation – they formed a potent resistance which engages the US in an increasingly prolonged war of attrition. The US intervention did not secure an oil monopoly; it has jeopardized its supply of oil in the Middle East by intensifying instability in Saudi Arabia. The war has soured US oil dealings in the Caucuses and resulted in speculative oil price increases, increasing the US trade deficit. Equally significant while the US is immersed in the Iraq War, China, India and Japan secure strategic oil and gas contracts in Asia and Latin America.

The Zionists were wrong in envisioning that the US would proceed to a series of successful wars with Israel's other enemies in the Middle East – Iran, Syria, Lebanon and Saudi Arabia. The Iraq invasion has tied down the vast majority of US active ground troops in a losing war with high casualties, thus at least, temporarily limiting its capacity to start new wars on behalf of the Empire or Israel. This has not prevented the Pentagon Zionists and their AIPEC allies from pushing for a new military attack on Iran and Syria.

Apart from England, Israel has been the major supporter and ally in the US conquest of Iraq for good reason: They are the principle beneficiaries.

The Pentagon Zionists and their zealous ideological allies have weakened the US economy by widening the trade deficit (via higher oil prices) and increasing the budget deficit (because of war spending). Israel has not suffered at all — on the contrary military sales to the US increased as well as revenues from the Pentagon for military advisory and training, missions to Iraq and elsewhere.

The US war in Iraq has several particularities as well as common characteristics with other wars. In the first place it demonstrates how a highly organized, ideologically coherent, financially powerful minority with highly placed co-thinkers in the top policy-making institutions of the imperial state can twist policy to suit the needs of a foreign power over and against established economic interests. Secondly the decisions about imperialist wars, though they usually serve the long-term interests of the dominant sectors of the capitalist class, are "made" by politicians, who have their own agendas, ideological and political loyalties which may or may not benefit (or prejudice) the ruling class.

The war in Iraq is a clear case in which the loyalties of the key architects of the war were distinct from those of the ruling class, who were barely taken into account, let alone consulted. The ruling ideology of the architects of war was 'Israel First, Last and Always'. To cover the Israel-centered war plans, the Zionists fabricated a series of "threats" to US interests which were made to parallel those faced by Israel: threats of weapons of mass destruction, terrorism and Muslim fundamentalism. Anti-Arab and anti-Muslim hate literature circulated in the mass media, in influential journals and talk shows as an army of Zionists ideologues went into an ideological frenzy -- infecting the US body politic – and setting off a secondary wave of vituperative froth from fundamentalist Christians, neo-conservative allies and liberal congress-people.

The generalized attack by the Zionists against Arab states and people was directed toward the strategic goal of extending Israeli domination beyond Palestine ("Greater Israel") not through direct colonization but via a series of client regimes beholden to the US – a US whose major foreign policy institutions would be subject to Zionist influence. The ideological formulae adopted to promote US-Israel dominance in the Arab world was "A Middle East Common Market" based on a campaign to "democratize the region". Both formulae served as the ideological basis for permanent war in the Middle East, the installment of dual purpose puppet regimes willing to serve both US energy interests and Israel's market penetration.

The Zionist ideologues' manipulation of "free market" and "democratic" rhetoric resonated widely among liberal and conservative imperialists, even as the US imperial state and Israel was denying Iraqi and Palestinians their elementary democratic rights and domestic markets. The tactics of the influential Zionists and their extensive networks in the US were directed at fusing Israeli expansionist interests with US imperialist goals, in order to legitimate their pursuit of Israeli state policies – a position echoed by President-elect Bush.

In the real world however, as the US continued to suffer heavy casualties in Iraq and the war debt grew by billions of dollars a day, and as its 'coalition partners' abandoned the war, the Zionist influentials inside and outside of the government intensified their pressure on the US to escalate its troop commitments in Iraq and to engage in new Middle East wars. The acid test of Zionist loyalties to Israeli interests is found in the fact that they pursued the war policy even as it weakened the US strategic global position, heightened discontent in the military and in elite civilian circles and increased the probability of an economic crisis resulting from the war deficits and weakening dollar. The Zionists in power are so embedded in the Israeli matrix, that they are totally impervious to the effects which their policies have on the US Empire, domestic economy or civil society.

In effect the US imperial attack of Iraq can be understood as a surrogate war for a regional power, designed and executed by influential policy-makers whose primary allegiance is to defend the interests of the regional power. The Zionist zealots have incorporated the same pathological style of mass paranoid politics prevalent in Israel to the US: the politics of permanent terrorist threats, of pervasive fear, of a hostile world, of unreliable allies... The Zionist zealots have led the ideological charge poisoning relations with France and other European countries which fail to respond favorable to the bloody repression of occupied peoples. No policy group has done more to weaken the sustainability of the US Empire than the Zionist zealots in government and the massive well-financed pro-Israel networks through the US. The Congress, the Executive branch, state and local governments, and national and local media have all come under the influence of the Jewish "lobby's" pro-Israel agenda to the point that none or few dare to criticize Israel or its US representatives.

The overweening power of the pro-Israel power configuration has inevitable provoked opposition – mainly from non-elected officials. The FBI (Federal Bureau of Investigation) is preparing to indict several high official from AIPEC, the most powerful representative of Israel's interests in the US, for spying on the US for Israel. Almost all the major Jewish organizations are preparing to defend AIPEC and its practice of twisting US policy toward the "Israel First" agenda. By early 2005, it was clear that the Zionist power structure had paralyzed the investigation. Numerous retired military and CIA officials have denounced Zionist power in designing and promoting the interests of Israel over US imperial interests. Meantime the Zionists along with the neo-conservatives successfully purged or "neutralized" independent analysts in the CIA, Defense and State Department who questioned the doctrine of sequential wars against Israel's adversaries in the Middle East. The Second Bush administration is completely controlled by the neo-conservative-Zionist extremists.

The conventional wisdom which perceives world imperial powers dictating policy to lesser regional powers clearly fails to deal with the US Middle East Wars. The reason why this common sense notion is inadequate is because it fails to deal with a series of unique (at least in modern history) phenomena affecting the policy-making structure of the US Empire – the active role of a privileged and influential minority deeply embedded in the decision-making structure and whose primary loyalty is to another state. It is as if the State of Israel has 'colonized' the main spheres of political power in the imperial state. These 'colons' however are not exactly transplants or emigrants from their "mother country". Rather they have mostly grown up and have been educated in the imperial center, they have pursued lucrative careers in the US and have, in most instances, been strong supporters of US imperial expansion and militarism. They have risen to and influenced the highest spheres of political power. They have not been discriminated against, nor have they suffered any economic, social or political exclusion. They have not been marginalized - they are integrated in the centers of power. Yet they have set themselves apart from the rest of the US citizens and conceive of themselves as having a special mission — of being first Jews who unconditionally support the State of Israel and all of its international projections of power. How can we explain this irrational embrace of a militarist state by a set of individuals who only vicariously share its life and destiny?

War in the 21st Century: Atavistic Behaviour

Schumpeter in his book, Imperialism and Social Class, written shortly after the First World War, attempted to square his argument that capitalism is opposed to war by citing the re-emergence of residual "atavistic" traits, embedded in previous feudal warrior societies, as the cause of war. While I do not share Schumpeter's view of the peaceful evolution of capitalism, particularly in the face of a series of imperialist wars in Asia, Africa, Latin America and Europe, his concept of atavistic behaviour is useful in explaining the irrational embrace of Israel by otherwise affluent, educated and highly influential Jews. Their embrace of Israel is certainly not for reasons of monetary remuneration, though Israel financially rewarded American-Jewish spies like Jonathan Pollard. What causes a modern or post-modern elite group to exhibit patterns of fanatical loyalty to a foreign militarist colonial power engaged in ethnic cleansing?

The Jewish-led and financed Zionist movement and its influential and wealthy supporters and leaders are a highly cohesive and disciplined group which exhibits zero tolerance against any Jewish dissidents or other critics of the warrior state or of their supporters anywhere in the world. What accounts for the apparent anomaly of highly educated professors, doctors, lawyers, investment bankers, media moguls and billionaire real estate tycoons giving unconditional support to a state engaged in primitive vindictive acts, of mass torture of prisoners, of collective punishment and guilt (destroying family homes of guerrilla suspects, taking family members hostage), systematically destroying farmland and uprooting hundreds of thousands of farmers, communities for almost six decades? They embrace ancient land claims and the vindictive and gratuitous humiliation of subjugated people based on mythological religious beliefs. The primitive belief in a "superior" or special people used to justify blood crimes harks back to the ritual barbarities of ancient tribal justice. This atavistic behavior is, however, tied to the most modern military technology in the hands of highly trained technical experts. The combination of tribal cohesion, religious mythology, high-tech weaponry and an overweening desire to exercise power on behalf of a military state based on 'racial-religious' exclusivity, is a potent concoction for US Zionists to inhale. Yet there are immense psychological satisfactions from being part of a powerful closed in-group, with a vision or fantasy of the revival of a lost 'kingdom', a sense of being part of superior people, members of a survivalist culture which has endured a unique suffering, and therefore possesses the righteousness to commit violence and use power to strike down adversaries anywhere and not to be bound by conventional international laws which only serve to limit the prerogatives of a 'righteous people'.

Tribal loyalties have tight rules of conduct for all who are considered members, whether they are active practitioners of Zionist politics or even critics of the State of Israel – home of the chosen people. Tribal rules are interpreted in different ways by different segments of the Jewish Diaspora. For the Presidents of the Major Jewish Organizations and their functionaries there are Five Commandments: (1) 'thou shalt not criticize any action by any Israeli leader at any time, no matter how heinous the crime, nor how often it is repeated, irregardless of how vast or intense world opprobrium', (2) 'Thou shall not allow any others to criticize or act contrary to Jewish State interests or to organizations which embrace the Zionist ideal,' (3) 'Every weapon, financial, physical, psychological, ideological and economic can be legitimately wielded to weaken, isolate, discredit or stigmatize critics of the Tribal Homeland or any of the overseas Tribal Organizations,' (4) 'Thou shall raise funds from all sources (legal or illegal), public, social or private to finance the military machine of the Tribal leaders – tribute secured from lesser "others" must enhance the security and living standards of the chosen people' and (5) 'Thou shall declare loyalty first and foremost to the tribal identity, then to the powers which support "our tribe" and lastly to "universal values"'.

Despite sharp criticism from a minority of dissident Jews, both in Israel, the US and elsewhere, there are certain unstated codes which are observed even by the most critical commentators. One is to never criticize or identify the power of the Jewish organizations in the US and their influence in the government. Jewish progressives de facto denial of Jewish power in shaping US war policy in the Middle East severely restricts the effectiveness of the anti-war movement by exonerating one of the key ideological props of the imperial war machine. The second unstated code followed by the "observant" progressive Jewish intellectuals is a denial that Israel has an important influence on US Middle East and global policy via its tribal loyalists in the US. Jewish progressives deliberately and systematically exclude any mention of Jewish power and influence in shaping US policy in the Middle East by focusing exclusively on "oil interests" or "neo-conservative ideologues" (who just coincidently are mostly tribespeople and their camp-followers). In deference to or more precisely because they share a deep underlying identity with the tribe –

they refuse to include any systematic study of the very obvious and blatant exercise of power in every branch of government, electoral processes and media reports. Likewise with the Middle East, Israel is considered by progressive Jews as an "instrument" of US imperialism even as the instrument cuts both ways – as Israel uses the US to savage its adversaries, to build up its military machine and to manufacture its commercial weapons systems to sell even to US competitors (i.e. China).

The emergence of atavistic behavior and its extension among the Zionist elite is a relatively recent development (over the past two decades) and goes contrary to the universalistic, secular and socialist values and practices as well as the traditional religious and communal practices and beliefs of many Jewish communities during previous centuries. The embrace of imperial power, the turn from religious communitarian values toward the embrace of the militaristic state of Israel, the shift from internationalism and socialism toward an unconditional embrace of a narrow exclusivist ideology has activated the latent atavistic behavior associated with vengeful killing of adversaries and blind singular loyalty to the idea of Israeli supremacy in the Middle East. Translated into the US context, it means virulent pro-war propaganda, advocacy of concentration camps for Islamic believers (as proposed by Daniel Pipes and others) and collaboration with Mossad agents in promoting Israel's strategic military, economic and political goals; by utilizing all the instruments of power within the US and with its overseas clients (Kurdish regions of Iraq, for example).

Atavistic behavior secures its goals through the shrewd manipulation and artificial inflation of "fears" emanating from Israel's enemies. The purpose is to create mass support in the US for wars on Israel's behalf. US Zionist ideologues, drawing heavily on the self-induced political isolation which the Israeli State has brought upon itself through its savage destruction of Arab Palestine, have elaborated and preached a paranoid view of the world, in which all international organizations (the UN, the World Court etc.) and forums, international opinions surveys, Europe, Asia, Latin America and Africa are accused of "anti-Semitism" because they recognize and condemn Israel's violation of Palestinian political and human rights.

The greater the "justifiable" violence of Israel, the wider the condemnation of its behavior, the more hysterical and strident the vituperation emanating from the major Zionist centers, the greater the concerted efforts to discredit the international bodies and to heighten US support. Just as an imaginary Neanderthal might bellow loudly and grab a heavy club when others protest his trespass of territory, so too do the Zionists reach for the club of US military power to pummel those who challenge Israel's transgressions.

"Atavistic behavior" is not confined to affluent Zionists, it is found among civilian militarists, Christian Zionists and other religious fundamentalists, who are defenders and practitioners of unrestrained violence and permanent imperial wars. Under the veneer of civilized discourse and moderate tonalities, is the barely restrained lust for unlimited power, total warfare and uncompromising savage torture. Atavistic behavior increasingly threatens to overwhelm the rational basis of economic calculation. The civilian militarist who may have originally been seen by many capitalists as one tool among others for conquering markets and seizing strategic resources have gradually taken a life of their own, subordinating capitalist interests to their raging quest for unlimited power. Atavistic behavior is both the apogee of US imperial power and its ultimate regress to the dark ages.

Contemporary and future wars in the Middle East cannot be explained merely by reciting an inventory of economic resources and matching them with imperial strategic designs. This rationalist-economistic reductionism fails to take account of specific ideological, irrational political determinants which have demonstrated greater explanatory power.

Privatization and War

One of the strategic goals of imperialist policy-makers is the privatization of public resources as an "end" in itself and as a means of securing political, social, economic and cultural control over a country in order to enhance empire-building.

Privatization strategies are pursued by political as well as military means, either through military invasions or via military coups by surrogate military juntas. Privatization is a first step toward de-nationalization and re-colonization of the economy and state.

De-nationalization of the economy usually follows the imposition by imperial lending agencies of a macro-political strategy dubbed structural adjustment policies which include among other measures privatizations of public enterprises – especially strategies sectors such as energy, petroleum, metals, telecommunications, finance and banking. The move toward de-nationalization follows one of two paths – either th direct purchase by foreign companies of national assets or a two-step process, whereby the nationalist capitalists first buy the public enterprise and then re-sell it to foreign capital.

Whether directly or indirectly, privatization means foreign control over essential economic decisions (investment, marketing, transfer of profits etc) in strategic sectors of the economy. Foreign control of strategic industries means the power of decision over local industries and exploitation of natural resources.

Beyond the economic consequences of privatization/ de-nationalization (P/D), it is a political instrument of empire-building strategies:

1. P/D involves the recruitment of 'national executives', financial officers, publicists, managers, economists who become an active political base in backing and promoting deeper and more extensive colonization as well as political submission to imperial power.
2. The chief executive officers of P/D enterprises play a leading role in influencing and directing sectoral organizations (automobile and parts manufacturers, banking associations, mine-owners' consortiums, etc.), thus "hegemonizing" the national capitalists within the associations and securing their acquiescence in imperial-colonial projects.
3. P/D firms can work in tandem with the imperial state to pressure a regime to follow imperial policies by decreasing economic production or by dis-investing. For example, in the 1960's the State Department ordered the US-owned oil refineries to refuse to process Cuban oil imports from

Russia in order to overthrow the Castro government.

4. The US government frequently plants 'agents' (CIA and FBI) in US-owned multi-national corporations (MNCs). The MNCs provide a "legal cover" for intelligence agents involved in destabilization campaigns, espionage and recruitment of local business and trade union leaders to serve imperial interests.
5. P/D firms provide imperialist policy-makers with additional leverage to pressure a regime to submit to IMF policies and to support colonial rule via ALCA.
6. P/D provide a pretext for imperial intervention and conquest, using the excuse that the invaders are "protecting the property rights of US citizens.
7. P/D provide a "beach head" for multiplying privatization using local allies and political influence, following the initial takeovers. P/D have a "falling dominoes" effect, leading to cumulative power, from enterprise to enterprise, from sector to sector, from economy to media, from economy and media to political control. P/D has a catalytic effect in strengthening imperial policy-makers and forcing the hand of any recalcitrant regime.

The Dialectics of Privatizations/De-nationalization and War

Wars are motivated by and result in the privatization and de-nationalization of publicly owned properties. Likewise, privatizations lead to war in order to protect and prevent the re-nationalization of strategic industries. Privatizations are frequently accompanied or followed by the granting of military bases, thus strengthening the colonial presence and weakening the sovereignty of Third World countries. At a minimum, privatizations almost always are accompanied by military "co-operative agreements" and "mutual defense agreements" which, in effect, allow for the presence of US military advisers in the Ministries of Defense, the indoctrination and training of military officials and a "legal formula" allowing US military intervention if and when a client regime is threatened. In other words, privatization and de-nationalization weakens the Third World state – deprives the state of economic resources, revenues and levers of power, while severely restricting its sovereignty. Weakened clients often supply mercenary soldiers for future imperial wars and colonial occupation, such as in Iraq, Afghanistan and Haiti.

Colonial Wars in the 21st Century

In the 21st century, imperial wars, especially multiple colonial wars requiring military occupation of a colonized country, can only be sustained by recruiting mercenary soldiers from client regimes. The US imperial armed forces are incapable of sustaining a colonial occupation in the face of a prolonged peoples war without large-scale mercenary support from client regimes. This is very evident today in Iraq (and Afghanistan), where the US colonial officials and their puppet regime are desperately trying to assemble an army of Iraqi and Afghan mercenaries to take the brunt of "security duties" (repression of the colonized people). The US colonial army, particular the Army Reservists, is demoralized and has experienced a sharp decline in re-enlistment.

Given the imperialist involvement in two countries (Iraq and Afghanistan), Washington turned to recruiting military mercenaries from its Latin American client regimes to provide several thousand officers and soldiers to prop up the US puppet regime in Haiti. Since the imperial strategists particularly the neo-conservatives and Zionists have made military conquest the centerpiece of imperial expansion, it is the military which has paradoxically become the "weakest link" in the imperial chain which extends from imperial war to colonial occupation and control, to P/D to economic pillage.

In the past the US imperial state engaged in external and internal wars to P/D strategic industries. The US overthrow of the Arbenz regime in Guatemala (1954), the Mossadegh regime in Iran in 1953, the failed effort to invade Cuba in 1961, the CIA engineered coup in Chile (1973), the US Contra-War in Nicaragua (in the 1980's) were all directed toward P/D of the economies as well as serving imperial geo-political strategies.

In recent years however, the imperial state has increasingly relied on financing civilian electoral politicians and pressure from the international financial institutions to implement P/D. Only in the Middle East where Zionist-Israeli power is factored in has military invasion become the policy of choice. The reliance on war to privatize and colonize continues to operate where imperial-financed civilian electoral strategies have failed. Two recent cases come to mind.

The US 'internal' war in Venezuela, where a US-financed and directed coup briefly (48 hours) overthrew the elected President Chavez is a case in point. In that short period of time, the puppet Carmona regime immediately broke relations with Cuba, withdrew from

OPEC and began to draw up plans to privatize the state petroleum company before popular power restored Chavez and rescinded the decrees. The US-sponsored coup and subsequent 'bosses lock-out' in the oil industry were part of an internal war strategy designed to circumvent an unfavorable setting for a manipulated electoral outcome.

Likewise in Yugoslavia, the US, in alliance with European imperialism, launched an unprovoked military invasion, using Croatian and Kosovar terrorists to destroy the Yugoslav nation and set up mini-states in which former self-managed enterprises were P/D'd, major military bases were established and mercenary troops were recruited for the Middle East colonial wars.

Privatization and de-nationalization whether it occurs through imperial wars or via subsidized client electoral politicians however entails inter-imperialist competition and conflict over which the imperialist states will seize the most lucrative ex-public firms. The experience in Eastern Europe and Latin America suggests that US political successes resulted in European powers securing most of the privatized firms and most lucrative oil, telecommunication and financial enterprises. Similarly in the Yugoslav break-up, the Europeans secured influence and control over the richest mini-states, Croatia and Slovenia, while the US colonized the poorest, mafia-states – Kosovo, Macedonia, Montenegro and Bosnia.

The turn to unilateralist imperialist wars reflected this reality of unequal benefits from co-operative US-EU imperial wars. The US unilateral invasion of Iraq was designed to maximize US control of the forthcoming privatization and de-nationalization of Iraqi oil industry and to undercut European benefits from the post-war "reconstruction" as well as to privilege Israeli interests in the Middle East.

If imperialist expansion is linked to P/D, the competition and conflict between US and EU imperialism shapes the forms and methods through which that expansion takes place. The US resort to unilateral (forms) and military (means) is related to its "comparative advantage" in military weaponry and the predominance of militarist civilian decision-makers. The doctrines of "total war", "offensive wars", and unipolar world supremacy were all designed and implemented by a special elite of political ideologues, with specific set of political attributes – they lack direct ties to the traditional military hierarchy and have demonstrated contempt for the military and intelligence commands. These civilian militarists conceive of themselves as an elite chosen to carry out the mission of terrorizing real or imagined adversaries overseas and punishing, expelling or silencing traditional military and intelligence rivals within the state. Their extremist militarism is directly related to their distance from the actual "blood and guts" of mass killing of civilians and ground level military casualties and their proximity to the Israeli State.

Their arrogance in exercising power is matched by their abject ignorance of the political and economic conditions and consequences of their decisions. Their blind subservience to serving Israel's interests led them to "miscalculate" the massive degree of Iraqi opposition to the war and occupation. Their quest for world domination led to unsustainable multiple military invasions, leading to the weakening of the US Empire. Their militarist logic revealed their abysmal ignorance of the enormous destruction of lucrative Iraqi assets and the cost of war of war to the US economy. These policies forced sharp divisions within the imperial state. In response, the extremists in the Pentagon have seized control over intelligence functions and special forces operations, involving clandestine operations. The Second Bush administration is more extreme and even more aggressive than the first. The political conflict within the State is extending into civil society where over half of the population opposes the plans for new wars. Instead of adopting an empire-building strategy mixing economic, political and diplomatic pressures with selective wars, the civilian militarists have, in the Middle East, relied exclusively on military strategies. Even within this one-sided military approach, they have chosen the most extreme measures, unilateral permanent wars, as opposed to coalitions (and joint colonial spoils) and limited wars (in time and place). Military extremism in pursuit of unsustainable colonial war is no virtue.

Israel's dirty little colonial war, despite its daily civilian assassinations, terror bombings and ritual torture and humiliation of the Palestinians has not succeeded in 60 years of warfare against 3 million Palestinians even with universal conscription and life-time military reservists. The civilian militarists in the imperial state have learned nothing from Israel's failures: For them Israel can do no wrong, it can never fail, it is their living ideological model of the military will to conquer. Our own civilian militarists, in their exalted hubris believe that 150,000 colonial forces could defeat 200,000 armed resistance fighters backed by over 20 million fellow citizens.

The Mind of the Civilian Militarists

One of the key aspects of the civilian militarists' rise to power has been their ability to apply organizational principles which further their political programmes. Their procedures, while not usually spelled out in a written document, can be deduced from their organizational behavior. For brevity of space, we can spell out their modus operendi:

1. Precipitate war thus precluding public debate and systematic analysis of who benefits and who loses, and the tactical gains and strategic costs. Given that the civilian militarists came to power with an already fixed doctrine and a disciplined cohort, it was not difficult for them to impose their views over their fragmented and dispersed rivals and opponents within the military and government bureaucracy. Taking advantage of the notion of "civil supremacy" they were able to impose their extreme militarist war doctrines on their critics within the traditional military leadership, whom they attacked as being "too bureaucratic and cautious". In effect their ultra-voluntarism military doctrines conflicted with the more rational-calculated policies of the established military strategists.

2. Facilitating an apocalyptic event was an essential element in the ascendancy of the civil militarist in imperial policy-making positions and the seizure of war making powers. Massive documentation and critical analysis drawn from official intelligence sources reveal that the civilian militarists were knowledgeable and actively involved in facilitating the terrorist

attack on September 11, 2001. The civilian militarists, on the day of the terrorist event, set in motion their Middle East war agenda and proceeded to propound and implement their extremist "offensive war" agenda. They deliberately induced and magnified a paranoid style of politics which centered on an immediate world-wide terrorist threat to millions of defenseless civilians based on nuclear, biological and chemical warfare (despite that fact that 9/11 terrorist attack was carried out with cheap plastic box-cutters). This unprecedented bizarre ideological "terror campaign" orchestrated by the civilian militarists resonated strongly with the paranoid politics of the Israeli regime which urged a Judeo-Christian Crusade against a worldwide Islamic terrorist threat.

3. Messianic missions are a constant component of the civilian militarist mentality. These are partly cynical exercises in the manipulation of universal democratic ideals and partly the result of a fervor for US world supremacy. Messianic missionary zeal has the intended consequence of providing a self-justification for gross violations of human rights, international and domestic laws. The civil militarists know that their military invasions willingly destroy democratic rights of self-determination, that their advocacy of military occupation lead to the denial of the rights of democratic self-government, yet they proclaim their goal is to "democratize the Middle East", a claim which is echoed in the mass media. Cynicism aside, the Messianic mission fuels the vituperative attacks against real or imagined

critics which accompanies authoritarian repressive measures aimed at intimidating critics, and inciting arbitrary arrests, indefinite jailing and the use of torture against suspects.

4. Moralistic military campaigns have the virtue of not having to provide facts to justify violent assaults on peoples and nations. The issue for the civilian militarists is not whether an attack or a military threat really exists. The essential element for them is that there is a self-defined world of "good" and "evil" — a virtuous world power (US) united with its regional accomplice (Israel) against an evil "other" (Muslim, Third World, independent state) hostile to US empire building and Israeli colonization. Moral crusaders among the civilian militarists believe that the masses need to be deceived by a "Noble Lie", because the masses are incapable of understanding the "higher truth" of the virtues of permanent war to secure US world supremacy and a "Greater Israeli" regional mini-empire. Many progressive critics have spilled gallons of ink refuting the lies of the civilian militarists regarding Iraq's weapons of mass destruction, Saddam's links to Al Queda. This is a worthy enterprise but one which is irrelevant to the civilian militarists, because, for them "truth" is embodied in their (military) actions and not in the pretext (lies) that they expounded. Insofar as the lies "worked", that is insofar as they were able to launch a war, prepare for other wars, terrorize the population into supporting war, and seize control of the levers of power, a "higher truth" became a reality: the beginning of permanent offensive warfare.

5. The doctrine of "living space" is intimately related to the civilian militarist practice of permanent war. In their paranoid voluntaristic vision, no place and no time is secure. Threats exist in a series of concentric circles from the Middle East Islamic people (surrounding Israel) outward toward Asia, North Africa, and Western Europe... Security threats are present among "Old European States" and Third World countries which refuse to subordinate themselves to US security forces. In order to achieve "living space" in the US and wherever its business interests, military bases and operation can (or should) have a dominant presence, the issue of "security" becomes a code word for perpetual overt or clandestine military, political and ideological warfare. Ultimately, for the civilian militarists, only a world in which the US exercises absolute supreme sovereign imperial power will result in secure living space.

To enhance their power in the imperial state, the civilian militarists have pursued a number of organizational reforms. For illustrative purposes we can cite at least three types of "reforms" and their stated rationale and real purpose:

1. *Organizational decentralization:* Civilian militarists argue that there are too many bureaucratic and political constraints on timely and efficient decisions in a time of imminent threats of terror. In a time of national emergency, established "bureaucracy" becomes part of the threat rather than part of the solution. This is the formal rationale to disguise the real purpose which is to concentrate power in the hands of

civilian militarists in the Pentagon elite and among the neo-conservatives in the National Security Council. The "reform" is designed to bypass existing lines of command until they can be purged and replaced by civilian militarist loyalists.

2. *The establishment of non-traditional sources of information (intelligence):* Civilian militarists argue that the traditional existing intelligence agencies are ineffective, inaccurate and cumbersome. They argue for "broadening" the basis of intelligence gathering, "diversifying" sources and by-passing cumbersome bureaucracies and securing "direct lines" from the field in order to take decisive action in a timely fashion. The real purpose of the civilian militarists is to create their own parallel "sources" to fabricate intelligence in pursuit of their permanent war doctrine.

3. *Greater 'cooperation' with acknowledged friendly states with a long-term, in-depth experience in the area of terrorist warfare:* The formal rational for this "reform" advocating "special relations" with overseas experts is that the imperialist state can save time, build on existing expertise, avoid making mistakes through trial and error and duplication by creating new bureaucracies. In addition the civilian militarists, especially the Zionists, look at the Israeli "anti-terrorist" apparatus as a successful model, despite the fact that Israel is the most likely site of terrorist action. The real purpose is to strengthen ties with the State of Israel, to increase biased information and disinformation flows in order to

mold US imperial policies around Israel's Middle East interests. Since the Pentagon Zionists have the best and most intense relations with Israel who is better placed to facilitate joint cooperation than these very same ideologues

Conclusion

War, specifically US imperialist war, doctrine is made up of several sub-tests and key concepts such as a "unipolar world", offensive, permanent wars and extra-territorial jurisdiction. The doctrine is based on the belief of imperial invincibility – based on mass media imagery of successful US warriors-supermen representing a righteous superpower.

The key to understanding the source and practitioners of these doctrines is found in the ascendancy of a "new class" of civilian militarists (CM) and their think-tank auxiliaries and civil society supporters who have triggered catastrophic events to facilitate their dominant position in the imperial state. The ascent of the CM has not gone uncontested both from inside the imperial state and from without, especially from former traditional military and intelligence leaders.

In the new millennium a combination of circumstance and timing as well as calculated long-term positioning, has enabled a specific group of civilian militarists to achieve strategic positions in the imperil state – namely Zionist ideologues intimately involved in long-term relations with the state of Israel.

These ideologues and their civilian militarists cohort have pushed to the limit their psychological warfare designed to terrorize the mass of the population to follow their extremist doctrine and make the financial and human sacrifices for on-going wars.

This paper demonstrates that the decisions to launch imperial wars today are not simply the result of the economic interests of US multi-nationals (petroleum or otherwise). In the case of the Middle East, many of the decision-makers did not consult nor were they influenced by oil or other economic interests – most of the multinationals had on-going, lucrative and stable working relations with conservative oil producing Arab elites. At most some oil companies were promised future benefits via privatization of public oil facilities.

Imperial war was designed and driven by a set of policymakers with little interest in or no notion of the economic costs of war. The driving force for the war is found among civilian militarists who facilitated and capitalized on a catastrophic event (9/11) which allowed them to bypass traditional military and intelligence hierarchies. Internal consent for extremist militarism was induced through massive, intense and continuous fear propaganda fomented by the civilian militarists to consolidate their power. The psychological-ideological campaign allowed for vast expenditures of resources and civilian militarist monopoly over imperial policy. War took on a special meaning for the Zionist component of the civilian militarists – serving as a prop for enhancing Israel's regional power.

While the ideological dominance and psychological control exercised by the civilian militarists over the masses is formidable it is profoundly vulnerable. The constant and irreversible defeats suffered by the US colonial army in Iraq have demonstrated that the US imperial army is not invincible. The incapacity for the

US to move on to new ground wars has temporarily challenged the doctrine of permanent offensive wars. The mass discontent within the colonial army has undercut and exposed the irrationality of the civilian militarists. Their proposals for increasing troop levels in Iraq, augmenting the recruitment of soldiers, that is, deepening US involvement in an un-winnable war is leading to greater casualties, deeper discontent at home and greater resistance in Iraq, and severely straining the crisis-ridden US economy. Escalation of war to Iran based on irrational voluntarism will bring the civilian militarists into greater conflict with traditional economic and military power centers. Capitalist rationality, based on cost-benefit calculations, is likely to challenge the atavistic behavior of the civilian warlords, leading to greater internal divisions within the empire and without.

Inter-elite conflicts may serve to activate sectors of the 'rational' middle class concerned with the long-term, large-scale interests of empire against the civilian-militarists and their associated power worshipers. "Living space" security doctrines will continue to be played out but in more select locations and within the boundaries of imperial capacity to recruit clients and imperial allies. Wars, which endanger the military status of the imperial state, will be recast in terms of spheres of influence – in which big powers interests will marginalize the exaggerated and inflated role of Israel in world and regional politics. Today the future of the US Empire and particularly the future of its civilian militarists depend on how decisively the empire is defeated in the Middle East. As goes the war in the Middle East, so go the future methods of imperial expansion.

The total military debacle of the civilian militarists and their Zionist core in the Middle East will probably result in a rethinking of the meaning, purposes and goals of imperial wars. Most likely, the economic costs and benefits of imperial wars will return to the center of elite debate, without the bias of third countries interests. These elite debates will attempt to forge a new more limited and 'rational' model of world empire.

The issue of turning from empire toward a more 'republican' style of politics can only be taken up in another venue, within mass-based anti-imperialist movements which will begin among the colonial subjects of imperial centers but may include the excluded and exploited within the imperial capitals.

4

The House of Horrors: Torture and Genocide

James Petras - June 12, 2004

When future historians write of the US empire, they will emphasize the process of empire building, methods of rule, the principle ideologues, and how at a particular moment in time a small, dependent state – Israel – was able to shape US war policy to suit its needs.

Empire Building

Military violence, direct and through surrogates, was crucial to the expansion and consolidation of the empire in South and Central America and the Caribbean – from 1964 to 1990 US-backed surrogate military regimes and paramilitary forces took power in Argentina, Brazil, Peru, Chile, Uruguay, Bolivia, Dominican Republic – and later in Guatemala, El Salvador, Honduras, Nicaragua and Panama. Over 500,000 people were slaughtered in order to impose the imperial centered system of accumulation (later called "neo-liberalism"). Imperial strategy of invasion and intervention established the parameters for long-term consolidation: An economic system 'open' to imperial penetration and control ("free market economies") and a state apparatus (judiciary, military, central bank etc.) capable of deepening and consolidating the imperial centered economy. Subsequently the domesticated electoral politicians accepted the imperial parameters and Washington encouraged political competition. In the case of Mexico, voter fraud ensured the election in 1988 of "President" Salinas who proceeded to "integrate" Mexico via NAFTA into the US Empire.

A similar process took place in Africa. Between 1970 to the 1990's, massive US military intervention and support of "surrogate" mercenaries aided by US strategic ally, South Africa, killed millions in Angola, Mozambique, Guinea Bissau, Congo, destroying the economic and political basis for development and establishing client regimes. These mineral and oil rich countries were incorporated into the empire. In the case of South Africa the leadership of the African National Congress was coerced and then co-opted and became an integral part of the Euro-US imperial system. Similar processes took place in Asia where imperial wars were followed by economic 'openings' extending imperial dominance throughout the region...at the cost of over seven million dead Koreans, Indochinese, Filipinos, Indonesians and Timorese.

Between the 1990's to the present the US empire expanded into the Balkans, Eastern Europe, the Baltic countries, Central Asia and the Caucuses by aggressive ideological intervention aided by the corruption and deep rot in the dominant Communist parties ruling in those countries. The Middle East, Southwest Asia and the Balkans were next, in part, because they are integral to exploiting oil resources, building pipelines and building military bases. Yugoslavia, Afghanistan and Iraq were invaded. Satellite regimes were established in Kosovo, Macedonia and Serbia. A US puppet regime in Kabul rules in alliance with opium-subsidized mercenary warlords. Iraq was invaded, occupied and ruled by a US pro-consul. The US Empire is built on wars, using its own military forces, surrogate mercenaries and paramilitary forces.

Imperial Consolidation

To sustain power in the face of mass anti-imperial resistance, the US state has repeatedly violated all international conventions and laws: Torture of prisoners, mass killings of civilians, destruction of infrastructure and historical sites, the pillaging of natural resources, and the establishment of a client colonial state and imperial-centered economy.

The US conquest of Iraq is the latest example of empire building with its own particularities. The most salient feature of the imperialist conquest of Iraq is the exposé of the brutal methods of imperialist rule.

We have all read and seen photos of large scale, systematic torture of thousands of Iraqi citizens, suspected of being freedom fighters. Torture has been the principle source of "information" to buttress colonial rule. The model of rule via mass torture and sexual violence is heavily influenced by the Israeli experience, where nearly half of the male adult Palestinian population has been incarcerated and subject to "legalized" Israeli torture. This is not a circumstantial coincidence. The main ideologues defending torture include the most prestigious Zionist academics and policy makers in the United States. Harvard Law

Professor Alan Dershowitz, Princeton Professor Bernard Lewis, William Kristol, Yale Professor Robert Kagan, John Hopkins Professor Eliot Cohen, to name only a few of the Zionist totalitarian ideologues, defending Israeli terror and US imperial force. Mass systematic torture in Iraq was the first but not the most important revelation of imperial rule. Within the Pentagon the top leaders, Rumsfeld, Wolfowitz and Feith specifically ordered the use of torture while the Justice and Defense Departments insisted that the President could override any laws – international or national and the US Constitution – in defending the empire. In other words, torture was seen as a special Presidential power beyond any legislative or legal restraint. Ruling an empire knows no legal restraint. De facto and de jure dictatorial powers of the President are assumed in securing 'Imperial Security'.

The third revelation resulting from the exposé of torture exposed an empire operating with a highly organized network of assassins throughout the world, killing, kidnapping and torturing "suspects" and sympathizers of resistance movements. 'Murder Incorporated' is called the *Special Agency Program (SAP)* and is composed of highly trained Special Forces (Army), SEALS (Navy), and DELTA Force. The SAP violate the sovereignty of every country in the world, engages in criminal behavior conducive to capital crimes including frequent arbitrary extra-judicial murder of suspected "terrorists" or sympathizers. Their model is the Mossad policy of "selective assassinations" of suspects. As the empire expands and the anti-imperialist resistance grows worldwide, the SAP acts as an international death squad of the US imperial terror network.

Ideologues of Imperial/Colonial Terror

The destruction of Iraq's historical existence as a sovereign nation – the pillage of its archeological museums and historical sites, libraries and archives, the violent intrusions into sacred sanctuaries, the humiliation of its people via torture, collective punishment and sexual violence are all designed to destroy the country's historical identity as an Arab nation. The purpose is to create mini-states based on tribes, religion and ethnicity, to divide and rule. The model is the Israeli policy toward the Palestinians. Israel's practice of sexual humiliation of Palestinians (and Lebanese) has been routine (rapes, stripping and hooding of prisoners). Collective punishment and taking family members hostage are legally condoned and extensively practiced in Israel. The recent Rafah/Jenin invasions demonstrate the extremities of colonial savagery and inhumanity.

The Israelis deny the Palestinians their past as a nation, their land as a place to live, and their right to govern themselves. So do the US Imperial rulers in Iraq. They constantly work to ethnicize the conflict, deny the existence of the Iraqi nation, the people and their history. The US, like Israel, has taken land, resources and built fortresses and walls of segregation. A group of extremist Zionist scholars have contributed to the totalitarian denial of Arab culture led by the virulent Bernard Lewis (see From Babel to Dragomans). Recently Martin Wolf of the Financial Times justifies imperial wars throughout the world, rejecting national sovereignty and defending US-European and Israeli conquest of "failed states". (Financial Times, June 9, 2004 p. 5).

Conclusion

We, in the United States, live in a House of Horrors – where empire building via torture and assassination is executive policy, where White House approved torture is exposed in the media but continues to be state practice. The mass media promoters and publicists of the House of Horrors, count on our short memory: They praise Ronald Reagan, whose infamous presidency marks a decade of genocide against Mayan Indians in Guatemala (300,000), in Nicaragua (50,000), El Salvador (75,000), Honduras (several thousands). It was Reagan who publically defended General Rios Montt, the butcher of Guatemala, from criticism for human rights abuses ("He's getting a raw deal".) and who praised the butchers of Afghanistan's secular society as "The moral equivalent of our founding fathers". The White House, Pentagon, State Department, CIA, each in its turn has its own "side show" of horrors: Colin Powell's blatant lies in the United Nations on weapons of mass destruction, the Pentagon promoting torture, the CIA practicing assassinations.

The continuity of torture and mass murder, between the past Reagan regime to the present Bush regime is not merely due to many of the same political criminals (Wolfowitz, Abrams, Cheney and Rumsfeld) but to the politics of imperial conquest, destruction and extermination.

The House of Horrors does not merely replay the past scenarios for the same ideological and political interests. Today's horror show has many of the same cast but with different directors and producers. In Central America and Southern Africa, fanatical anti-Communists were in command. Today it is the extremist Zionist militarists in the Pentagon who direct the US

Horror Show in Iraq. Unlike Reagan's Cold Warriors, today we have prestigious professors who provide the justification for unrestrained state terrorism. More than ever in recent US history there is a long list of distinguished professors who line up to defend the House of Horrors, the Prisons of Torture, the Seminars on Dehumanizing Arabs. These prestigious professors turn millions of victims into terrorists, all the better to justify their brutalization. All of them are unconditional supporters of Israel, its paranoid politics, its routinized torture, its nuclear threats to humanity, its savage assaults of Palestinians. They appear constantly in all the mass media, spewing their ideological venom: Perle, Abrams, Wolfowitz, Stern, Dershowitz, Cohen, Kagan, Kristol, Rubin, Adelman, Lewis, Pollock and many more. Their primary loyalty is in joining US imperialism and Israeli colonialism into one marvelous House of Horrors, under the big tent of a "Mid East Democratic Reform Initiative". Zionist influence on Washington's criminal policies in the Middle East in favor of Israel is transparent. We should remember however that the "House of Horrors" has a history which preceded the Zionist ascendancy and will certainly continue after their influence has declined. The deeper problem is empire building – imperialism –, which provokes popular resistance to which the empire responds with torture and genocide. To end torture and defeat colonial powers overseas, we must resolutely confront their supporters and ideologues at home, whatever their ethnic or religious affiliations. We must not let their ideological fanaticism and aggression silence us from engaging a growing majority in the Americans opposed to the war and Zionist terror.

5

US–Iraq–Israel–Zionist Connection

James Petras and Robin Eastman-Abaya
May 25, 2004

Why did the US go to war against Iraq in March 2003 with further plans to attack Syria, Iran and probably Lebanon? None of the reasons thus far given provide a shred of evidence. No weapons of mass destruction have been discovered. No ties between Iraq and Al Queda have been established. No threats to US security existed. Many of the US past and present allies have equal or worse human rights records than Iraq. The war, the conquest, occupation, killing and vile systematic torture and imprisonment of thousands of Iraqis has aroused the hostility and indignation of hundreds of millions of Christians, Muslims and free thinkers throughout the world, justly discrediting the whole political establishment in Washington and overseas. US oil companies have been unable to benefit in the face of a growing anti-colonial resistance, their investments throughout the Middle East and South Central Asia are under siege. The OPEC countries for a time rejected US and EU pressures to pump more oil to lower sky-high prices – partly a hostile response to the US invasion of Iraq.

Who benefited then from the US war? By examining the beneficiaries we can get an idea who had a motive for promoting this crime against humanity. The only major beneficiary of the war is the State of Israel, which succeeded in having the US destroy its most consistent Arab adversary in the Middle East – the regime that extended the greatest political support to the Palestinian resistance. Together with Iran and Syria they formed the core resistance to Israeli expansionist plans to expel the Palestinians and conquer and occupy all of Palestine. The plan to "democratize" the Middle East proposed by US Zionists in the government in essence meant a joint control by the US and Israel over the entire Middle East via a series of wars.[1]

What were the obstacles to Greater Israel? First the Intifada, the uprising of Palestinians who refused to be driven out of their country and was able to inflict losses on the self-styled Chosen People of God (Israel is by law an exclusively Jewish state, inhabited by immigrants mainly from Europe and their children and governed by exclusionary religious dogma). Secondly Hezbollah had inflicted a strategic military-political defeat on Israel, forcing them and their client Lebanese Maronite Christian mercenary allies to evacuate from Southern Lebanon. Thirdly Iraq, Iran and Syria, the three countries which were most consequential in their opposition to Israeli annexation and regional domination, were developing economic and political ties with a multitude of countries and especially in the case of oil contracts, signing trade and exploitation agreements with Japan, China, Russia as well as Western European corporations. Israel's hopes for sharing Washington's co-prosperity economic sphere of domination based on servile, client Arab regimes were increasingly doubtful. Fourthly the Iraqi regime was slowly recovering, despite the decade long US-European boycott and constant military aggression. With time running out, the Israelis and their Zionist agents in the Bush administration realized that an agreement to end the boycott and normalize relations with Iraq was on the horizon. Finally there was a deepening internal crisis in Israel over the economic costs and personal insecurity accompanying the policy of the criminal settlements and savage repression in the occupied territories. Israel's out-migration exceeded its in-migration, its Jewish based welfare policies were in tatters, and hundreds of active reservists refused military duty in the dirty colonial war.

A series of US wars against independent Arab regimes, beginning with Iraq, was clearly in the interests of the Israeli state and so it was perceived by the Sharon regime, its secret police (Mossad), the Israeli military and right-wing Zionists in positions of influence in Washington.

How was the Israeli state able to influence the US imperial state into pursuing a series of wars, which would imperil its own imperial economic and security interests and further those of Israel?

The most direct answer is to be found in the role played by key pro-Zionist officials in and around the most important policymaking positions in the Bush administration. These US officials had long-standing ideological and political ties to the Israeli state, including policy advisory positions. Throughout most of their political lives they had dedicated themselves to furthering Israel's state interests in the US. While the design and execution of the US war strategy was in the hands of Zionist civilian militarists in the Pentagon they were only able to succeed because of the powerful support exercised by Sharon's acolytes in the major Jewish organizations in the US. The Presidents of the Major Jewish Organizations, the Anti-Defamation League, AIPAC, and thousands of their activists – doctors, dentists, philanthropists, real estate brokers, financiers, journalists, media moguls and academics – acted in concert with key Jewish politicians and ideologues to press the case for a war, because they would argue, it was in the interest of the state of Israel to destroy Saddam Hussein and the secular Baath Party state apparatus.

Israel and the US: A Unique Relationship

U.S.-Israel relations have been described in a variety of ways. Politicians refer to Israel as the U.S.'s most reliable ally in the Middle East, if not the world. Others speak of Israel as a strategic ally. Some speak of Israel and the U.S. sharing common democratic values in the war against terrorism. On the Left, critics speak of Israel as a tool of U.S. imperialism for undermining Arab nationalism, and a bulwark against fundamentalist Islamic terrorism. A few writers point to the "excess influence" which the Israeli governments exercise on U.S. government policy via powerful Jewish lobbies and individuals in media, financial and governmental circles.

While there is a grain of truth in much of the above there is a unique aspect in this relationship between an imperial power like the U.S. and regional power such as Israel. Unlike Washington's relation with the EU, Japan and Oceana, it is Israel which pressures and secures vast transfer of financial resources ($2.8 billion per year, $84 billion over 30 years)[2]. Israel secures the latest arms and technology transfers, unrestrictive entry into U.S. markets, free entry of immigrants, unconditional commitment of U.S. support in case of war and repression of colonized people and guaranteed U.S. vetoes against any UN resolutions.

From the angle of inter-state relations, it is the lesser regional power which exacts a tribute from the Empire, a seeming unique or paradoxical outcome. The explanation for this paradox is found in the powerful and influential role of pro-Israel Jews in strategic sectors of the U.S. economy, political parties, Congress and Executive Branch. The closest equivalent to past empires is that of influential white settlers in the colonies, who through their overseas linkages were able to secure subsidies and special trading relations.

The Israeli "colons" in the U.S. have invested and donated billions of dollars to Israel, in some cases diverting funds from union dues of low paid workers to purchase Israel bonds used to finance new colonial settlements in the occupied territories. In other cases Jewish fugitives from the U.S. justice system have been protected by the Israeli state, especially super rich financial swindlers like Mark Rich and even gangsters and murderers. Occasional official demands of extradition from the U.S. Justice Department have been pointedly ignored.

The colonized Empire has gone out of its way to cover up its subservience to its supposed ally, but in fact hegemonic power.

The U.S.-Israeli relationship is the first in modern history in which the imperial country covers up a deliberate major military assault by a supposed ally. In

1967, the U.S. Liberty a communications and reconnaissance ship was bombed and strafed by Israeli fighter planes in international waters for nearly an hour, killing and wounding hundreds of seaman and officers. Intercepted Israeli messages as well as the clearly displayed U.S. flag demonstrate that this was a deliberate act of aggression. Washington acted as any Third World leader would when faced with an embarrassing attack by its hegemon: it silenced its naval officers who witnessed the attack and quietly received a compensation and pro-forma apology. Apart from the fact this was an unprecedented action in U.S. military and diplomatic relations with an ally, there is no case in record of an imperial country covering up for an assault by a regional ally[3]. On the contrary, similar circumstances have been followed by diplomatic and bellicose responses. This apparent anomaly cannot in any way be explained by military weakness or diplomatic failures: Washington has far superior armaments and its diplomats are capable of forceful representation to allies or adversaries, when the political will is present. The Jewish-American lobby, Congress people, media and Wall Street moguls strategically located in the U.S. political economic system ensured that President Johnson would act as a docile subject. No direct pressures were necessary, for a hegemonized political leadership, acts, seemingly on its own beliefs, having learned the rules of the political game. Israel-U.S. is a unique relationship that not even an unprovoked military attack should call into question. Like all hegemonized powers, Washington threatened the U.S. Naval witnesses with a court marital if they spoke out, while they coddled their attackers in Tel Aviv[4].

Another illustration of the asymmetrical relation is found in one of the most important espionage cases during the Cold War involving an Israeli agent, Jonathan Pollard and the Pentagon. Over several years Pollard stole and duplicated bagfuls of top-secret documents about U.S. Intelligence, counter-intelligence, strategic plans, military weaponry and turned them over to his Israeli handlers. This was the biggest case of espionage carried out against the U.S. by any ally in recent history. Pollard and his wife were convicted in 1986. The U.S. Government privately protested to the Israeli government. The Israeli's on the other hand, through their Jewish-American allies organized a lobby to propagandize in his favor. Eventually all top Israeli leaders and Jewish-American lobbyists campaigned for his pardon, and almost succeeded with President Clinton.

The unequal relation is clearly evident in the case of a major fugitive from justice, Marc Rich. A financier and trader, he was indicted in the U.S. federal court on several counts of swindling and defrauding clients. He fled to Switzerland and subsequently obtained an Israeli passport and citizenship, investing hefty sums of his ill begotten wealth into Israeli industries and charities. Despite the seriousness of his offense, Rich hobnobbed with top political leaders in Israel and its economic elite. In the year 2000, the Prime Minister of Israel and numerous pro- Israeli Jewish personalities, including Rich's ex-wife convinced Clinton to pardon him. While an outcry was raised about a linkup between the Rich pardon, and his wife's $100,000 plus contribution to the Democratic Party, the underlying relationship of subordination to Israeli influence and the power of the Israeli lobby in the U.S. were clearly more important. It is worth noting that it is extraordinarily unusual for a U.S. President to consult with a foreign ruler (as Clinton consulted with Barak) in dealing with an accused swindler. It is unprecedented to pardon an indicted fugitive who fled his trial and never served any sentence.

The power of Israel is manifested in the numerous annual pilgrimages that influential U.S. politicians make to Israel to declare their loyalty to the Israeli state, even during periods of intensive repression of rebellious subject people[5]. On the contrary, U.S. satraps of the Israeli's mini-empire applauded the Jewish state's invasion of Lebanon, its bloody repression of the Intifada I and II and opposed any international mediation to prevent further Israeli massacres, sacrificing any credibility in the United Nations.

In votes in the United Nations, even in the Security Council, despite overwhelming evidence of human rights violations presented by EU allies, Washington has toiled in the service of its hegemon. Sacrificing international credibility and deliberately alienating 150 other nations Washington labeled criticisms of Israeli racism as "anti-Semitism". This does not mark the high point of Washington's servility to Israel.

The most recent and perhaps the most important instance of U.S. servility occurred in the months preceding and following the September 11 attack on the World Trade Center and the Pentagon. On December 12, 2001 Fox news learned from U.S. Intelligence sources and federal investigators that 60 Israelis engaged in a long-running effort to spy on U.S. government officials were detained since 9/11. Many of those arrested are active Israeli military or intelligence operatives. They were arrested under the Patriot Anti-Terrorism Law. Many failed polygraph questions dealing with surveillance activities against and in the United States.

More seriously federal investigators have reason to believe that the Israeli operatives gathered intelligence about the September 11 attacks in advance and did not share it with its Washington ally. The degree of Israeli involvement in September 11 is a tightly guarded secret. A highly placed federal investigator told Fox news there are "tie-ins". When asked to provide details, the federal investigator refused "Evidence linking these Israelis to 9/11 is classified. I cannot tell you about evidence that has been gathered. It is classified information[6]."

Nothing exemplifies the power of Israel over Washington as this case of Israeli espionage. Even in the case of the worse bombing in U.S. history, Washington suppresses federally collected evidence linking known Israeli spies to possible evidence about prior knowledge. Clearly this evidence might raise questions about the links and ties between political and economic elites as well as undermining strategic relations in the Middle East. More important it would pit the Bush Administration against the Jewish American lobby and its powerful informal and formal networks in the media, finance, and in government. Fox News obtained numerous classified documents from federal investigators probably frustrated by the cover-ups of Israeli espionage by political leaders in Washington. These documents unearthed by Cameron reveal that even before September 11, as many as 140 other Israelis had been detained or arrested in a secret investigation of large scale, long term Israeli espionage in the United States. Not one of the major print or electronic media reported on these arrests. Neither the President nor any Congressional leaders spoke out on Israeli's pervasive and sustained effort to obtain key U.S. military and intelligence information.

The classified documents detail "hundreds of incidents in cities and towns across the country," that investigators claim could be an Israeli organized intelligence gathering activity. Israeli agents targeted and penetrated military bases, the Drug Enforcement Administration, the Federal Bureau of Investigation and dozens of government facilities and even secret office and unlisted private homes of law enforcement and intelligence personnel according to the Federal documents, cited by Fox News. The General Accounting Office (an investigatory arm of the U.S. Congress) document referred to Israel as "Country A"; it said "the government of Country A conducts the most aggressive espionage operation against the U.S. of any U.S. ally." A Defense Intelligence report said Israel has "voracious appetite for information...It aggressively collects military and industrial technology and the U.S. is a high priority."

The Fox News Report written by Carl Cameron appeared on the Fox News internet site briefly (Dec. 12, 2001) and then disappeared - there was no follow up. None of the other mass media picked up on this major espionage report. No doubt the powerful pro-Israeli influentials in the mass media played a role. More significantly than direct "pressure" Israeli hegemony "persuades", "intimidates", the media establishment and political leaders to operate with maximum discretion in limiting reporting about Israel's appropriation of strategic information.

While the web of Israeli agents are sometimes subject to arrest, interrogation and expulsion, the Israeli state and the ministers in charge are never publicly condemned, nor are there any official diplomatic riposte such as the symbolic temporary withdrawal of the U.S. Ambassador.

The closest parallel to U.S. behavior toward Israeli spies is the response of poor, dependant Third World countries to U.S. espionage. In that context docile rulers quietly ask the Ambassador to rein in some of the more aggressive agents.

Unanswered Question: September 11 and the Israelis

Following September rumors circulated throughout the Arab East that the bombing was an Israeli plot to incite Washington to attack Muslim-Arab adversaries. These stories and their authors provided nothing more than circumstantial evidence, namely that Bush's anti-terrorism campaign legitimated Sharon's "anti-terrorist" repression of Palestinians. The stories implicating Israel were completely dismissed by all the media and political leaders across the spectrum. Now U.S. federal investigators reveal that the Israeli's may have known about the attack before it occurred and did not share it.

This raises the question of the relationships between the Arab terrorists and the Israeli secret police. Did the Israelis penetrate the group or pick up information about them[7]? Federal investigators' confidential information could probably clarify these vital questions. But will the confidential information ever become public? Most likely not. For the very reason that it would expose Israeli influence in the U.S. via its secret agents and more importantly via its powerful overseas lobby and allies in government and finance. The lack of any public statement concerning Israel's possible knowledge of 9/11 is indicative of the vast, ubiquitous and aggressive nature of its powerful Diaspora supporters [8]. Given the enormous political and economic importance which the mass media have given to 9/11, and the sweeping powers, funding and institutions created around the issue of national security, it is astonishing that no mention has been made about Israel's spy networks operating in the U.S.'s most delicate spheres of counter-terrorism.

Of course it is not astonishing if we understand properly the "unique relationship" between the U.S. Empire and Israel, a regional power.

Theoretical Issues

The relationship between the U.S. - a global imperial power - and Israel, a regional power provides us with a unique model of inter-state relations. In this case the regional power exacts tribute ($2.8 billion annually in direct contributions from the U.S. Congress), free access to U.S. markets, protection of overseas felonious Jews from prosecution or extradition to the U.S., while engaging in pervasive espionage and money laundering. Moreover Israel establishes limits on U.S.-Middle Eastern policy, in the international forums. Israel's hegemonic position has endured under both Democratic and Republican presidencies for almost half a century. In other words it is a structural historical relation, not one based on personalities, or particular transitory policymaking configurations.

Several hypotheses emerge from an examination of this unique relationship.

The first stems from the fact that the territorial Israeli state has little power of persuasion, economic reach or military clout in comparison to the major powers (Europe and the U.S.). The power of Israel is based on the Diaspora, the highly structured and politically and economically powerful Jewish networks which have direct and indirect access to the centers of power and propaganda in the most powerful imperial country in the world. Tribute is exacted via the influence of these "internal colonialists" who operate at the level of mass media opinion makers and via Congress and the Presidency. Close to 50 per cent of the funding of the Democratic Party comes from pro-Israeli Jews. For every dollar spent by the Jewish networks in influencing voting outcomes, the Israeli state receives $50 in aid to finance the building and arming of colonial settlement in the Occupied Territories complete with swimming pools, Rumanian gardeners and Filipino maids.

Through the overseas networks the Israeli state can directly intervene and set the parameters to U.S. foreign aid in the Middle East. The overseas networks play a major role in shaping the internal debate on U.S. policy toward Israel. Propaganda associating Israeli repression of Palestinians as the righteous response of the victims of the Holocaust has been repeated and circulated throughout the mass media. From the heights of the network to the lawyers boardroom, and the doctor's lounge the supporters of the network aggressively attack as "anti-Semites" any critical voices. Through local intimidation and malicious intervention in the professions, the zealots defend Israeli policy and leaders and contribute money, organize voters and run for office. Once in office they tune in to Israeli policy needs.

The phenomenon of overseas expatriates attempting to influence an imperial power is not an exclusively Jewish phenomenon. The Cuban exiles in Miami exercise significant influence in both major parties. But in no other case has linkage led to the establishment of an enduring hegemonic relationship: An empire colonized by a regional power, the U.S. paying tribute to Israel and subject to the ideological blinders of its overseas colons.

Many questions remain to be answered as the Empire aggressively pursues its military expansion and the internal voices of repression narrow the terms of public debate.

As the colons extend their influence throughout the political and intellectual spheres, they feel more confident in asserting Israel's superiority to the U.S. particularly in the areas of political coercion and war. They brazenly boast of Israel's superior security system, its methods of interrogation including its techniques of torture and demand the U.S. follow Israel's war agenda in the Middle East. Israel has acknowledged state-sanctioned physical and mental abuse of prisoners in interrogation, which has broad public support [9].

Seymour Hersch urges the U.S. FBI and Intelligence Agencies to follow the Israeli secret police's tactics and use or threat to use torture of family members of terror suspects[10]. The US follows suit by imprisoning the wives and daughters of wanted Iraqi Baathists. Richard Perle, highly influential in Rumsfeld's Defense Department, advocates the Israeli tactics of offensive bombing of adversaries. "In 1981 the Israelis faced an urgent choice: should they allow Saddam Hussein to fuel a French built nuclear reactor near Baghdad or destroy it? The Israelis decided to strike preemptively. Everything we know (SIC) about Saddam Hussein forces (SIC) President Bush to make a similar choice: to take a pre-emptive action or wait, possibly until it is too late.[11]"

Another prominent colon, Senator Joseph Lieberman called on the U.S. to bomb Syria, Iraq and Iran immediately after 9/11, echoing Primes Minister Sharon's policy advice to President Bush. Alan Dershowitz, Harvard Law professor, publicly endorsed both torture and repressive legislation in the U.S. - modeled on the Israeli system of unlimited detention of Palestinians[12].

The colon's subordinate U.S. policy to Israel's foreign policy needs, independent of circumstances and the extremities to which Israel's colonial policies push it. Moreover as representatives of the hegemonic power in the U.S., they even try to micro manage security measures - torture in interrogation - as well as becoming vociferous advocates of a generalized Middle East war. The colons have successfully influenced the U.S. government to block any EU initiatives toward international mediation, as well as the U.S. sponsored Mitchell Plan, advocating peace observers in the occupied territories. In a word, the U.S., despite its occasional inconsequential criticism of Israel's excesses, has not only been an unconditional supporter of Israel, but it has done so, in the context of a prolonged bloody, repression and occupation of Palestinian territories, to which Washington is a party to securing. Israeli hegemony over the U.S. via its colons is a formidable weapon for neutralizing the U.S.'s NATO allies, Arab petroleum clients, the vast majority of the general Assembly in the United Nations and even its own public on certain Middle Eastern issues.

Even more dangerous is the irrational paranoia which the colons transfer from Israeli politics to the U.S. All Arabs are suspect. Middle Eastern adversaries should be threatened if not bombed. Secret military tribunals and summary justice should be meted out to suspected terrorists. The mass media is especially tuned to pick up the Israeli paranoid syndrome: magnifying every threat, featuring Israeli resolution and efficiency against Arab "terrorists". The paranoid style of politics had led to Israel's attacks on Arab countries in the Middle East, espionage on the U.S., illegal purchase of nuclear devices in the U.S. and unremitting violence against Palestinians and Lebanese. The danger is that the assimilation of the paranoid style by the U.S. has vast consequences not only for the Mid-East but for the rest of the world and to democratic freedom in the U.S.

What the intellectual colons and other Israeli publicists forget to mention is that Israeli security policy in the occupied territories is a total disaster: Israeli bus stations, public malls, five star hotels, pizzerias and all of its frontiers have been attacked and hundreds of Israeli citizens have been killed and injured. Tens of thousands of educated Israelis flee the country precisely because of insecurity and the proximity of violence, which neither the Shin Ben, the Army or the settlers are capable of preventing. Israeli intellectuals are especially embittered by the enormous costs of the settlement movement[13].

Blind to Israel's security failure, the colons insist on creating conditions for internal repression and external war. Given their influential role in the mass media, their prominence in the editorial and opinion pages of the most prestigious newspapers, the colons message reaches far beyond their limited numbers and the mediocrity of their intellect. Location and money can make up for their psychological and political pathologies as well as override any qualms about dual loyalties.

Israel's Colonial Style: The US Pays Tribute to the State of Israel

In the face of Israel's defiance of world public opinion, and its refusal to permit any international humanitarian organization to examine the results of its murderous destruction of the towns and refugee camps in the Occupied Territories, who is financing the Israeli state and why does that financing continue in the face of world opprobrium?

The attempt by the United Nations to investigate Israel's near total destruction of Jenin in the spring of 2003 has evoked the hostility of the entire Israeli political class. Shimon Perez (the self-styled labor moderate in Sharon's government) accused the 170 plus member United Nations Organization of "blood libel" presumably including the U.S. which voted in favor of the resolution creating the investigatory commission.

The question of who is financing the Israeli state is basic because, Israel as we know it today, is not a viable state without massive external support. Billions of dollars are raised from a variety of Jewish and non-Jewish institutions to sustain the Israeli war machine, its policy of generous subsidies for Jews enticed to settle in colonies in the Occupied Territories and in Israel, with the world's 20th highest living standards for Israel's Jewish citizens[14]. Without external aid Israel's economy would require severe cutbacks in living standards and working conditions, leading to the likely flight of most Israeli professionals, businessmen and recent overseas immigrants. The Israeli military budget would be reduced and Israel would be obligated to reduce its military interventions in the Arab East and the Occupied territories. Israel would cease being a rentier state living on overseas subsidies and would be obligated to engage in productive activity - a return to farming, manufacture and services minus the exploitation of low paid Asian maids, imported Eastern European farm workers and Palestinian construction labourers.

Europe continues to privilege the importation of Israeli exports and financial services, despite overt and malicious attacks by leaders of both Israeli parties. Prominent Jewish organizations in France and England, linked to major parties have muted any efforts to use the "trade card" to pressure Israel to accept European Union or United Nations mediation. European trade and financial ties to Israel however are not the basic prop for the Israeli war machine. The principle basis for long-term, large-scale financial support is found in the U.S., among public and private institutions.

In the United States there are essentially four basic sources of financial, ideological and political support for the Israeli rentier economy:

1. Wealthy Jewish contributors and powerful disciplined fund-raising organizations.
2. The U.S. government - both Congress and the Presidency.
3. The Mass media - particularly the New York Times, Hollywood and the major television networks.
4. The trade union bosses and the heads of pension funds.

There is substantial overlap in these four institutional configurations. For example, Jewish supporters in the Israeli lobby work closely with Congressional leaders to secure long-term, large-scale

U.S. military and economic aid for Israel. Most of the mass media and a few trade unions are influenced by unconditional supporters of the Israeli war machine and its rentier economy. Pro-Israeli Jews are disproportionately represented in the financial, political, professional, academic, real estate, insurance and mass media. While Jews are a minority in each and every one of these categories, their disproportionate power and influence stems from the fact that they are organized, active and concentrate on a single issue - U.S. policy in the Middle East, and specifically in securing Washington's massive, unconditional, and continuing military, political and financial support for Israel. Operating from their strategic positions in the power structure, they are able to influence policy and censor any dissident voices from circulating freely in the communications and political system.

In the political sphere, pro-Israeli politicians and powerful Jewish organizations have joined force with pro-Israel ultra right-wing mass based Christian fundamentalists and powerful political leaders tied to the military - industrial complex like Secretary of Defense Rumsfeld and Vice President Cheney.

Israel's unconditional support of Washington's Cold War and subsequent anti-terrorist military offensive has strengthened ideological and military ties between U.S. right-wing political leaders, pro-Israeli politicians and the leaders of the leading Jewish organizations. The politics of Washington's new imperialism coincides splendidly with the Sharon-Peres conquest and destruction of the Occupied Territories. It is not surprising that four of the leading Pentagon advocates of Washington's permanent war doctrine and Israeli aggression are Paul Wolfowitz, Douglas Feith, Elliot

Abrams and Richard Perle, both staunch supporters of right-wing Jewish-American organizations.

The mass media in the U.S., particularly the "respectable" New York Times has been in the forefront of propagandizing Israeli conquest and destruction as a "defensive", "anti-terrorist war". Not a single voice or editorial in the New York Times has spoken of the mass killing of Palestinians civilians and Israel's destruction of priceless historical and religious sites that go back over 2000 years[15]. While Israel's war machine destroys ancient monasteries and the heritage of world culture, the pro-Israeli mass media in the U.S. focus their critical lenses on the scandals of the Catholic clergy. The Church's protests at the Israeli shelling of the Church of the Nativity and the murder of those seeking sanctuary are thus silenced.

Wealthy and organized Jewish organizations, compliant Congressional representatives and right-wing fundamentalist organizations are not the only financial supporters of Israel. U.S. taxpayers have been funding the Israeli war machine with over $3 billion a year of direct assistance for over 35 years (over $100 billion and continuing). Rank and file trade union members might be surprised to learn that their pension funds have been invested in Israel bonds with below normal rates of return and higher risk. Despite the poor investment quality of Israel bonds, some of the U.S. largest trade unions, employee pension funds and major multi-national corporations have collectively loaned billions of dollars to the Israeli regime. In all cases, the decisions to purchase a foreign government's bonds are made by the trade union bosses and corporate fund managers without consulting the membership or stockholders[16].

Nathan Zirkin, a financial director of the Retail, Wholesale and Department Store Union when asked if his union would continue to purchase Israel bonds despite Israel's repression and arrest of Palestinian trade unionists and activists, replied "Absolutely. The Palestinians didn't have a damn thing until Israel came in.[17]" The bonds proceeds are used to fund Jewish settlements in the West Bank and Gaza. Most of the rest of the bond revenues are transferred to the ordinary budget to be spent on the military and the Israeli intelligence agencies.

Many of the trade unions, which are purchasers of Israeli bonds, are controlled or influenced by the Mafia. The teamsters unions is the biggest purchaser of Israel bonds; it is also the union which has seen more senior officials indicted for Mafia ties, illicit use of union funds and massive robbery of membership pension funds. In this case the trade union Mafioso were buying favorable propaganda from the mass media and support from the "respectable" Jewish organizations via the purchase of Israel bonds.

Union pension funds have also been used by trade union bureaucrats to purchase Israel bonds. The most notorious case is the former International Ladies Garment Workers Unions (ILGWU), now called UNITE, a union whose workers are 95 per cent Black, Hispanic, and Chinese, most earning at below the minimum wage. UNITE's leadership and staff is overwhelming Jewish and earning between $100,000 to $350,000 a year plus expenses[18]. By channeling over $25 million in pension funds to Israel, the U.S. workers are deprived of access to loans for housing, social services, legal defense, etc. Clearly the Jewish trade union bosses have a greater affinity for the state of Israel and its oppression of

Palestinian workers, than they has with their own poorly organized workers, employed under some of the worst working conditions in the U.S.

Israeli bond promoters, with support from Mafia - influenced corrupt trade union bosses, have sold hundreds of millions of dollars of Israel bonds to 1500 labor organizations at interest rates below those of other available securities and well below what most investors would expect from loans to an economically troubled foreign government like Israel.

Three factors account for the U.S. trade union bosses channeling their members pension funds and union dues into Israel bonds: political protection and respectability in being associated with Israel and its lobbyists - this is especially important to Mafia-linked and corrupt officials. Ideological and ethnic ties between Jewish trade union leaders and Israel is a second factor. Thirdly, the use of Israel bonds to launder funds obtained illicitly by union bosses. The main organization selling Israel bonds managed to settle money-laundering accusations brought by the U.S. Securities and Exchange Commission "out of court."

Accomplices to Genocide

In April 2002, over 100,000 mostly Jews and Christian fundamentalists marched in support of the Sharon regime in the midst of the siege of Jenin. In Israel two out of three Israelis (65 per cent) polled in late April 2002 supported Sharon and almost 90 per cent believed the regime's propaganda that the U.N. commission to investigate Israeli devastation of the Occupied Territories "will not be fair to Israel." The Israeli public, the U.S. trade union bosses, and political and financial elites who finance Sharon are accomplices to the crimes against the Palestinian people. Obviously the shrinking minority of Jews in Israel who oppose the military machine have little or no influence in policy, in the media and in securing overseas financial support.

The wealthy and powerful reactionary overseas Jews gravitate toward Sharon. Seven of the eight billionaire Russian Mafia Oligarchs have donated generously to the Israeli state and are on excellent terms with Sharon and Shimon Peres and have no use for dissident military reservists.

Because of powerful unconditional external financial and military support primarily from influential Jews in the U.S., Christian Fundamentalists, the military industrial complex, the Pentagon extremists, and corrupt U.S. trade unionists, Israel is able to defy world public opinion, slander humanitarian organization and human rights leaders, and brazenly continue its genocidal policies. Israeli leaders know "their people": they know they have unconditional supporters who have already been tested. They know that their bankers, professionals and fundamentalists will back them up to the last murdered Palestinian: the march of the 100,000 in Washington in the midst of the Jenin massacre proved it. The huge turnout of politicians at the annual AIPAC conference during the massacres in the Rafah refugee camp in the Gaza strip confirms that they support the butchers of Rafah.

Fabrication of the Iraq War Threat: US Zionists in Action

There is growing debate and criticism in the US Congress and media of the Bush Administration's fabricated evidence of Iraq's possession of weapons of mass destruction. Even more serious the investigation and testimony of top US military and civilian officials in the Pentagon and State Department reveal profound differences and divisions between themselves and the "political appointees". The testimony and evidence of the professionals' revelations are crucial to understanding the structure of real power in the Bush Administration. It is in times of crises and divisions in the governing class that we the public are given insights into who governs for whom. The debate, criticism and division in Washington today is just such an instance.

After years of UN inspections, and almost five months of thousands of searches and interviews by over thousand US military, intelligence and scientific inspectors it has been definitively demonstrated that Iraq did not possess weapons of mass destruction (or even of useful national defense), a point now practically conceded by some members of the Bush Administration. This raised the next key question – Who in the Bush regime provided the fabricated evidence and for what purpose.

The initial response of the Bush apologists was to attribute the fabrications to "bureaucratic errors" and "communication failures" or as Wolfowitz cynically claimed to "secure a consensus for the war policy"[19]. CIA Director Tenant became the self-confessed scapegoat for the "mistakes" and eventually had to "resign". As the investigations progressed however, testimony from a multiplicity of high level sources in the Bush regime revealed that there were two channels of policy making and advisers, the formal structure made up of career professional military and civilians in the Pentagon and State Department and a parallel structure made up of political appointees. From all available evidence it was the "unofficial" political advisers organized by Wolfowitz, Feith and Rumsfeld in the Office of Special Planning (OSP) who were the source of the fabricated evidence, which was used to "justify" the invasion and occupation of Iraq. The OSP was headed by Abram Shulsky and included other neo-conservatives, who have virtually no professional knowledge or qualification in intelligence and military affairs. Douglas Feith, Undersecretary of Defense, and Paul Wolfowitz set up the OSP. Shulsky is an avid follower and protégé of Richard Perle, the well-known militarist and long time supporter of military attacks on Arab regimes in the Middle East.

According to the testimony of a Pentagon insider, Lieutenant Colonel Karen Kwiatkowski who worked in the office of the Undersecretary of Defense for Policy, Near East and South Asia Division and Special Plans in the Pentagon, the "civil service and active duty military professionals were noticeably uninvolved in key areas" of interest to Feith, Wolfowitz and Rumsfeld, namely Israel, Iraq and Saudi Arabia. Lieutenant Colonel Kwiatkowski goes on to specify that "in terms of Israel and Iraq all primary staff work was conducted by political appointees, in the case of Israel a desk officer appointee from the Washington Institute for Near East Policy and in the case of Iraq, Abe Shulsky." Equally important, the ex-Pentagon official describes the existence of "cross-agency cliques". She describes how the members of a variety of neo-conservative and pro-Israel organizations, (Project for a New American Century, the Center for Security Policy and the American Enterprise Institute), who are now in the Bush regime only interact among themselves across the various agencies. She points out that major decisions result from "groupthink" – the uncritical acceptance of prevailing points of view and the uncritical acceptance of extremely narrow and isolated views". She was forced to resign by her chief after she told him that "some folks (the cliques and networks) in the Pentagon may be sitting beside Hussein in the war crimes tribunal" for their destructive war and occupation policies[20].

What is very clear is that the OSP and its directors Feith and Wolfowitz were specifically responsible for the fabricated evidence of the "Weapons of Mass Destruction" that justified the war.

The OSP and the other members of the networks that operated throughout key US agencies shared a right-wing pro-militarist ideology and were fanatically pro-Israel. Feith and Perle authored an infamous policy paper in 1996 for Likud Party extremist, Benjamin Netanyahu, entitled "A Clean Break: A New Strategy for Securing the Realm", which called for the destruction of Saddam Hussein and his replacement by a Hashemite monarch. Syria, Lebanon, Saudi Arabia and Iran would then have to be overthrown or destabilized for Israel to be secure in a kind of 'Greater US-Israel Co-Prosperity Sphere.' The OSP was an arm of the Wolfowitz-Feith policy of furthering the policies of the most extremist groups of the Sharon regime, forging close ties with a parallel ad hoc intelligence operation in the Israeli regime according to a report from the British newspaper, The Guardian[21].

The finger clearly points to Zionist zealots who directed the OSP, like Abram Shulsky and Feith, as the source for the "phony intelligence" which led to the war that Wolfowitz and Rumsfeld were seeking. The manner in which the Zionist zealots organized and acted – as a clique of arrogant like-minded fanatics hostile to any contrary viewpoints from the professional intelligence, civilian and military officials suggest that their loyalties and links were elsewhere, most evidently with the Sharon regime in Israel.

To understand the central role of the Zionist ideologues in shaping US foreign policy in the Middle East it is important to frame it in the context of US-Israel relations and the powerful influence of the pro-Israel lobby inside of the US. As Patrick Seal describes in the liberal US weekly The Nation, "The Friends of Ariel Sharon (among the Jewish pro-Israel zealots) loath Arabs and Muslims... What they wished for was an improvement in Israel's military and strategic environment"[22]. The US invasion of Iraq and its aggressive military posture toward most Arab regimes in the Middle East has made the names of these Zionist policymakers known to the world. Wolfowitz and Feith are second and third in command of the Pentagon. Their protégés in the OPS include Abram Shusky, Richard Perle of the Defense Policy Board, and Elliot Abrams (a defender of the Guatemalan genocide of the 1980's) senior director for Middle East affairs for the National Security Council. Washington's most influential pro-Israel zealots include William Kristol and Robert Kagan of the The National Standard, the Pipes family and a large number of pro-Israel institutes which work closely with and share the outlook of the rightwing Zionists in the Pentagon. The growing consensus among US critics of the Bush Administration is that "9/11 provided the right-wing Zionists zealots with a unique chance to harness US Middle East policy and military power in Israel's interest and succeeded in getting the United States to apply the doctrine of pre-emptive war to Israel's enemies".

Concerned more with Israeli supremacy than US military losses, the zealous Zionists plan new wars – Perle, Feith and Wolfowitz are now targeting Iran, Lebanon and Saudi Arabia, raising a whole new series of "intelligence reports" accusing the Arab countries of funding, protecting and promoting terrorism. And the pre-fabricated intelligence flowed from the members in the OPS and their cliques and networks so well described by Lieutenant Colonel Kwiatkowski.

As US military casualties mount daily in Iraq, with over 10,000 wounded and over 800 deaths by June 2004, as the military costs of the war undermine the US economy, the US public is becoming disenchanted with the Bush Administration. If and when the identity and political loyalties of the architects and propagandists of the US war against Iraq and for Israel's supremacy are made public, there is likely to be a harsh and righteous backlash by the general public against the neo-conservative Zionist ideologues and their networks in and out of the government. Up to now their role has been the worst kept secret in Washington.

The Zionist Power Configuration in the United States

C. Wright Mills once wrote that he US "power elite" ruled by denying it held power; the Zionist elite follows this formula, but defends it by accusing its adversaries of being "anti-Semites" and pursuing retributive measures that would please former Senator Joseph McCarthy. The Zionist power configuration (ZPC) cannot be understood merely as the "Jewish lobby" or even the AIPAC, as formidable as it is with 150 full-time functionaries. The ZPC can best be understood as a complex network of inter-related formal and informal groupings, operating at the national, regional and local levels and directly and systematically subordinated to the State of Israel, its power holders and key decision makers. Influence is wielded via direct influence by Zionist representatives in the Government (most notably in the Pentagon under Bush) both in the Executive branch, as well as in the Congress; indirectly via its use of campaign funds to influence the selection of candidates within the two major political parties and to defeat critics of Israel and reward elected officials who will toe the Israel line. The parameters of political debate on Israel-related issues – which have broadened over time – are shaped by Zionist and Jewish organizational pervasive influence in the mass media, censoring and virulently attacking critics and pushing pro-Israel "news" and commentaries. The fourth circle of influence is through local and sectoral organizations (professional bodies, trade unions, pension funds etc), both those affiliated with national apparatus and those embedded in local "civil society". This is probable the most serious threat as it inhibits average US citizens from voicing their doubts and criticisms of Israeli policy. All over the US, local editors, critical intellectuals and activists and even doctors have been branded as "neo-Nazis" and have suffered threatening phone calls and visits by local pro-Israel zealots – including 'respectable' members of the Jewish community. The consequences usually stop discussion and/or to intimidate local citizens advocating an independent and democratic foreign policy. Zionist power is cumulative as each sector complements the others giving the minority great influence overall.

Moreover the ZPC's formal and informal structure has a crucial dynamic element to it: Each power center interacts with the rest, creating a constant "movement" and activity, which converges and energizes both leaders and followers. Secondly those non-Jewish or even non-Zionist political, media and civic leaders influenced by the ZPC in turn influence their constituency, multiplying several fold, the initial influence of their "hegemons". The relative absence of an informal, organized and active grass-roots democratic foreign policy movement, particularly in relation to Mid-East policy gives the ZPC a clear field with virtually no competitors. Over time the same pattern of Zionist influence has manifested itself in US executive agencies. The State Department's "Arabists" are bring replaced by pro-Zionists as is the case with senior civilian militarist in the Pentagon, in the Mid East think tanks and the Council of Foreign Relations, among others. It should be noted that the so-called "single issue" (US-Middle East Policy) focus of the ZPC of the past has been replaced by the new Zionist strategies in the Pentagon and right-wing think tanks who link the expansion of Israeli power beyond Palestine, to US-European relations (especially French bashing), US nuclear policy and US military and energy strategy. This analytical framework is useful in understanding the US-Iraq war, macro-imperial policy as well as micro-colonial practices.

The ZPC in Action: The Iraq War

The major theoretical strategist of US World Empire is Paul Wolfowitz who first presented a detailed outline of action in 1992. The argument for permanent wars, unilateral action and colonial conquest was spelled out for the first Bush Administration, and later supported implicitly during the Clinton Administration's continued military attacks against Iraq, its unconditional backing of Israel's war against the Palestinians, the Balkan wars, the de facto takeover of the ex-Communist states of Eastern Europe, the Baltic states and the South-Central Republics of the ex-USSR. The Clinton Administration's vigorous intervention in favor of Yeltsin's seizure of power and backing of the Russion Oligarchs played a major role in dismembering and weakening its former adversary to world domination. Clinton's unconditional support for Israel and more important the formulation of a Mid-East strategy convergent with Israeli foreign policy was tied to three sets of policies: Destroying the military and economic power of one of Israel's main critics in the Mid East (Iraq) via economic boycotts, arms inspections and unilateral disarmament of Iraq, while Israel stock piled nuclear and other weapons of mass destruction; financing and arming Israeli expansion and colonization of Arab Palestine; maintaining an economic boycott of Libya, Iran (supporters of the Palestinians) while subsidizing Arab client states friendly to Israel (Egypt and Jordan). Direct Zionist influence over US Mid East policy was shaped by Secretary of State Madeleine Albright who, while a convert from Catholicism to the more elite Episcopalian Church, had benefited from her newly discovered Jewish ancestry when she justified the US induced deaths of 500,000 Iraqi children during her tenure in office, declaring "It was worth it." Secretary of Defense Cohen was instrumental in promoting Israeli military dominance in the Middle East and Richard Holbrooke, a closet Zionist was one of the most influential Clinton advisers on the Middle East "peace negotiations". President Clinton and the Democrats laid the basis for the eventual capture of US foreign policy making by the Zionists in the subsequent Bush administration by accepting Zionists in strategic foreign policy positions influencing Mid-East policy and shaping US policy to fit Israeli expansionist aims. To be sure Clinton and his "moderate" Zionists did not threaten Israel's critics like Saudi Arabia or the rest of the Arab countries with military attacks – as did the Bush regime dominated by the ultra-Zionist militarists. Nor did his regime follow the Israeli line of accusing all of Europe, especially France, of being anti-Semites for criticizing Israel's slaughter of Palestinians. The Clinton regime and its moderate Zionist influentials believed it was possible to establish US dominance by consulting with Europe and conservative Arab regimes and sharing the economic benefits of imperial spoils in the Mid-East while supporting Israeli expansionism.

The Bush regime represented a qualitative advance in Zionist power in US policies, both foreign and domestic. The key economic policy maker was Greenspan, head of the US Central Bank (Federal Reserve Bank), a long time crony of Wall Street financial interests and promoter of the major pro-Israeli investment houses – responsible for the speculative boom and bust economy of the 1990's. Paul Wolfowitz, Under-Secretary of Defense was the architect of the US war policy for the Middle East. Richard Perle, the vituperative influential civilian militarist whose hatred of Arabs was matched by his blind tirades against the professional military commanders and intelligence agencies who refused to subordinate US military policy to Israel's regional interests, was head of the Defense Policy Board. Douglas Feith, Assistant Secretary of Defense, a fanatical Zionist and lifetime defender of Israel's interests, consultant with right-wing Israeli regimes and was the principal planner and successful propagandist for the US attack on Iraq. David Frum, the major policy speech writer for Bush and author of Bush's infamous "Axis of Evil" speech which made explicit and operational "Bush's policy" of permanent wars against Arab nations and other critics of Israeli power is a Canadian Zionist. Elliot Abrams, a racist Zionist (he condemns American Jews who marry Gentiles[23]) and a long term proponent of the Israel First doctrine within the Zionist elite was put in charge of Middle East Policy despite being a convicted felon for his role in the Central American Iran-Contra (Drugs for Guns) Scandal, and an intellectual architect of the Guatemalan genocide of 1981-1983. Their influence on US Middle East policy far exceeds their formal positions because they are backed by an array of influential Zionist academic ideologues (Kagan, Cohen, Pipes), political pundits (Kristols, Krauthamer, Peretz etc) and directors of war think-tanks (Pipes, Rubin) who are given constant access to the opinion pages of the major US newspapers, or interviewed as Middle East "experts" on pro-Israeli television and radio shows –advancing their war propaganda designed to promote US defense of Israel's Middle East agenda. These policy and opinion makers, backed by the mass media have been working in close consultation and in tandem with the major Jewish organizations in the US and in close "consultations" with top officials in the Sharon regime. Mossad agents, Israeli diplomats and key officials in the Sharon regime have free access to the offices of the Zionists officials in Washington and interchange information on how to optimize Israeli interests.

Prior to the US invasion of Iraq, all the Zionists in key policy positions and their counterparts in Congress backed a US war with Iraq; after 9/11, Wolfowitz and Senator Liebermann immediately proposed a war against Iraq – demanding that the Intelligence agencies "find" the connection and accusing the military of being cowards, for not engaging in war to "protect" Israel.

Despite Herculean efforts by Feith et al, to twist CIA and MI reports to serve their pro-war Israeli line their bellicose rhetoric lacked substance. They then invented the, now admitted, BIG LIE (by Wolfowitz) of the Iraq weapons of mass destruction threat to US security. To pursue this line the Zionist in the Pentagon by passed the traditional military/intelligence agencies and created their own propaganda – "intelligence" agency or "Office of Special Plans) run by fellow Zionist fanatic Abram Shulsky , under the control of Douglas Feith, which worked closely with Chalabi and the Mossad in "cooking" the data on WMD to fit the plans of their Zionist bosses in the Pentagon. The Mossad was later chastised for "intelligence failures" by the Israeli Knesset after release of the Steinitz Report on March 29, 2004, but their Zionist counterparts in the Pentagon, Shulsky, Wolfowitz, Feith and Abrams were never called to account, their collaboration with the Mossad never questioned, nor was an investigation of their pursuit of Israel's interests ever even raised. Only the Gentiles in the Military and the CIA were questioned. Zionist power manifested itself first in the making of the war and then in imposing impunity on the crimes of the war makers in the government. The Zionists then painted a totally unrealistic and false picture of the war, its consequences and the response of the Iraqi resistance to an Israeli style conquest and colonization. The Zionist were initially able to marginalize the high military officials who questioned the war, like General Anthony Zinni, and who opposed the way the war was launched and the length and breadth of the engagement. The Zionists shut out all debate of who would benefit and who would lose from the war: US soldiers killed, rising oil and energy costs, huge budget deficits, and of course massive loss of life and property among the Iraqis.

Wolfowitz claimed that the invading army would be welcomed as liberators (evoking the liberation of Paris). Perle claimed "the Arabs" would offer little or no resistance (being a "tribal" society). Kagan claimed that "one big bomb" would silence the Arab street and public opinion. Feith and Wolfowitz promoted the massive purge of the entirel Iraqi civil service, professions, universities, schools and hospitals of Baathists: as well as the dismantling and dismissal of 400,000 Iraqi military and police personnel – over the shocked objections of experienced senior US military officers who had expected to work with the surrendered military and administrative structure of Iraq to control the colony. This opened the way for the pillage of Iraq's complex infrastructure and historic treasures and libraries, as well as the growth of criminal gangs involved in theft, kidnap for ransom, murder and rape – activities virtually unknown under the tight Baathist regime. Rumsfeld dismissed the massive destruction of Iraqi society as the "messiness of freedom".

Many top US military officials objected, as did the first US pro-consul, former General Jay Garner. But the Zionists in the Pentagon and their partners in crime, Rumsfeld and Cheney, were determined to dismantle the secular Iraqi state. This was the result of a policy to turn Iraq into a desert kingdom - loose collection of at least three "tribal" client mini-states based on ethnicities, religious-tribal loyalties and forever incapable of opposing Israeli expansionism, particularly in Northern Iraq[24]. Instead of easy conquest, the 'Israel First' Pentagonistas provoked a massive popular opposition, unified the religious and secular groups in opposition to the US occupation, and swelled the ranks of the armed resistance with thousands of discharged armed professionals. In the course of pursuing a policy of strengthening Israel's regional position, the Zionists weakened the US colonial occupation and medium term plans to convert Iraq into a US oil colony. The result has been thousands of US military and client collaborators dead, maimed and wounded, and a burgeoning worldwide opposition, particularly in the Arab East, and among several hundred million Muslims.

The Israel First Pentagonistas successfully promoted the idea that the Israeli military and intelligence experts had a lot to teach their ignorant American counterparts on "urban warfare" and "information gathering" drawing on Israel's wealth of experience: Over 50 years, Israel expelled and destroyed Palestinian communities and developed interrogation and torture techniques on Palestinian and Lebanese captives[25]. The purpose of the Pentagon Zionists was to deepen the ties with Israel's security apparatus as part of a middle term goal of making "the cause of Israel as the cause of America" (as prostrate Presidential candidate Kerry has pledged[26]). The long-term goal was to leverage military security and co-manufacture of military weaponry between the US and Israel into the Grand Scheme of a Greater Middle East US-Israel Co-Prosperity Sphere. Imperial Israel would then have access to water, oil, capital and markets, which the heavily subsidized rentier militarist state lacks at the present.

The torture-interrogation techniques taught by the Israeli instructors converged nicely, updated and refined the older CIA torture manuals, more specifically introducing specificities pertaining to torturing Muslims and especially Arabs[27]. Once again the Zionist-Israeli priorities undermined US imperialist policies: The photo revelations of US soldiers torturing, raping and humiliating Iraqi prisoners discredited the US occupation worldwide, heightened Arab and Muslim resistance throughout the Middle East and discredited the Bush regime. Congressional hearings and mass media reportages even provoked a burst of public disapproval of the invasion of Iraq and Bush's handling of the occupation. Throughout the country there were calls, including from members of Congress, for Rumsfeld's resignation. Curiously enough, there were virtually no calls for the resignation of the Israel First Pentagonistas – who were equally implicated and responsible for the mass torture of Muslim detainees. According to Newsweek, Douglas Feith was in charge of setting policy on Iraqi detainees[28]. Even in the face of this horrible crime against humanity, even in the general national outcry to investigate, impeach and hold responsible those involved, the top Zionist co-architects of the war, the responsible heads (number 2 and 3) of Pentagon intelligence in the Iraq war involved in ordering the torture have escaped critical scrutiny, protected as they are up to now by the pro-Israel pundits, political fundraisers, presidential campaign fundraisers and influentials,(see the appendix on the exposé of Seymour Hersh).

Nevertheless, the widespread condemnation of these war crimes, the media exposure of the systematic lies of the Pentagonistas and the fear that the highly influential and visible role of the Israel Firsters has raised alarm bells among some of the most astute Congressional Zionists, fearful of an anti-Israel backlash[29]. Senator Frank Lautenberg (Democrat-New Jersey) a committed Zionist called for the "replacement" of Wolfowitz and Feith. "The men in charge have let down the soldiers in uniform. Simply replacing Secretary Rumsfeld will change little at the Pentagon if his discredited team of advisers remains in high-level positions. It is time for us to bring in new civilian leadership at the Defense Department" (Newsday May 13, 2004). Lautenberg makes it abundantly clear that the Pentagon Zionists are central to the whole US war effort, from beating the war drums, to cooking the data, designing the war strategy, to micromanaging the business of interrogation-torture.

Several former top US military professionals objected to the Zionist control over US policy and their close network of collaborators. Colonel Karen Kwiatkowski has given us an inside picture of the Feith/ Shulsky operation whose links to the Mossad seemed closer than to the US military. The Rumsfeld-Zionist group's monopolization of military policy, war strategy, military calculations and military promotions all alienated the military high command. Some who clearly foresaw the disastrous consequences of the policies of the Israel First crowd on US global ambitions were silenced and marginalized. It is likely that the torture photos release to the media was deliberately encouraged or promoted by highly placed military officials or former officials as a way of discrediting Rumsfeld and the Pentagon Zionists[30]. This move severely undercuts the war effort, which more and more of the military high command sees as destined to fail and are determined not to become the Neo-Cons' scapegoats. However to gain an "honorable" withdrawal they must know that they have to remove Rumsfeld and his Zionist colleagues, whose criteria for evaluating the war has less to do with the aims of the US military and more to do with Israeli expansionist goals in the Middle East.

While the Pentagon Zionists and the powerful network of pro-Israel Jewish organizations have seen their Iraqi serial war strategy collapse, they have succeeded in securing Presidential economic sanctions against Syria and bind US political support to Sharon's destruction and annexation of the remnant of Palestine. Moreover the leading Jewish organizations were able to secure a near unanimous vote in Congress (407 to 9) in favor of Bush's declaration supporting Israel's "new borders" in Palestine[31]. Once again the Zionist lobby has demonstrated its power – even turning Bush and Congress into self-effacing political idiots before Sharon. After Bush put all of his limited credibility in Mid East politics in his "Roadmap" for a Middle East peace accord, Sharon unilaterally declared a policy of "annexation and separation" and told Bush to swallow it. All the major Jewish organizations back Sharon's plan. Bush submits and endorses this, alienating virtually every European country, all Arab countries and clearly demonstrating the slavish complicity of US policymakers who once again renounce US Middle East imperial interests in order to accommodate Israel's expansion into the remnants of Palestine. Bush's policy reversal was backed by the vast majority of Congress who are forever fearful of Zionist-Jewish retaliation for the least deviation from unconditional and total support for Israel.

During the invasion and occupation of Iraq, some Congress members have been critical of the war. Hundreds of thousands of people have demonstrated their disapproval. Many Jewish Americans have participated in the protests and in some cases have led the protests. Mass media outlets have on occasions (especially after the torture exposé) publicized adverse news on the war (tortures, civilian victims, wedding parties bombed and homes and orchards bulldozed). While the US pursues the war in Iraq, the Israeli government has been equally brutal: engaging in premeditated assassination of Palestinian leaders, systematically destroying thousands of homes, farms, orchards, stores, schools, mosques and factories, and killing and maiming thousands of Palestinians activists, civilian women and children. They resort to the routine hooding, manacling and torture of detainees. All the major pro-Israel Jewish groups in the US, high and low, have defended all these crimes against humanity, successfully pressured both major parties, the Congress and President to say nothing: no protest, no investigation, no punishment. More perversely in the face of the Israeli mayhem they secure $10 billion dollars more in aid and lucrative joint-venture military contracts (no outcry about Halliburton-type contracting). The leaders of the peace movement, both Jews and non-Jews reject any effort to include Israel's genocidal war against Palestine – for fearing of alienating the "public" (read the major Jewish organizations) and the self-styled progressive Jews, who are ever protective of everything Jewish – even war crimes. Worse still, with a few rare exceptions, the "progressive" Jewish critics of the war and Israel are forever and adamantly determined to avoid criticizing the role of powerful Zionist policy makers in the government, their ties to Israel and the powerful support they receive from the major Jewish organizations in all matter which pertains directly or remotely to Israeli interests. With blind simplicity they all see Israel as simply a "tool" of the US for weakening the Arabs in the service of US oil interests. Apparently they have never consulted US petrol CEO's, advisers or investment brokers, who all agree that US support of Israel is destabilizing the region, threatening oil supplies, boosting prices to US consumers and creating enemies out of Arab client rulers who invest in the US, buy US currency to keep it from collapsing and raise

OPEC quotes to help lower US prices. By its blind support for Israeli colonial brutality the US has alienated several hundred milion Muslims, millions of Arabs of all faiths, the great majority of Europeans, Africans and Asians, heightening US global isolation. With imperial tools like Israel, who needs to organize an anti-imperial movement: its embedded in the policy. Even the crude virulent anti-European ideology propagated by Israeli ideologues and their transmission belt Jewish organizations in the US and Europe has influenced the US government. At a time when Muslims and Arabs are conquered and persecuted, thousands jailed and many "disappeared" by the US, Israeli and European governments, Secretary of State Powell convenes a meeting in Europe on the rising danger of ... "anti-Semitism"!! And the UN, under Kofi Annam, follows suit with its own meeting on 'anti-Semitism' during the ongoing devastation in the Rafah refugee camps in the Gaza Strip. The major Jewish organizations repeat the Sharon line "anti-Zionists" are "anti-Semites" – and it becomes established policy in the US and in some countries or Europe... to the point that individuals critical of Zionism are fired, cultural institutions pressured into censoring anti-Zionist events and creating a general culture of fear of offending the hegemonic Jewish organizations. Even Webster's recent dictionary equates anti-Zionism with anti-Semitism. In the midst of this, the major Jewish organizations in France openly condemn the manufactured hysteria as an Israeli mechanism to encourage the migration of French Jews to Israel.[32]

Jew in North America, South America and Europe are disproportionately in the highest paid positions and the most influential ethnic group, with the highest proportion in the exclusive, prestigious private universities, with disproportionate influence in finance and the media, memberships of country clubs and exclusive – it is clear that "anti-Semitism" is a very marginal issue.

The tragic myopia, or perverse refusal of leftist Jews to face up to the prejudicial role of the major Zionist and Jewish groups promoting the Israel First policy and imposing it in the electoral agendas substantially undermines their and our efforts to secure peace and justice in the Middle East and to forge a democratic US foreign policy.

Conclusion

The problems of peace and war, humane treatment of all racial and ethnic groups, of allocating foreign aid to those in the Third World who need it most and not to an aggressive colonial state with the 20th highest per capita income are foremost on our agenda. Confronting Zionists, the colonial state and its overseas loyalists requires us to face up to the inter-related challenges of opposing US military and economic imperialism and its class and ethno-religious backers, regardless of their claims of being a special people with a unique history, cause or claims on humankind. Many profound questions are pending and will be certainly raised after the Iraqi military debacle, which cost so many US lives and bled the budget of so many billions that should have been spent on tens of millions of US citizens and residents without health care and adequate living standards. There will certainly be a call for Congressional investigation to answer questions about "Who lost Iraq?" "Why did the US launch the war?" Why did the US "lose the war?" And above all – "Who was responsible?" There will be one series of questions however which will provoke the most vehement and concerted opposition and that would focus on the role of the Pentagon Zionists, their advisers, collaborators and supporters in and out of the Bush regime.

This line of inquiry will predictable be opposed by the neo-conservatives, liberals and philanthropic Jewish organizations and their non-Jewish allies in and out of the government, including those who did a magnificent job of exposing the non-Zionist militarists in the Bush Administration, but curiously enough forgot to even mention the Zionist cohorts and their ideological and organized backers in "civil society"[33].

The inquiry could serve as an educational experience in informing US citizens on the profoundly undemocratic nature of decision-making in questions of war and peace, the threats that civilian-militarists represent in relation to international law and the rights of national self-determination and the real threat of highly organized internal elites who become transmission belts for colonial mini-states carving out regional empires.

There are two lines of inquiry with regard to the Zionist disastrous influence on US war policy in the Middle East. One line is from the "nationalist" empire builders who see the problem of Zionist power in terms of the negative effect that the war had on US empire building[34]. They are likely to testify that the Israel loyalists, isolated the US from its European and conservative allies, by pushing for a unilateral military conquest strategy, instead of engaging in joint diplomatic and economic strategies and pressuring Israel to act like a "normal state", by negotiating a 'peace for land' two state solution. These conservative empire builders will seek to publicize the role of the Zionists in the Pentagon and their slavish adherence to Israeli state interests, its devastating effects on US world political, economic position, by focusing on the US's loss of leverage over Arab and Muslim oil producers, and particularly the mindless threats to Saudi Arabia. In particular the professional military and intelligence officials will seek to demonstrate how the Zionists seized control over decision making, marginalized and manipulated them, ignored internal intelligence reports in favor of "cooked reports" by their specially invented cohort and Israeli intelligence in order to maximize Israeli interests. The professional officials will especially emphasize the deliberate and wanton disregard of internal experts who warned against the war, the futility of looking for weapons of mass destruction, the irrationality of a series of Middle East invasions, and the likelihood of greater resistance during a colonial occupation. The NATO oriented military will point out how the Israeli-oriented policy makers, deliberately provoked needless hostilities to their European allies in empire building, by orchestrating virulent "anti-Semitic" campaigns against France and Belgium because they were critical of Israel's territorial expansion and ethnic cleansing.

In a word, the conservatives (political, military and intelligence officials) will argue that the Zionists by putting Israel in the center of their policy making undermined US empire building, draining troops, resources, money and public support to support Israel's quest for regional domination[35]

Another line of inquiry, from the left or progressive side, is likely to address the question of Zionist power over war and peace in the Middle East and elsewhere by focusing on the usurpation of democratic rights of

US citizens in the making of foreign policy: the fact that a small elite of several thousand highly organized, affluent and well-funded lobbyists can control the voting behavior of congress members, intimidate or defeat political representatives who criticize Israel's colonial policies, and who buy, silence and/or intimidate media outlets and public spokespeople who dare to raise questions about Iraqi-Israeli inter-connects. The progressive critique will be directed not only at the role of the Pentagon Zionists in twisting US war policy to favoring Israel but their whole world view drawn on the Israeli view of its relation to the world: A paranoid and self-serving vision of eternal external enemies everywhere and unreliable allies, of perpetual repudiation of international law, covenants and Geneva Accords, of shrill polemics and deep penetration of ostensible allies' military and intelligence apparatuses. Progressives will attack the Israeli view that labels adversarial states mortal enemies who only understand force and that considers negotiation a cynical device to neutralize critics, to disarm adversaries in order to create new "facts on the ground" through forces and violence. Progressives will have to courageously make the connection between the Pentagon Zionists, their affinity for Israeli ideology and their destruction of diplomacy, international law and co-operation. The inquiry will have to point out that a great deal is at stake beyond law and peace: That the architects of the Iraqi war planned a series of aggressive wars of conquest based on the principle of domination by violence, torture, collective punishment, total war on civilian populations, their homes, hospitals, cultural heritage, churches and mosques, means of livelihood and educational institutions—these are the highest crimes against humanity. Crimes against humanity are inevitable in "total wars" based on ideologies of exclusive ethno-religious loyalties, whether Jewish, Christian, Hindu or Muslim. The worst crimes are committed by those who claim to be a divinely chosen people, a people with "righteous" claims of supreme victimhood. Righteous victimology, linked to ethno-religious loyalties and directed by fanatical civilian militarists with advance weaponry is the greatest threat to world peace and humanity. Progressives must forcefully reject "righteous victimology" by exposing its contemporary imperialist agenda and the fact that many descendants of victims have now become brutal executioners. They must reject "special exemptions" in naming Zionists power brokers and decision makers, especially by their Jewish colleagues on the Left. Selective criticism not only weakens the political substance and credibility of the critique, but is morally reprehensible as it denies an important truth – the politics of the Zionist architects of US imperial policy making. The progressives must reject all imperial politics with or without Israeli design. It must return to republican principles, but in so doing progressives have to point to the incompatibility between a democratic republic and empire building, between narrow, explicit or implicit, ethno-religious loyalties and internationalism, between expansionist capitalism and democratic socialism. In order to pursue the progressive line of inquiry and alternative political perspective we should expect a prolonged, vitriolic and irrational assault.

The first line of ideological attack, particularly by the ZPC's, will be the "labeling" tactic – hard hitting critical analysis will be labeled "anti-Semitism" to inhibit readers and listeners from discussing the evidence and substance of the issues. The examination of linkages between the Israel-centered Pentagonistas and the

Israeli state will be labeled "pages from the 'Protocols of Zion'" and other such spurious analogies.

The second line of attack will be to conflate Zionist power today with the not too distant past (1940's-1950's) when Zionism was only one of several views among US Jewry and when it was less organized and influential in politics, the media and economy. The purpose of this dishonest amalgamation is to polemicize by citing past examples of relative Zionist weakness and to falsely attribute to the critics a worldview of a worldwide, long-term Jewish conspiracy.

The third line of attack and the most morally reprehensible is to conflate the victims of the Holocaust with the state terrorists of the Israeli state and their intellectual apologists and supporters among US Zionists. The use of "blood ties" to make this connection when there is no social-economic-political similarity only reveals the irrational mystical and reactionary nature of the current ideology of the Zionist right. The purpose of course is to secure public acquiescence with Israeli and US Zionist crimes against humanity by presenting their actions in terms of "defensive" or "survival" tactics in the face of another holocaust-in-the-making. No evidence is needed – just breathless, vicious invective about the holocaust-in-the-making deniers. For the Zionist ideologues Israel is presented as the incarnation of universal values of democracy, liberty and justice and those who criticize Israel are then labeled as supporters of "Arab" dictatorships, repression, injustice and terrorism. The stated universal values are worth upholding but abundant evidence exists that they are not practiced in Israel – where Arabs, both Muslim and Christian – are treated as second-class citizens, and death, destruction and ethnic genocide is daily fare for the Palestinians, and Israel's nuclear arms threaten its Middle East neighbors[36]. Finally one will hear from Zionists the "relativist" argument: "Israel's crimes are no worse than many countries in the world". Except that few countries (except the US) are engaged in colonizing a neighbor, bombing adversaries with impunity (and killing massive number of innocent bystanders), storing nuclear warheads with an offensive doctrine, securing 2/3 of US foreign aid including its most advanced technology, controlling US congressional voting on Mid East issues, shaping the Mid East political agenda for both Presidential candidates, routinely torturing thousands of political prisoners (and sending advisers throughout the world), and practicing the totalitarian law of collective punishment for popular resistance.

There are many and profound reasons to single out Israel for condemnation, because while many countries practice some of the Israeli injustices, Israel and its overseas network in the US contain a whole configuration of power relations which threaten not only the oppressed people of Palestine but the rights of people throughout the world.

Facing this ideological attack will not be easy because media access is totally unequal. The opposition is well organized, strategically located and well financed. But the crimes and failures of policy particularly as the Iraqi debacle deepens and many more Americans are open and increasingly involved in seeking answers, the critics of the Israel-Zionist-Pentagon connection have a grand opportunity to expose and weaken the ties that bind. Moreover outside the US we have mass public opinion in our favor. Latin America, Europe, Africa, Asia - the great majority see Israel as a threat not a force for peace. Secular, democratic Jews anywhere else in the world have no problem criticizing US Zionists and their leading policy-makers in the Pentagon. Nowhere except in North America do the Israeli-centered Zionists have such power as they have in the US. Even in Israel there is a minority of Jews who openly despise the Pentagon-Zionists and their proposed serial wars; they especially despise Zionist ideologues like Richard Perle and Douglas Feith, who from afar, are willing to sacrifice the last Jewish soldier for their megalomaniacal idea of "Greater Israel".

In this battle of ideas we have many allies around the world, our ideas and questions are relevant and will resonate in this time of deep anxiety among the American people. Let's move ahead and de-colonize our country, our minds and politics as a first step in reconstituting a democratic republic, free of entangling colonial and neo-imperial alliances!

References

1. *A Clean Break: A New Strategy for Securing the Realm,* Richard Perle, Douglas Feith, David Wurmser, et al, Institute of Advanced Strategic and Political Studies. 1996.

2. *US Financial Aid to Israel: Facts, Figures and Impacts,* Washington Report on Middle East Affairs. 2004.

3. James Bamford, *Body of Secrets: Anatomy of the Ultra-Secret National Security Agency* (Doubleday, New York, 2001)

4. James Ennes, *Assault on the Liberty*, (Random House 1980.

   See also Statements by Ward Boston, Jr., Captain,

JAGG USN (Ret), January 9 2004 and Admiral Thomas Moorer, USN (Ret) January 11, 2003.

5. Washington Report on Mid East Affairs, *Pro-Israel PAC Contributions to 2002.*

Congressional Candidates, June 2003.

See Carl Cameron Investigates (Parts 1-4) Fox News Network, Dec. 17, 2001.

7. Richard Reid, the ex-con and would-be shoe bomber, convicted for trying to blow up an American Airlines passenger jet over the Atlantic in December 2001, managed to enter Israel on an El Al flight despite his unusual background, BBC News, Dec. 28, 2001.

8. See Gordon Thomas and Martin Dillon, *Robert Maxwell, Israel's Superspy: The Life and Murder of a Media Mogul*, (Carol and Graf, New York, 2002) for in depth discussion of the powerful media links with Israel.

9. Frankel, Glenn, *Prison Tactics A Longtime Dilemma for Israel,* Washington.

Post, June 16, 2004; page A01.

10. National Public Radio Interview, October 2004.

11. NY Times, December 28, 2001, p. 19.

12. CBS News September 20, 2002.

13. Gideon Levy, *Compensate settlers for what?,* Haaretz, June 15, 2004.

14. *US Financial Aid to Israel: Facts, Figures and Impact.* Washington Report on Middle East Affairs.

15. William Dalrymple, *From the Holy Mountain,* Harper Collins 1997. Chapter 5 chronicles the systematic devastation of the ancient Orthodox Christian communities in Israel and the Occupied Territories, including the Armenians.

16. *Israel Bonds Raise $130 million from US Labor,* Jerusalem Post, July 25, 2001. see also Forward, Feb. 21, 2003 – *El Al Moves to Avoid Tiff with Big Labor – Sharon Steps in.*

17. Russel Mokkiber, *Bonds of Affection,* Multinational Monitor 1988 (multinationalmonitor.org.)

18. Rachel Donadio, *Talking the Talk at Jewish Labor Diner,* Forward, March 22, 2004., see also Robert Fitch, *The Question of Corruption,* Metro Labor Press Association, October 21, 1999, and Robert Fitch, *Testimony, House of Representatives, Hearing on Workplace Competitiveness,* March 31, 1998.

19. Paul Wolfowitz in Vanity Fair interview, July 2003, "the issue of weapons of mass destruction" was chosen "for bureaucratic reasons because it was the one reason (for invading Iraq) that every one could agree on."

20. Jim Lobe, *Insider fires a broadside at Rumsfeld's Office (Air force Lt. Col. Karen Kwiatkowski,* Asia Times, August 7, 2003. Col. Kwiatkowski remarked "I suggested to my boss that if this (evidence for invading Iraq) was as good as it got, some folks on the Pentagon's E-ring may be sitting beside Hussein in the war crimes tribunal."

21. Julian Borger, *The Spies who Pushed for War,* Guardian, UK, July 7, 2003.

22. Patrick Seale, *A Costly Friendship,* The Nation, July 2, 2003.
23. Elliot Abrams, *Faith or Fear: How Can Jews Survive in Christian America,* The Free Press, June 1997.
24. *A Clean Break: A New Strategy for Securing the Realm*, Richard Perle, Douglas Feith, David Wurmser, et al, Institute of Advanced Strategic and Political Studies. 1996, see also Lelie Gelb, *"The Three-State Solution"*, New York Times, November 25, 2003 and Seymour Hersh, *Plan B* , New Yorker, June 28, 2004 on Israeli activity in Kurdish Northern Iraq.
25. Glenn Frankel, *Prison Tactics A Longtime Dilemma for Israel*, Washington Post, June 16, 2004.
26. John Kerry, *Perspectives: An Israel Review,* Brown University Publication, November 19, 2003.
27. Matthew Clark, *Concrete, razor wire, ID cards,* Christian Science Monitor, December 8, 2003.
28. *Newsweek Magazine*, June 7, 2004, p. 35.
29. see *Haaretz*, April 24, 2004 where Israeli deputy ambassador to UN, Arye Mekel complained that criticisms "only enhance suspicions ... linking us with Iraq where we nave no business." and Nathan Guttman, *Prominent US. Jews and Israel Blamed for Start of Iraq War,* Haraatz, May 31, 2004.
30. Martin Sieff, *Army, CIA want torture truths exposed,* United Press International, 5/18/2004.
31. *Sharon praises U.S. on West Bank Refugees,* Haaretz, June 25, 2004.

32. Xavier Ternisien, *Des responsables communautaires protestant contre un "plan" isralien incitant les juif francais a emigrer,* Le Monde, June 17, 2004.

33. In the entire body of exposés by Seymour Hersh in the New Yorker during April-June, 2004: the role of the Zionist Pentagonistas is not discussed.

34. On June 16, 2004, 27 retired top diplomats and top military officials released a statement calling for Bush's electoral defeat and in May 2004 a more specific open letter to President Bush signed by 60 retired diplomats referred to the damage the US-Zionist relationship had done to US prestige and influence in the Muslim world and in Europe.

35. U.S. Senator Ernest Fritz Hollings, *Bush's failed Mideast Policy is creating more terrorism,* May 6, 2004 and *Why we're in Iraq,* June 23, 2004.

36. Yulie Khromchenco, *Poll: 64 per cent of Israeli Jews support encouraging Arabs to leave,* Haaretz, June 22, 2004. Citing a survey by the Hiafa University National Security Study Center, a remarkable 25 per cent of Jewish Israeli would support the banned racist Kach Party in an election.

6

Experts on Terror: Looking in the Mirror

James Petras – June 2004

After reading hundreds of books and articles and listening to scores of speeches and interviews by experts on terrorism and terrorists from the US, Canada, Israel, Europe, Latin America, Asia and South Africa, I have come to the conclusion that there are recurring patterns. They use a common language to describe their subjects and their environment, they are extremely ideological under a thin veneer of scientific jargon, they possess a keen sense of selective observation, they always pretend to possess a psychological understanding though few if any have dealt close up with their subjects in any clinical sense except perhaps under conditions of incarceration and interrogation. Their style is righteous, highly moralistic, vitriolic, given to hyperventilation and yet facile with euphemisms to describe the violence of their partisan states. Their analysis is almost always filled with highly charged personalistic – individualistic invective, which is devoid of any political motivations. Psychobabble provides a "legitimate" sounding channel for expressing deep-seated hostility, a way of assuming a state of civilized superiority in the face of their dehumanized subjects.

The dehumanization process is central to the whole terrorist-political-academic enterprise — for the purpose is to present "the terrorist" with no redeeming features, with no 'place' in the world, no 'time' to exist – in other words worthy of physical extermination.

The Terrorist Experts are the "set-up" people. They motivate the colonial and imperial conquerors and reinforce their idea that the "terrorists are not worthy of ruling or being ruled in regions of wealth or even of living in any territory contiguous to civilized or "chosen" people.

The Terrorist Experts project the violence of the rulers, their ambitions to conquer, their greed to seize land and resources, their savage destructive impulses on to their victims; the responses of the victims, the survivors are clothed in the rhetoric of pathologic behaviour. The really clinical pathologies are found in the minds of the verbal assassins – who cannot distinguish the repeated rapes and tortures committed by their patron-states from the desperate cries of the excluded, displaced and exploited.

Almost all the terror experts have a chronic psychological blindness to the systematic and comprehensive violence inflicted by the West and Israel on particular groups. Today it is the "Arabs", at others times it is all insurgents who respond to imperial violence with violence.

The all-pervasive practice of torture is a means of breaking and converting militants, and then infiltrating resistance movements. This interrogation method receives ideological justification and moral support from the Terror Experts. In their writings insurgents or 'terrorists' are described as beyond the human pale– they are described as sub-human, in a "trance". Their leaders are described as cynical profiteers and manipulators who have no human values. Their communities are "lawless pockets". Once committed, they know no law, no justice – only death, murder and martyrdom. They live in failed states. They have no history or culture (or at least one inferior to 'Western', 'Judeo-Christian' civilization). In a word the world will be better without them. To the torturer this means his or her work is in the best interest of civilization. Of course the Terror Experts are offended when the practitioners are exposed, their handicraft of brutality photographed and published throughout the world's media. The Terror Experts are grieved, not for the acts of moral degradation, but because it confirms what the "terrorists" have been saying – they revolt out of the outrage and humiliation they suffer in the hands of their US/Israeli/European torturers, soldiers, mercenaries and bosses. Terror Experts protest at the public exposure: that the dirty secrets absent from their analysis have become public knowledge. They attribute feelings of "anger", "humiliation" to the personality disorders, childhood or family or cultural/religious dysfunctions of the "terrorists". The statements of the Terror Experts become less convincing faced with the publicized facts of physical humiliation by the armies and states of the chosen civilizers.

An Emblematic Terror Expert

A lead article published by the Weekend Financial Times by Professor Jessica Stern "How Terrorists Think" (FT June 13, 2004) is emblematic of the Terror Expert genre. Stern is identified as a lecturer at Harvard's John F. Kennedy School of Government and the author of a recent book, Terror in the Name of God: Why Religious Militants Kill (Harper Collins, 2003). Published in the most prestigious business newspaper, employed by a leading elite private university, with a book edited by a major publisher, Stern has all the right credentials to be a Terror Expert.

Method

The Terror Experts operate and see themselves on two levels: as 'scholarly researchers' and as political prosecutors and 'security' advisors.

As 'experts' their work is of dubious quality despite the self-declared wealth of sources they claim to have consulted.

Many of the alleged "terrorists" interviewed were in jail where they were most likely tortured, drugged and their conversations monitored. They are hardly in a position to speak with the minimum conditions to give a fair interview. Secondly the Terror Expert can be expected to edit out any excerpts that provide a political context for their actions: they are likely to pay more attention to their own jaundiced "impressions" of how the 'terrorist' looks, speaks or listens, usually fixing on their own preconceived "meanings" of particular facial expressions or body movements.

The Terror Experts excel in selecting the worst case sample as "representative" of the leadership of the terrorists, the boastful, the moneygrubber, the affluent. They omit the norm of persecuted resistance fighters who are modest, sacrificing, in solidarity with their people, upon whom they have many times to depend for food, medical care and refuge.

There are "fundamentalist" Moslems who in every way pursue modern professions, use Western critiques of colonialism and imperialism; who find it compatible to seek self-determination, majority rule and practice their religion.

There are fundamentalist Muslims who are pietistic – they seek solace in spiritual practices, who live in a narrow circle of work, mosque and family, who have experienced the violent disruption of their pietistic life and respond, not only because the imperialists have transgressed the sacred, but because they have destroyed the family network and intergeneration codes of existence. Pietistic Muslims avoid political engagement until their intimate human and spiritual circle is violated.

In the midst of the chaos, violence, dislocation, pillage and occupation of a country, a whole people are adversely affected. As they reach out to respond, to protest, to survive, they seek movements and institutions that have some resources, a modicum of power. In the past there were powerful nationalist, socialist and communist parties, dynamic trade unions and peasant movements. In a few countries they are still active and a force to be reckoned with. In many regions however, they have been decimated by US client regimes, local secular or religious dictators, and by the disintegration of the Communist Parties. Under harsh conditions requiring clandestine activity and mass support, many secular activists have jointed politically oriented religions movements, which embrace anti-colonial, anti-imperialist and social warfare programs. The secular "conversion" to Muslim-inspired movements is based on politics, not religion. Leon Trotsky once advised his followers during the Nazi occupation of

Europe that it might be necessary to join the Catholic Church if that was the only space available for political action. Given the mass base of the Muslim movement, given its engagement in the anti-colonial struggle, it is no surprise that many secularists (who may be leftists, nationalists and democrats) have joined these movements – and may later turn to other political movements.

To subsume the rich mosaic of resistance fighter to one ideological formula because of formal affiliations as these Terror Experts do, is an egregious error. They are eager to prescribe a general repressive solution to the "terror" problem, truckling to the political interests of their paymasters in the big foundations or state apparatus. They repress inconvenient complexities, diverse motivations, conjunctural convergences between secular and spiritual. Terror Experts evoke the emotive phrase 'Islamic Fundamentalist Terrorists' to end debates and considered analysis which might require the public to reconsider their support for imperial wars, Israeli conquests and their opposition to Iraqi nationalists and Palestinian resistance fighters.

Interrogation: Questions for the Terror Experts

Terror Experts (TE) claim that objective conditions, or what they refer to disparagingly as "exploitation", "oppression" or "imperialist" (predicable always with quotes), are only a veneer covering some deeper "personal need". The TE then proceed to "unmask" the "true" motives – with a stream of psychobabble. In fact the resort to crudely conceived and applied psychological categories, are the principle method that the TE use to suppress the "objective" world, which impinges on the action of the resistance fighter.

The external world, in which violent resistance movements emerge are by any measure very hostile. The US and Israel, for example, are recognized the world over as very aggressive, normless actors consider themselves unaccountable to any and all international laws. The TE can avoid this fundamental 'fact' impinging on the resistance fighters' behavior by focusing on their supposed "inner world", and "immediate" face to face relations. This allows the TE to avoid the unpleasant aspects of their own state loyalties. The Terror Experts' primitive, tribal, clan, ethnic, religious, colonial, imperial loyalties underlie their veneer of respectability, their phony defense of civilization and humanity.

The TE were horrified by the photos of US torture in Iraq – not the acts. The revelations unmasked the savagery of their accomplices, the practitioners of their prescriptions, the whole underworld of crime and punishment that is logically derived from the totalitarian pseudoscience of the Terror Experts. It brings the TE of Harvard, Princeton, Yale and Johns Hopkins closer to the savage scenes of homo and heterosexual rape, mass sequential genital violence. The TE, of course, strike the pose of indignation at the brutal guards, interrogators, the military commanders. They are silent as their current paymasters are pilloried – Rumsfeld, Bush – knowing full well that the next President will also employ their services. In any case who is going to look deep and far form the scenes of torture and identify the torture accomplices among the TE?

The TE simply pronounce their diagnosis of the armed resistance fighters: incurable psychopaths, extremely dangerous when at large. The politicians dictate the commands: capture, confine, torture or kill. The Special Forces break doors in the middle of the night, cut throats or take prisoners. The prison commandants establish the rules of "interrogation". The guards torture. This is s very coherent international division of labor, in which the TE play an important part in elaborating the rationale. They ply the secular version of Jihad: a morally and scientifically justified war-unto-death of the "untermensch" the "inferior" peoples, the "fundamentalist Arab Muslims", the "suicide bombers", the "Terrorists". A common language is spoken between the TE and their state patrons, and then promoted in and by the mass media.

Questions for the TE: (1) Why do the imputed terrorists' "personal needs" find expression through politics (and not in a thousand and one personal, cultural, familial, civic channels)? Why do the terrorists' "personal needs" find expression against a certain enemy (the dominant power) rather than a host of other objectives, less dangerous, easier to access, more direct? Why do the terrorists' "personal needs" express themselves in favor of a particular group (family, neighborhood, nation or class) and not another (foreign powers, exclusive elites, etc?) Why do the terrorists' "personal needs" find expression at a particular time (during invasions, occupations, etc.) and place (locus of imperial power, military and political institutions, mercenary police stations)?

Obviously the "personal" has multiple forms, objects, places and times for expression. To explain specific political actions one must examine the political, ideological, class relations, state and international configuration of power.

The second question is a refinement of the first: Why do "personal needs" not express themselves in other non-violent forms of political action such as elections, for example, instead of as a guerrilla, suicide bomber, etc.? More specifically what political obstacles or literal or figurative walls prevented other than violent forms of political action? We can hypothesize that the greater closure imposed on the political system (colonial and neo-colonial rule, long-term military occupation, racist exclusive ideology and practice, systematic widespread torture of "suspects"), the greater the degree of uprooting or ethnic purging, the more likely the choice posed by the ruling power: subject yourself or revolt. Under the circumstances there is a greater likelihood of violent resistance, individual or collective.

Suicide bombings are a form of individual sacrifice, of individual resistance taken in the name of a collective. In Western society, individual sacrifice to defend the nation in war merits the highest military medals – the distinguished medal of honor, with distinctive military and religious ceremonies. In the Middle East, similar honorific activities accompany the suicide bombers: they are cited as 'martyrs' to the cause of national liberation. Why do the TE ascribe pathological behavior to the Middle Eastern resistance fighters and not to their own military heroes who died for the bloody empire? Why is one culture which honors its sacrificial martyrs called a democracy and another a fanatical violent fundamentalist culture?

This question is especially relevant because throughout history in all nations facing superior arms, organization and technology from an imperial conqueror, resistance includes sacrificing one's life in the course of inflicting the highest number of casualties on the enemy. Just think of Leonides at the pass of Thermopylae, with a few hundred soldiers facing the advancing Persian imperial army, was he engaged in a form of "suicide" defense of Athens? Why is it 'glorious' to be the equivalent of a suicide bomber in ancient Greece and not in modern Palestine?

History teaches us that there have been and always will be self-sacrificing individuals or collectives (nations/ people etc.) defending nation and home when faced with superior arms. Countries (especially imperial states) with superior arms rarely practice, either individually or collectively the use of the human body as a missile or weapon. Japanese kamikaze fighters were not used in the conquest of China or the Philippines – they only came into practice faced with the superior air and sea power of the US.

TE attempt to denigrate the politics of popular resistance by attributing the struggle to the manipulation by leaders with unworthy motives. This overlooks all mass movements, which have by their nature a whole range of leaders, activists and sympathizers. Terror Experts imagine leaders who are in search of "money, "status", "power", "jobs" etc. Once again the "unmasking" technique fails to explain obvious facts. Overwhelming evidence throughout the world, past and present, demonstrates that those who struggle against a dominant colonial, imperial power suffer severe material losses of life, family, jobs, income, houses and property. In the case of the Palestinians, the Israeli Jews punish the whole extended family, steal personal belongings and heirlooms and destroy generations of old orchards and cultivated fields. With resistance movements ,it is very rare that "leaders" enrich themselves in the midst of a life and death struggle. Most leaders who do enrich themselves usually do so after the struggle has ended, especially if they turn to embrace the neo-colonial paymasters of the TE. In fact it is the Terror Experts' closest collaborators and their informants who enrich themselves by spying and turning in the patriots who the experts call 'terrorists'.

Repeatedly the TE engage in role reversal turning the victims into executioners and the executioners into victims. This has been a common ploy used by totalitarian imperialist ideologues to justify the use of force from the Nazis to the present day US, European and Israeli colonialists.

To justify their preposterous claims, the TE comb the world to find some group and individual leaders who will fulfill their stereotype and titillate their readers in New York, Tel Aviv, Washington or London. The Terror Expert meets a leader (Muslim of course) who just happens to lead a "group known for beheading foreigners and for its close alliance with Osama bin Laden". The TE has touched all the right buttons to evoke the conditional response – only they are the wrong buttons. Millions engaged in violent resistance do not "behead" foreigners – only a very small handful do and then under questionable circumstances. Osama bin Laden has very few allies among the major liberation movements, even within Muslim countries.

The selective vitriolic libeling of a subject prepares the Western reader to accept the emotionally charged imputation of pathologic behavior. Harvard academic, Jessica Stern provides us with a typical example – almost a parody – of these polemical ejaculations. She describes the purpose of her study "to identify some common themes that might help to explain how violent Islamic nihilism continues to spread beyond the lawless pockets and failed states where terrorists tend to thrive and into the cities of the west". (Jessica Stern, *How Terrorists Think,* Financial Times , June 12/13, 2004, w1-w2). Nihilism presumes no goals, no values, and no alternatives. Most observers would disagree based on a simple reading of most of the Islamic revolutionary or radical web sites: they have goals – replace Western dominance with nationalist Islamic rulers. Their values include both traditional religious and modern variants and their alternatives to submission is guerrilla, mass or individual resistance. The neighborhoods, cities, and communities where the putative "nihilists" originate are far more stable, norm-guided and law-abiding before the forceful intrusion of imperial and colonial power, which tear asunder the networks that bind collectivities. "Lawless pockets", to the degree in which they exist, are products of the unwillingness or incapacity of the conquering powers and their proxies to establish a just and stable social order. Moreover, one can observe in many cases that "lawlessness" is selective: occupied peoples disobey colonial 'laws', 'edicts' or 'fiats' while abiding by the laws or rules declared by their legitimate authorities. Moreover, it is generally the case that newly liberated areas run by guerrillas are more lawful than under previous military or colonial occupation with their drugs, brothels and bars.

The notion of "failed states" has achieved a certain notoriety among Western pundits, academics and especially the TE. Its exponents use it to describe the collapse of nations, which have been devastated by surrogate pro-Western militarists, pillaged by Western banks under the tutelage and protection of the IMF and the World Bank. No doubt there have been gangster rulers in the former Soviet Union, Eastern Europe and the Third World – but they have more often than not been trained by Western foundations or universities and send their ill gotten fortunes to Western, Israeli or "off shore' banks. The Terror Experts in labeling their former progeny as failed rulers, disown their own offspring. What Imperial ideologues mean by "failed states" is the failure of clients to establish a stable neo-liberal regime, necessitating "successful" Euro-US imperial intervention to create "prosperous democracies". Like in post-invasion Kosova, Afghanistan, Iraq and Haiti where white slavery, drug trafficking, warlords, deathsquads rule with the aid of US helicopter gunships hovering over and firing into unruly neighborhoods.

Stern and other verbal assassins strip the victims of their humanity ("nihilists"), denigrate their place of birth ("lawless pockets"), deny the historical authenticity of their nations ("failed states"), all the better to oversee their extermination, their ghettoization, their torture.

Through the eyes of the Terror Experts Euro-US and Israeli bombing of population centers is seen as doing "humanity" a great favor: preventing the 'spread' of terrorists into the cities of the West.

The shrill anti-Arab/Muslim rhetoric of the TE encourages 'moderate', Western politicians to impose more rigid and humiliating administrative and legal measures against Arab, Middle Eastern and South Asian travelers, immigrants, visitors, religious leaders, academicians and businesspeople.

Targeted by and subject to systematic denigration by the Western mass media, state functionaries, immigration police, hostile embassy personnel, academic terror experts, the secret police and special assassination teams, oppressed people are forced to transform themselves to meet a chronic "national emergency". Ruler-ruled relations are a series of perpetual impositions, unwelcome visits by colonial operatives granted license by the imperial Terror Experts. Faced with a systematic effort to lower their self-esteem, the oppressed people "find" themselves in their own organizations, public and clandestine, religious and secular. This reaffirmation finds expression in a reassertion of a religious or secular identity, embodied in a mosque, church, political movement or resistance organization.

Colonial/imperial power disrupts the daily routine of the general population: 'going to work' faces roadblocks, work places are destroyed, fruit trees are uprooted. "Taking care of the family" becomes a daily life and death struggle of securing food at black market prices, facing unpredictable hostile fire in the marketplace. 'Enjoying leisure' becomes a memory of the pre-colonial/pre-imperial past. Now there is 'forced leisure' – jobless, policed, futureless – in the street, where individual discontent is socialized by local opinion leaders who provide a focus for action. Taking sides, addressing the oppression, the hardening of attitudes is a fundamental effort to recover the 'daily routine'.

The complex interweaving of powerful spiritual loyalties, family responsibilities and workplace displacement leads to a commitment to direct action and a political movement. This is a rational and complex process. The Terror Experts colonial preconceptions blind them to this reality. For example, Stern sees the committed resistance fighter as being in a "kind of trance" – irrational, dogmatic and simplistic.

The Terror Experts repeat ad naseum that the "terrorists" join their organizations in their search for strength – a common response of all those who engage in politics and social action. The TE turn a commonplace observation which has a lineage of over 3,000 years or more into a particular feature of "terrorists". The resistance fighters do have a sense of altruism and an idea of the public good – which the Terror Experts refuse to take serious. To do so would require a profound re-examination of their loyalties, and collaboration with imperial/colonial powers, and a deep critical self-examination of their institutional location and motives. This would be a difficult psychological and material experience for Terror Experts since their prestige, income, status, and influence might be threatened. Their critical introspective analysis might lead them to question their paymasters, their institutions, their colonial/imperial states. What foundations would pay to have a 'renegade' Terror Expert bear witness to their prejudices, falsifications and close ties to politicians who sanction torture and murder? Would their former colleagues describe the renegade as being in a "kind of trance", "victim of the Stockholm complex" (accepting the views of their captors)?

The colonial practitioners and their academic experts specialize in verifying each other's stereotypes of resistance fighters. They oversimplify their motives, decisions and commitments. They rely on blanket categories that obscure deeper structural realities in favor of subjective labeling. Above all they banish any objectivity. Relations of power and dominance, state violence, violent intrusions into Arab, Muslim, Latin American countries, towns and villages are described by the TE as "defensive", "retaliation". As the limbs and body parts of Palestinian babies, women and grandparents are exploded over the ruins of homes and neighborhoods, Harvey Morris , the Zionist Bureau Chief of the Financial Times in Israel writes of Israeli "retaliation", after killing dozens of children and old people. Banishing objectivity means the incapacity to empathize with the human condition of the colonized victims – for that reason the experts must present the victims as sub-human. Because the Terror Experts are condemning the most abused victims in the name of the most vicious powers, they convince themselves that their vitriolic diatribes are merely a service to truth and science. The TE have invented a new paradigm — scientific diatribes in the service of intellectual dishonesty.

The TE are masters of euphemism, especially in dealing with the muck and gore of empire building. Imperialists become "one worlders". Colonial occupation is called "nation building". Murderous sequential destructive offensive wars become "humanitarian interventions".

Above all the Terror Experts celebrate triumphal imperialism: the defeated colonial peoples, we are told, are "resentful" – "those who feel they can't keep up". Of course with a hood over their head and shackled legs and feet and a cattle prod burning their genitals – they can't keep up, they can't turn around and express gratitude to their torturers.

How is a Palestinian farmer going to "keep up" with a Jewish settler who seizes his land, water and , supported by local thugs and Israeli soldiers, blocks his access to the market? Anything short of resentful would be masochistic. Is it any wonder that the deraccinated and dispossessed risk their lives to convert resentment into resistance? By all means. When the tanks roll into

Iraqi neighborhoods after shelling homes and mosques, is it any wonder that furious neighbours swarm around an ambushed tank and dance on the shards of smoking metal and corpses? Is it a frightful spectacle of pitiless terrorists or jubilant neighbours, who have silenced the sound of shells bursting over their heads and into some neighbors' homes?

The Terror Experts existed before the Iraqi resistance and they will exist after it. Wherever the oppressed rise and effectively resist imperial rule there will be academic chairs, foundations grants and Centers for International Studies for the ambitious upwardly mobile TE. The Imperial state will demand their services, the prestigious Councils of Foreign Relations will offer membership and universities will reward them with distinguished professorships. They will be celebrities – the mass media talk shows will feature them. They will be far from the killing fields but their spirit will be there, on the front lines and in the torture chambers, guiding the hands that place the hoods over the unredeemable, nihilists, Muslims, Marxists or national patriots.

Bibliography

1. Jessica Stern, "How Terrorists Think", *Financial Times Weekend*, June 12/13, 2004 W1-2.

2. Alan Dershowitz, *Why Terrorism Works*, R.R. Donnelley and Sons, 2002.

3. Scott Altran, "Genesis of Suicide Terrorism", *Science* March 7, 2003 pp. 1534.

4. Rafael Patai, *The Arab Mind*, WW Norton and Co., 1973 with preface by Norvell B. De Atkine.

5. Harvey Morris, "The State They're In", *Financial Times Weekend*, July 3-4 p. W1-2.
6. D. Long, *The Anatomy of Terrorism*, Free Press, New York, 1990.
7. E. Stout (ed), *The Psychology of Terrorism*, Praeger, Westport CT, 2002.
8. Hector Qirko, "'Fictive Kin' and Suicide Terrorism", *Science*, April 2, 2004 p 49.
9. "The Sociology and Psychology of Terrorism", Federal Research Division, Library of Congress Washington DC, Sept. 1999.

7

The Suicide Bombers: The Sacred and the Profane

James Petras
August 15, 2005

Introduction

One of the least discussed but most important aspect of the 'suicide bombers' (SB) attacks is the Angle-American (AA) systematic and profound degradation of that which the Islamic religion holds most sacred: its code of ethics, its mode of spiritual practice, its religious rituals, its sacred texts and its respect for the observant believer.

The neo-conservative, liberal and pro-Israel propagandists, both journalists and academics focus on what they choose to call the "pathologies" of young Muslims, the fanaticism of their beliefs, their gratuitous violence, the "generational anger", the "frustration" of living in "failed states" and a long litany of irrational behaviours which exonerates the AA and Israeli violence and torture.

A progressive school of thought emphasizes the "reciprocal nature of violence" – Anglo-American wars, invasions and occupations which engender Arab or

Islamic terror as part of a spiral of violence. In some versions – the religious element is subordinated to the political concern for self-determination in explaining the behavior of SB.

While the latter approach has the advantage of advancing beyond the vitriolic psychobabble of the neoconservative and Zionists 'experts' of the "Arab Mind", it fails to account for the depth and scope of the suicide bomber phenomena, especially the sharpening intensity during the occupation.

Beyond the general mayhem induced by Anglo-American wars, invasions and occupations, there are two forms of violence derivative from the general conception of war, which stand out as the direct determinants of suicide bombing.

The AA have theorized and put in practice the idea of 'total war'– a war without legal, moral, geographic, temporal or spatial boundaries. As Bush, Rumsfeld and the Pentagon Zionists (Perle, Wolfowitz, Feith and Company) declared, this is a different war in which the 'enemy' is everywhere and attacking at all times. The final solution is to search and destroy them, their sanctuaries, their accomplices, their neighborhoods, families, religious institutions and any who might offer material or spiritual support, protection or encouragement. The theory and practice of "total war" obliterates the distinction between combatants and civilians, between military installations and civilian facilities, between military infrastructure and civilian transports systems, between the sacred and the profane.

The AA have imposed new norms of warfare and new practices for engaging the enemy which have been increasingly taken up by sectors of their adversaries. If AA imperialism can act with unrestrained violence against all military and civilian targets, so can the resistance – including the suicide bombers – whether they are Islamists or secular, poor or middle class. What determine the reaction of the adversaries of AA imperialism are their rules of warfare – the notion of 'total war'.

Total War: Content and Consequences

There are different forms of imperial conquest. In one variant the purpose is to work through local elites who become the tribute collectors and gendarmes of the colonial powers, which gain control of the agro-mineral wealth and finance their privileged position via local taxes.

In another variant, the imperial powers destroy the pre-existing society and governing system, frequently uprooting the population and in the process physically annihilate its members and culture in the course of seizing its wealth. The degradation of the sacred is a prelude to attempts to impose a new set of beliefs more conducive to submission and exploitation.

A third variant is a combination or a sequential process of destruction, degradation and exploitation followed by efforts to "reconstruct" a colonized military, police and political structure willing and able to repress and contain anti-colonial resistance.

The US invasions of Iraq and Afghanistan follow the third variant. In the initial phase, the imperial armies engage in total occupation, unrestrained pillage of historical sites, utter degradation of the population, destruction of cultural institutions, and the systematic assassination of leading members of the local political, civil service and professional classes. Following the growth of massive resistance by secular and religious forces, uprooted and divorced from their essential everyday living, under constant physical and spiritual assaults, the AA occupation regime moves toward the "reconstruction" of a colonial repressive apparatus and governing bodies — beyond the walls, barbed wire enclosures and watch towers of the colonial army.

'Total war' doctrine continues to wreck havoc with minor concessions to enclaves of collaborators, most of whom are 'dual citizens', exiles whose loyalties are first and foremost to the empire, whose homes, pensions and even families (not to mention bank accounts and English rose gardens) are located in the cities of the imperial countries.

Total War and the Resistance

The practitioners of 'total war' borrow heavily form the practice and doctrine of the Israeli colonial occupation of Palestine: practices of collective punishment, erasure of historical sites, destruction of homes, eradication of orchards and productive farms, bombing of small factories, building of ghetto enclosures (walls), massive forcible evictions, and especially torture and interrogation techniques designed especially to violate Islamic beliefs and the Arab identity. These techniques have been transmitted via Israeli advisers and training sessions to US interrogators and incorporated into their manuals. It is precisely the common methods of both Israeli and Anglo-US interrogation-torture techniques linked to the doctrine of 'total war', which has led to the common practice of SB against them.

Insofar as the interrogation-terror techniques strip their victims of all that is essential to their 'spiritual self', they also force upon the victims and their sympathizers a 'new morality', one that no longer abides by the older moral-religious precepts. In its place the 'new morality' is the mirror image of the practitioners of 'total war'. The SB act without concern for civilians, locations, time and circumstance. Like their interrogators, they seek to inflict the maximum damage to the "Western mind" – exposing their weakness, increasing their anxiety and fears, while undermining everyday routines. The key to the conversion of Islamists and even the secular opposition to suicide bombing and the practice of the 'new morality' is not merely the political-military colonial occupation and war, but the resort to the specific practices of degradation inflicted on the colonial victim.

Degradation: The Logic of Total War

The Israeli's have practiced torture by degradation for decades and have a powerful army of overseas supporters – professors, neo-cons officials, liberals, bankers, professionals, artists, journalists, and media moguls – providing justifications in the form of 'ameliorating circumstances' and 'moral equivalences'.

The Anglo-American practitioners of total war, impressed by the power of Israel to sustain its colonial occupation of Palestine and its impunity, overlooked the negative effects: the SB phenomenon, and Israel's repugnancy to the non-European world (and even among many Europeans).

Degradation is specifically designed to 'break' the 'Arab' or 'Islamic' Mind – as the Israeli psychological war experts labeled it – and secure an army of informers, agents and docile, terrorized released prisoners who would serve as exemplars to other would-be resistance fighters. While a few prisoners were 'turned' through torture and blackmail and others were released as 'broken' men and women incapacitated by profound psychological disorders, millions react with indignation, anger, and violence — and in some cases have taken the form of SB. The word from the victim-survivors of Israeli brutality and visual images provides a terribly graphic reality of systematic degradation of all that Arabs - Islamist or secular - hold sacred.

The perception of the victims, their families, their people, their fellow believers, and their nation is that degradation of Iraqi prisoners is the technique authorized and approved by the highest levels of power and executed by the terror experts, from elite psychologists down to the lowest jailers. Nobody can claim, "they didn't know". Nobody, in a volunteer army, can claim they were just obeying orders. Citizens in electoral systems who voted for the imperial executioners cannot claim innocence.

The Technique of Degradation: The Larger Meaning

The book of virtuous living for the Islamist and even, to a lesser degree, the secularist is the Koran. It is the 'divine book', which provides a moral guide and existential meaning to life. The torturers defecated and urinated on the Koran. They stomped on the Koran with muddy army boots. They flushed pages, held most sacred by the victims, down the toilet. They violated the most sacred single source of moral life.

The torturers systematically denied their victims water to clean themselves before prayer. Instead they defiled them with filth, scantily clad female interrogators smeared fake 'menstrual' blood on bound prisoners, forced them to defecate on themselves and ridiculed their victims' intense religious distress. They violated every taboo, every norm, including the deepest held moral codes. They forced (and photographed) deviant sex, prolonged nudity, raped men and women with cattle prods and other torture devices. They wrapped prisoners in the Israeli flag. Such humiliating techniques have lifetime psychological consequences preventing the victims from ever marrying and maintaining normal family relations. The torturers specifically told their victims that the films and photos of their degradation would be shown to their families and neighbors to intensify the anguish after their release. The torture techniques specifically focused on Moslems and Arabs, but in general defiling all normal men and women's sense of modesty. They used gross sexual humiliation designed to break all political bonds between the colonized people and the degraded victims. Women prisoners in Abu Ghraib reportedly sent out messages begging the resistance to kill them in their cells by mortar attacks. Mosques were destroyed or turned into slaughterhouses; wounded men huddled in the sacred halls were executed at point blank range.

The AA political leaders promoted Christian evangelical military chaplains who incited the executioners to 'fight Satan' as they encircled and destroyed the city of Fallujah.

Jewish and Christian 'terror experts' (often in the behavioral sciences) provided the emotional vitriol in pseudo-scientific jargon by transposing the psychopathic behavior of the executioners to the victims. The political psychologists as war criminals ... as creators of the Suicide Bombers...

Political Consequences of Defiling the Sacred

The profound systematic effects of 'total war' and its derivative defilement of the sacred has far-reaching effects on Muslims and Arabs, including secularists, in terms of geography, political practice, intensity of reflection and feeling about the practitioners, their government and their 'civilization'. The impact of defacing the sacred is strongest on those collectivities, which share the same ethnic, religious and cultural values as those who are violated. The degradation of the sacred texts and religious sanctuaries impinge on the spiritual and physical existence of the groups and individuals whose lives have been guided by the defiled texts. The message relayed to millions by the torturers and their leaders is that 'nothing is sacred' – everything and everybody is equally an acceptable instrument for conquest, domination and control. The whole process of degradation from the indiscriminant bombing of civilian communities, to the usurpation of public space, to the pillage of a cultural heritage, to the arbitrary arrest and assassination of passersby, culminates in utter depravity or literally turning the spiritual symbols and texts and moral guides into trash.

The denial of what is sacred to the oppressed is inherent to the process of creating a hierarchical chain – the greater the degradation of the 'other' the greater the power and self-esteem of the torturers. The lower the stature of the torturers – (those who, outside the torture chambers, have no access to the real spoils of conquest, the war profiteering, the 'reconstruction' racket or the military officers who can 'cream' the contracts) – the greater the inducement to achieve 'superiority' (symbolic rewards) by debasing the shackled and manacled, the naked and the humiliated, to please their superiors with tidbits of irrelevant 'intelligence'. Much of this is documented in General Antonio Taguba's report.

The chain of command dictates the license to torture; the word of the imperial executive informs the practitioners of degradation. The celebrants of imperial 'Judeo-Christian' values flaunt their impunity in the security of their technological and military might. The 'special people', the chosen nations, aggravate the experience of degradation. Imagine Rumsfeld and other officials and senators reviewing General Taguba's report describing the young son of an Iraqi Army officer stripped, smeared with filth and abused before his captive father (Seymour Hersch describes the shrieks of young boys being raped) — and projecting their own perversities on to the victimized people.

Suicide Bombers: A Response to the Desecraters

Some of the more intelligent of the generally benighted claimants of 'expertise' in terrorism have discovered that the SB are not necessarily poor, not necessarily 'direct victims' of imperial invasions, and are not necessarily Islamic fundamentalists. Most of them resort to psychobabble, citing 'alienation', 'generational conflict', and other behavioral pathologies. These Anglo-American and pro-Israeli 'experts', who pathologically ignore the monstrous crimes committed against the essential values and beliefs of the oppressed, see themselves, with all solemnity, as fit to diagnose the ills of others. A handful of the 'experts' claim that the terrorists, the SB, are political people and that these acts are 'political' – a response to the Anglo-American war, invasion and conquest. Closer to the truth, but still inadequate, some add the 'humiliation of a conquered people'.

What drives the SB is an effort to redeem the Sacred from the Desecraters. The 'Sacred' includes, but goes beyond, the material destruction inflicted by the Anglo-American invaders and Israeli colonists. Degradation and defilement of the sacred texts, the deep inner values and the disciplined customs produces a class of individuals who sense the bonds of humanity have been irrevocably broken.

The SB believes that spiritual wrath can counter the desecraters of the sacred. For the future SB, resistance, marches, protests, strikes, civil disobedience, even resistance in the homeland does not restore the 'Sacred'. The conflict rages in their neighborhoods, their houses; markets and transport are destroyed. The SB believes that only by reversing the violence, bringing it 'home' to the invaders will they redeem themselves, and respond in kind to the 'total war' advocates, apologists and innocent victims. Recognition of the licensed defilement of the sacred is now out of the box – whether it continues in one form or another, videoed or hidden in military archives, it is now embedded in the minds of tens of millions – it is their very cultural – psychological – moral existence. Everyday life has been put to the test.

Conclusion

From the 'Shock and Awe' bombing of cities, to the killing, maiming and destruction of millions, to the torture and profanation of the sacred, the orders have come from distant, faceless Generals, Presidents, Secretaries of War and have been executed, face to face, by average people, workers, employees, clerks...who 'elected' these leaders. The many faces of the enemy in the eyes of the SB are concentrated in the faces and acts of those who degrade the sacred and attempt to destroy what gives meaning to their everyday life.

To the SB, "the face of the enemy" is the face of "the people" – rich and poor, powerful and powerless, General and foot soldier. Hence the suicide bomber, whose bonds with the sacred and moral have been broken by systematic degradation, feels no compunction in attacking ordinary people, going about their everyday tasks in office buildings or subways.

Our analysis suggests a close relation between the Anglo-American practice of 'total war' and its derivative policies of systematic degradation and the emergence of 'suicide bombers' – one of the forms of rejection. If this analysis is correct, the demise of suicide bombers is most likely to occur when the practice of 'total war' is ended. This can only come about through a defeat of the 'colonial revivalist' strand of imperialism in both its US, European and Israeli variants. The question is how long it will take for domestic and external political discontent to coalesce a political alternative capable of formulating a strategy of military withdrawal and abiding by international law. Reconciliation between the Anglo-American and Islamic and Arab people can be achieved through a war crimes tribunal, similar to the Nuremburg Trials after the Second World War. The practitioners and proponents of crimes against humanity beginning with the President of the United States and the Prime Minister of Great Britain should be brought to trial and accorded exemplary punishment to prevent recidivism.

Peace and reconciliation is only possible if justice is meted to the architects and practitioners of total war and human degradation.

8

The War: New York Diary

James Petras
November 15, 2004

I am reading William Shirer's Berlin Diary, a journalist's account of Nazi political propaganda during the 1930's, as I read and watch the US 'news' reports of the violent assault on Fallujah. The US mass media 'reports', the style, content and especially the language echo their Nazi predecessor of 70 years ago to an uncanny degree. Coincidence? Of course! In both instances we have imperialist armies conquering countries, leveling cities and slaughtering civilians – ant the mass media, private in form, state appendages in practice, disseminate the most outrageous lies, in defense and praise of the conquering 'storm troopers' – call them SS or Marines. Both in Nazi Germany and contemporary US, we are told by the mass media that the invading armies are "freeing the country" of "foreign fighters", "armed terrorists", who are preventing "the people" from going about their everyday lives. Yet we know that of the 1,000 prisoners there are only 4 foreigners (3 Iranians and 1 Arab); Iraqi hospitals report less than 10 per cent of foreign fighters. In other words almost 99 per cent of the fighters are Iraqis – most of who were born, educated, and raised families in the cities in which they are fighting.

Like the Nazi media, the major US radio and TV networks only report what they call "military casualties" – failing to report the 100,000 civilians killed since the war started and the thousands of women and children killed and wounded since the assault of Fallujah began. Like in Nazi Germany, the US mass media feature unconfirmed reports by the US military of the bloody murders, beheadings and kidnapping "by the foreign terrorists". The unconditional support of Nazi/US mass media is best captured in their reports of the massive bombing of densely populated city districts. For the US networks NBC, the dropping of 500-pound bombs in the city of Fallujah is described as targeting an "insurgent tunnel network in the city". And the houses, markets, stores – the mothers and children above those tunnels – vaporized into "pink mist". Their existence never acknowledged by the leading reporters and broadcasters.

George Orwell in his famous essay "Politics and the English Language" once wrote that 'language' was one of the major casualties of imperial wars. The political language of the US killing machine in Iraq and their 'embedded' propagandists is nothing less than a collection of euphemisms in the service of the killing machine.

Almost the entire population of non-Kurdish Iraq is opposed to the US military and its puppet regime – yet the media refer to the patriots defending their country from the imperial invaders as – 'insurgents' minimizing the significance of a nation-wide patriotic liberation movement. One of the most surreal euphemisms is the constant reference to the 'coalition forces' – meaning the US colonial conquerors and the mercenaries and satraps that they direct and control.

The terror bombing of homes, hospitals and religious buildings by hundreds of airplanes and helicopter gunships are described by the media as 'securing the city for free elections'.

'Freeing the city of insurgents' includes the systematic murder of friends, neighbours and relatives of every Iraqi living in the city of Fallujah.

'Surrounding the insurgents' means cutting off water, electricity, medical aid for 200,000 civilians in the city and putting tens of thousands who fled under threat of a typhoid epidemic. 'Pacifying the city' involves turning it to absolute desolate poisoned rubble.

Why do Washington and the mass media resort to gross, systematic lying and euphemisms? Basically to reinforce mass support at home for mass murder in Iraq. The mass media fabricates a web of lies to secure a gloss of legitimacy for totalitarian methods in order that the US armed forces continue to destroy cities with impunity. The technique perfected by Goebbels in Germany and practiced in the US is to repeat lies and euphemism until they become accepted 'truths', and embedded in everyday language. The mass media by effectively routinizing a common language implicates the listeners. The tactical concerns of the Generals, the commanders directing the slaughter (pacification), and the soldiers murdering civilians are explained (and consumed by the millions listening and watching) by the unchallenged authorities to the compliant journalists and famous news anchors. The identification of the agents of mass murder and everyday US public is established via 'news reports': The soldiers 'paint the names' of their wives and sweethearts on the tanks and armored vehicles which destroy Iraqi families and turn Fallujah into ruins. Returning soldiers from Iraq are 'interviewed' who want to return to 'be with their platoon' and 'wipe out the terrorists'. Not all of US combat forces experienced the joys of shooting civilians. Medical studies report that one out of five returning soldiers are suffering from severe psychological trauma, no doubt from witnessing or participation in the mass killing of civilians. The family of one returned soldier, who recently committed suicide, reported that he constantly referred to his killing an unarmed child in the streets of Iraq – calling himself a 'murderer'. Aside from these notable exceptions, the mass propaganda media practice several techniques, which assuage the 'conscience' of US soldiers and civilians. One technique is 'role reversal' to attribute the crimes of the invading force to the victims: It is not the soldiers who cause destruction of cities and murder, but the Iraqi families who 'protect the terrorists' and bring upon themselves the savage bombardment. The second technique is to only report US casualties from 'terrorist bombs' – to omit any mention of thousands of Iraqi civilian killed by US bombs and artillery. Both Nazi and US propaganda glorify the 'heroism', 'success' of their elite forces (the SS and the Marines) – in killing 'terrorists' or 'insurgents' – every dead civilian is counted as a 'suspected terrorist sympathizer'.

The US and German military have declared every civilian building a 'storehouse' or 'hiding place' for 'terrorists' – hence the absolutely total disregard of all the Geneva laws of warfare. The US and Nazi practice pf 'total war' in which whole communities, neighbourhoods and entire cities are collectively guilty of shielding 'wanted terrorists' – is of course the standard operating military procedure of the Israeli government.

The US publicizes the cruel and unusual punishment of Iraqi 'suspects' (any male between 14-60 years) taken prisoner: photos appear in Time and Newsweek of barefoot, blindfolded and bound young men led from their homes and pushed into trucks to be taken to 'exploitation centers' for interrogation. For many in the US public these pictures are part of the success story – they are told these are the 'terrorists' who would blow up American homes. For the majority who voted for Bush, the mass propaganda media has taught them to believe that the extermination of scores of thousands of Iraqi citizens is in their best interests: they can sleep sound, as long as 'our boys' kill them 'over there'.

Above all the mass propaganda media has done everything possible to deny Iraqi national consciousness. Everyday in every way the reference is to religious loyalties, ethnic identities, past political labels, 'tribal' and family clans. The purpose is to divide and conquer, and to present the world with a 'chaotic' Iraq in which the only coherent, stable force is the US colonial regime. The purpose of the savage colonial assaults and the political labeling is to destroy the idea of the Iraqi nation – and in its place to substitute a series of mini-entities run by imperial satraps obedient to Washington.

Sunday November 14, 2004, I turn on the television to the popular program 60 Minutes and watch a replay of Mike Wallace's 'interviews' with Yasser Arafat. Like all US mass media 'stars', he ignores Israeli invasion of Lebanon and Sharon's murder of thousands of

Palestinians, the military occupation of Palestine and the wanton destruction of Jenin and Gaza City. Wallace accuses Arafat of being a liar, a terrorist, of being corrupt and devious. Thirty million US households watch this ugly spectacle of a self-righteous Zionist apologist flaunting the 'Western ideals', which are so useful in razing cities, bombing hospitals and exterminating a nation.

Yes, there are differences between Mr. Shirer's account of Nazi propaganda in defense of the conquest of Europe and the US media's apology for the invasion of Iraq and the Jewish State's slaughter of the Palestinians: One is committed in the name of the Fuehrer and the Fatherland, the other in the name of God and Democracy. Go tell that to the bloated corpses gnawed by dogs in the ruins of Fallujah.

9

Past, Present and Future of China: From Semi-Colony to World Power?

James Petras March 2006

Introduction

The general consensus is that China is emerging as the next great economic superpower. Despite growing awareness of severe ecological problems and occasional recognition of the growing social inequalities, many writers foresee China (and lately India) as the next world powers, challenging and surpassing Japan, Europe and the United States.

This essay raises serious methodological, conceptual, historical and empirical questions concerning the notion of China as the next world superpower. Without denying the tremendous increase in exports, investments and growth, this paper focuses on a more basic question: what is the character of the principal units of analysis responsible for this expansion, and how do they project into the future? This is not a semantic issue but one of method and conceptual clarity, without which we cannot comprehend exactly who are the 'agents' of growth and transformation. This requires that we go beyond simplistic national labels to identifying the socio-political character of the economic units acting within China and in particular the most dynamic of these units in terms of their future power.

The second section of the paper will provide a schematic historical analysis of the 'stages' of Chinese development, focusing on the continuities, ruptures, transitions and projections over the past half-century. The purpose is to identify the rise, fall and revival of social classes and the political economic project in which they are embedded.

The third section will focus on the performance of the Chinese political economy, both its growth and explicit and inherent contradictions.

The fourth section will focus on the impact of deepening liberalization on the economic and class structure, particularly the role of foreign capital. Specifically this section will discuss the long-term implications of the takeovers of Chinese enterprises by multi-national corporations and banks.

The fifth section will discuss the external political, economic and military threats and challenges, which China faces, as well as the internal conflicts, which are cause and consequence of China's insertion in the world capitalist system.

The final section provides an overview of the future trajectory of China's development. This section will be directed at the political and economic consequences of the cumulative purchases by foreign capital of the most dynamic sectors of the economy. It will examine whether the state is harnessing foreign capital to the Chinese growth engine or whether the Chinese state will become increasingly carved up into sectoral and regional fiefdoms by competing imperial capitals. This in turn will lead us to address the question of whether China's national and international capitalist classes will become protagonists of an emerging competing empire, partners and competitors of existing imperial powers or whether they will succumb and become satraps of old imperialists of the US, Japan and Europe.

The viability of Chinese capitalism ultimately rests not only on its growth rates and job generating capacity, but also on the social relations of production, circulation and reproduction. The ferocious exploitation of labor, the massive displacement of peasants, the firing of millions of skilled/semi-skilled industrial workers from state and bankrupt firms and their increasing propensity to engage in direct action foretells the emergence of large-scale class warfare pitting the new billionaire class of foreign and domestic capitalists and their 'protector state' against the hundreds of millions of dispossessed and alienated workers and peasants. The class struggle, its extent, intensity and political course will test the sustainability of the Chinese growth model of 'maximum exploitation' under autocratic control.

We will conclude by looking at the twin forces of growing foreign capital takeovers and intensifying class struggle as they intersect, to modify or transform Chinese society and economy.

Methodological and Conceptual Clarification

In any attempt to evaluate and analyze the Chinese economy it is essential to determine what it means to write of "China". The most obvious discussion focuses on the geographical border, which demarcate the country from other countries and the nature of the political regime. But a discussion of "China" requires us to go beyond this elemental designation, to a discussion of the principle economic activities and the ownership of the dynamic sectors of the economy. "Made in China" does not necessarily mean owned by Chinese. Insofar as the political-legal-territorial framework contains non-Chinese economic units engaged in large-scale, long-term trade, production, distribution, finance, and research and development, it is incumbent on the analyst to draw a distinction between the performance of "Chinese" and "non-Chinese" economic units and actors. To lump them altogether as simply "China" obscures differential performances and divergent middle and long-term consequences. Moreover it is important to delineate, the dynamic tendencies between Chinese and non-Chinese economic units to determine which will ultimately predominate.

Beyond the important quantitative differences in ownership between Chinese and non-Chinese units, is the question of whether non-Chinese units are 'harnessed' to a Chinese-directed growth strategy or vice versa? Almost all academics, journalists, consultants and officials from the international financial institutions (IFI) lump together the Chinese and non-Chinese economic institutions and actors in calculating exports, investments, production, financing, imports and so on. Moreover they generally overlook the fact that non-Chinese units are growing faster, increasing their share of exports (and imports), profits, royalty payments and control over new growth sectors of the economy.

This is particularly true since China joined the World Trade Organization, and deepened and extended its liberalization strategy. The growth of foreign owned enterprises means that investments, trade, exports, financing, location, and decisions are made according to the global needs of the MNCs and backed by their imperial states – outside of the framework of the legal entity called "China". As the presence of non-Chinese MNCs increases, so does their influence over the dynamic growth sectors of the economy, conversely the range of influence over the economy by the Chinese state declines. Even more important, given the close relation between strategic growth sectors and the state, the increasing presence of the MNCs is likely to change the nature of the state, making it less "Chinese" and more attuned and responsive to the policies of the foreign-owned MNCs.

Needless to day this is a middle to long-term process which depends on several factors beyond the dynamics of capital expansion. For example, intensified internal class and national conflict or external military economic threats and confrontations could weaken or even undermine the dynamic expansion and control of foreign MNCs.

In any case the method of measuring China's growth performance requires that the politically sensitive factor of Chinese versus non-Chinese is taken into account. The result is likely to downgrade or diminish the performance of China. On the other hand if we conceive of the MNC as extensions of the major imperial powers (US, EU and Japan), as dynamic outposts or enclaves of empire embedded in the Chinese economy, we should consider their expansion as part of the growth of empire.

In other words, political-legal "China" grows as the imperial powers expand – as is evident over the past quarter of a century and probably for the next several decades. This suggests that the arguments about Chinese power challenging the US, EU and Japan is based on a false premise, namely that what is "Chinese" is analytically and factually distinct from the principle economic units of the US and other imperial countries, which operate in China.

The assumption of growing Chinese power is based on the idea that Chinese-owned and controlled economic units in strategic sectors of finance, manufacturing and export are growing faster than imperial-based MNCs and international investment houses. As we will demonstrate in the text below, the data do not support such an assumption.

Another questionable presumption is the notion that foreign investment and MNCs are being subordinated or harnessed by the Chinese state to serve Chinese strategic goals just as the US used British investment in the railroads to expand US capitalism. There are several problems with this argument. First of all, the Chinese state, its policies and leadership are not fixed in time: initial foreign investment has led to accelerated entry in a wide range of sectors, both cause and consequence of increasing liberalization. Chinese governing elites have mutated over time from dominant partners to co-owners to minority shareholders in the latest investment ventures. The notion of 'harnessing' foreign investors to serve Chinese development strategy is losing relevance as MNCs capture the commanding heights of several sectors or at least lead management in key enterprises. As the Chinese state invests in infrastructure (railroads, ports, air transport and so on) the MNCs increase their role in the dynamic sectors of the market. China's 21st strategy reverses the US' 19th century strategy with regard to foreign investment – the lucrative growth sectors pass on to foreign capital, while the Chinese treasury funds the high cost, long-term, large-scale, low-return infrastructure.

The second general problem with regard to the notion of Chinese growth performance is the extremely limited geographical area and working population that it encompasses. One could almost write of "Two Chinas" – the coastal region and the interior. The fact of the matter is that China's productive grid is extremely limited to its port regions, with links to mining enclaves in the interior. Given the lack of national economic integration and the high level of integration (trade and investment) with external imperial powers (Japan, USA and EU) it is problematic to refer to China as a national economy. This is particularly the case when the coastal economic zones concentrate almost all of the foreign-owned or managed enterprises. In analytical terms what is termed Chinese growth is rather zones of expansion within which foreign-owned enclaves operate. Geographically speaking Chinese growth is profoundly circumscribed; within these circumscribed zones, the most dynamic enterprises are not Chinese.

State revenues and expenditures reinforce the "zonal" and enclave nature of what is effectively "China". At best the interior of China serves as a source of cheap labor, a declining share of food and raw materials, much as overseas labor and neo-colonies serve the imperial powers.

The third problem with discussing China's economic performance as an undifferentiated entity is the issue of the class-specific process of accumulation and distribution. The entire process of accumulation, reproduction, concentration and distribution is directed, owned and benefits an extremely limited class of foreign and domestic capitalists and state directors and their extended family networks.

The extreme and growing class inequities in power, wealth, ownership, access to state credit, contracts, licenses, incentives and land concessions is totally mystified by references to "China" invests, grows...etc. While the foreign and domestic ruling classes compete for government subsidies, concessions and market shares, they share at least two essential characteristics: one a common support for increasing capital's share of national income; and a common opposition to any efforts by labor to organize, protest or improve working and living condition. Conceptually this requires us to discard the undifferentiated notion of "China" and to focus on the class actors who act in the name of China, but who design or demand development policies compatible with their class interests. Otherwise the presumption is that the collective population embodied in the notion of 'China' is somehow implicated in the essential economic decisions or that those, who make the decisions, in some way "represent" the interests of the Chinese workers, unemployed and peasants rather than the class-controlled institutions in which they are embedded.

An equally important methodological issue arises from measuring the standard of living in China. Most analysts equate standard of living with monetary income and conclude that there has been a vast increase in living standards, a "historic" massive reduction in poverty and improved opportunity. These are very questionable inferences for several crucial reasons. Measuring the standard of living involves far more than a discussion of monetary income, especially in economies in transition from socialism to free-market capitalism.

The elimination of free education, health, paid vacations and pension in the transition signals a decline in living standards and should result in a major deduction from monetary earnings. Secondly capitalist displacement of millions of farmers, artisans and others with sideline earnings in kind (food, utensils and so on) means another deduction from monetary income. Thirdly the increase of living costs (rents, energy, electricity, water and so on) must be deducted from monetary income. Fourthly, the stress and physical abuse from the intensified exploitation of labor in export factories increases the likelihood of physical disabilities, workplace injuries and deaths, worsening conditions at the workplace means a further decline in living standards. The added multiple tax burdens on peasants by exploitative local officials, the delays and avoidance of paychecks by private owners, the eradication of workers neighborhoods and housing to benefit real estate speculators all have worsened living standards. While personal consumption has increased – very unequally over time and place – employment, land tenure, price and retirement insecurity are negative determinants of living standards.

If the estimates of mass living standards are distorted upwardly by reference to monetary income, they are understated for the new class of billionaire and millionaire capitalists and their progeny. Monetary income forms are important but partial measures of their living standards. Their access to the best private foreign and domestic health services, elite private foreign and domestic educational institutions, privileged and easy direct access to government policy makers, accumulation of a conglomerate of physical assets (productive and financial), their extended family privileges, capacity to inherit established wealth, their luxurious vacations, mansions, automobiles...to name only a few of their non-monetary assets, means that monetary measures of income underestimate the living standards of the capitalist class.

By any measure, the relative standard of living of the Chinese masses, as a share of the total goods and services and quality of life has declined precipitously. This is especially the case if we examine the 'ecology' of habitation and work and its unequal impact on classes. Scientists and all observers have written and spoken to the vast increase of air, water and ground pollution generated by unregulated capitalist expansion by private and state enterprises. What most observers fail to note however is that the sickness and deaths accrue overwhelmingly among the workers, peasants and low-paid salaried classes who are most exposed to pollution at their workplace, in their movements through the cities, their dependence on public water facilities and the location of their dwellings.

The ruling and upper classes live in less polluted locations, drink bottled water, have country and seashore villas to escape the contaminated air, have air-conditioned cars, homes, country clubs and are located far from the highly contaminated mines, factories, sewers, waste dumps and incinerators. The advent of capitalism has certainly increased respiratory illnesses and childhood diseases especially in "high growth" industrial zones. Ecological impoverishment is a major factor in reducing living standards because it adversely affects the quality of life.

Given the vast and growing inequalities, the worst measures of living standards are those, which rely on 'per capita income' (income divided by population). For reasons mentioned above, monetary income is a near useless or very limited measure. Per capita income obscures the elephantine inequalities between the top 5 per cent and the bottom 75 per cent of the population. The 'average' is a deceptive statistical artifact which obscures the real income levels of the vast majority. It would be more appropriate to average the monetary income by decimals, minus the costs of social services (health, education and pensions, rents, energy, travel and taxes). In addition, to convert the remainder of monetary income into a measure of living standards, we would have to counterpoise gains in purchases of consumer goods to losses in fresh air, leisure time, job security, near rent-free housing, paid vacations, benign working conditions and family separations.

The measure of monetary income and living standards is much more complex than what is argued by most orthodox economists. If we expand our discussion of living standards to what needs to be called the social pathologies, the argument in favor of rising living standards becomes even more dubious. The decline of public morality in the transition to capitalism is universally recognized. China ranks among the worst countries in the world in terms of corruption by public officials, usually but not exclusively in terms of transactions with the private sector. In terms of the monetary value of corruption and white-collar crime, China surely ranks at the highest level of the big US enterprises like World Com, Enron and the US savings and loan corporations. Tens of billions of dollars are illegally transferred (laundered) by Chinese elites overseas, purchasing real estate in the US, Canada and England, stocks, bonds and Treasure notes as well as financing expensive education and health care for progeny and family. Corruption permeates Chinese economic and public life down to local village officials –

reinforcing class privileges and creating new ones. While corruption existed during the Communist period, it was on a far lower scale and scope than the present, as most of the Chinese perceive and attest. Corruption has enormous class consequences: enhancing the power, property and privileges of the wealth while increasing the taxes for the peasants and deteriorating public services and eliminating public investments beneficial to the urban working class.

Equally important has been the massive increase of crime, including drugs, prostitution, sex slavery, and fraud and illegal public assaults on protestors deprived of land, jobs, pensions and homes. The geometric growth of street, office and state crime and the ensuing insecurity, loss of property, income and life, is a product of the new capital ethos of "get rich", which undermines the civic virtues of the collective good which reigned in the previous period, even as it was frequently breached in practice. Living with pervasive corruption, crime and arbitrary authority guided by motives of private gain at public expense is certainly a measure of declining living standards.

These methodological considerations will guide our discussion of the transition of the Chinese economy to 21st Century capitalism.

Stages of Chinese Development: From Semi-Colony to Revolution

Historical changes occur in unequal time frames: relatively slow processes involving small-scale changes and gradually emerging contradictions are followed by rapid and abrupt revolutions. China is illustrative of this proposition. Over the past half century China has passed through two major revolutions and two "transitional regimes" which have transformed property relations, the class structure and the nature of state power. Each political revolution has set in motion a re-organization of the economy and changed the nature of the class struggle, guided by a new configuration of socio-political power.

Each stage of development grows out of the previous period, carrying forth to the new political-economic regime some of the practices, values and classes from the old. Moreover the transition from socialism to capitalism, in particular, the high growth rates and many of the attractions for private foreign and domestic investors were products of the basic human and capital investments undertaken under the socialist regime. Each political-economic regime contains the seeds of its own destruction and the social agencies for the emergence of the new regime.

Stage One: From Colony and Neo-Colony to Revolutionary Socialist Regime

The Chinese socialist revolution (CSR) (1949) created the most basic political and economic conditions for any sustained and consequential economic development. The revolutionary movement played a major role in the military defeat of Japanese colonialism, ended the European enclaves and the coastal concessions in the course of creating national sovereignty. The CSR defeated provincial and local warlords and their allies in the Kuomintang thus creating a unitary state. It ended skyrocketing inflation, monumental corruption and pillage of the public treasury and financial system, laying the groundwork for a stable currency, fiscal discipline and a functioning economy capable of reconstructing the war devastated economy. It repulsed US threats to its frontiers during the US invasion of North Korea. Within the framework of a sovereign national state, free of intrusive imperial tutelage, the CSR organized vast infrastructure projects (roads, ports, airfields, railroads, irrigation, flood control, water and electrical linkages) that stimulated high rates of economic growth in industry, trade and agriculture, ending decades of mass starvation under Western and Eastern imperial domination. The CSR brought about several strategic reforms which provided the basis for long-term growth: it inaugurated a mass public literacy and health campaign at all levels of society – creating an educated, healthy labor force, and including millions of engineers, scientists and highly skilled machine/tool operators. Equally important it converted a mass of rural peasants into a disciplined skilled and productive urban industrial labor force, raising living standards in the course of creating a complex division of labour. Upstream industries in steel and coal and the capital goods sector created the basis for downstream light industries and inexpensive consumer items. In the countryside, fragmented and unproductive mini-agricultural holdings were consolidated leading to greater mechanization and facilitating the provision of social services to cooperative and later to larger collectivist units.

Without these profound structural changes, nation building and the emergence of productive economy would never have been possible. The development process was not altogether a linear, stable process: over-ambitious goals, which over-estimated the regimes organizational and technical capacity such as the Great Leap Forward (1957-58) led to temporary setbacks which had substantial negative consequences especially in the countryside. Equally important, the new system and regime, despite the radical changes in property relations, class structure and the new egalitarian norms, contained many of seeds of the past 'commercial-landlord-hierarchal-colonial' society, which preceded it. Party cadres acting on behalf of the state transferred the rural surplus extracted from the peasant coops to the central government engaged in rapid urban industrialization, using the same mixture of coercion and persuasion as the "tax collectors" in the semi-feudal past, even as the ends pursued were totally different. The vertical-centralized organizational structure of the regime in pursuit of egalitarian goals reflected the ruptures and continuities with the past, the combination of "feudalism" and socialism.

For nearly a decade after the revolution, a substantial number of capitalist enterprises continued to operate under the tutelage of the Communist regime. Subsequent to nationalization, many of the business leaders either fled the country or were incorporated into the economic, planning or industrial ministries. Some of these capitalist holdovers or their kin later made a comeback with the reversion to capitalism and the revival of private enterprise. Beyond the individual or class incorporation of capitalists into the public sector, the new enterprise directors adopted what they considered the "modern forms of production" – namely, mass production line, Taylorist production methods, unbalanced growth, emphasizing heavy industry and production goals over agriculture and consumption.

The influence of the Soviet model of economic development played a major role in defining growth and accumulation strategies, and the priorities and methods of economic development. Social consumption –

investment allocations to public health, transport and education took far greater precedence over individual consumption based on quality goods, including clothing, housing, recreation, food and household appliances.

The tensions between feudal-capitalist-Soviet methods and organization emphasizing vertical control and public-defined priorities increasingly came into conflict with mass demands for greater popular participation, horizontal solidarity and personal consumption. The latent and overt conflicts between the Party elite and the masses over participation took place within a general consensus over the iron rice bowl (guaranteed employment), universal free public education and health, 'affirmative action' (promoting individuals from worker or peasant background) and public ownership of the means of production. The major exceptions among the masses to this consensus existed in the countryside among peasants who cultivated small private lots for self-consumption, barter or occasional sale, and among a limited stratum of urban vendors. The most influential exception to the socialist consensus in the elite was among an important stratum of party leaders, ideologues and followers who argued for greater role for "the market", greater enterprise autonomy and the introduction of market reforms. The open class conflict between these forces eventually led to the "Cultural Revolution" (1966-1974), which sought to definitively set the revolution on a course toward deepening the socialist perspective. Paradoxically the outcome of the Cultural Revolution severely weakened the mass movements and led to the ascendance of what later became the "capitalist roaders" under the leadership of Deng Tsiao Peng.

The Cultural Revolution, at the onset, challenged the "feudal" extraction of the rural surplus, the Soviet style hierarchy and abuse of authority and the "Taylorist" organization of work. The struggle reaffirmed the primacy of the workers role in society thus precluding any openings toward the market, postponing at least for 20 years any liberalization. The urban mobilizations, especially of the young generation, was aimed at ending the abuse of power by public authorities and professionals who monopolized the public institutions of education, health, science and culture in order to bring them into line with egalitarian norms. The mass excesses and the conversion of the ideological/class struggle into an elite-bureaucratic conflict controlled from above, and the lack of any positive direction of the mass mobilization led to the exhaustion and disillusion of the mass movements.

The eventual ascendancy of the 'capitalist roaders' in the late 1970's was not so much a result of any decisive political-military victory as it was a byproduct of the demise and dissolution of the mass movements under the leadership of an aging Mao Tse Tung and what came to be called the 'Gang of Four'.

Stage II: From Communism to State Capitalism 1970-1989

The eclectic communism of the period (1949-78) period, and the demise of the renovating forces in the Cultural Revolution (1966-73) strengthened the bureaucratic elite favourable to opening up to the market, reinforced the capitalist remnants embedded in the regime, and more important opened room for advancement for economists, scientists, engineers and other party cadre educated or influenced by late Soviet experiments with profit-based enterprises and calculus. Equally important Mao's foreign policy right turn embracing Washington (Nixon and Kissinger) and a host of right-wing, anti-communist dictators and leaders from Pinochet in Chile, Marcos in the Philippines and Savimbi in Angola opened the entire party of a reassessment to its international politics and the centrality of the world capitalist market. This reassessment, in turn, strengthened the emerging new generation of professionals and cadres who came to maturity in the post-revolutionary period. Their thinking was shaped in sharp reaction to the plebian-egalitarian thrust of the Cultural Revolution and particularly by its excesses and its attempt to circumvent objective problems by 'creating facts' and by its frontal attack on scientists, experts and academics.

The new power configuration was made up of technocrats, market-oriented Communist leaders, aspiring private entrepreneurs, political ideologues of a new capitalist class and sectors of the old bourgeoisie restored to respectability. They developed a strategy of liberalization in stages. This new power elite sought to avoid a frontal attack on the social welfare system and collective property. Instead they adopted a series of 'staggered liberalizing measures throughout the 1980's. They substituted a de facto privatization of land via the dismantling of the collective farms, even those which were successful and imposed a 'family leasehold' system, encouraging private trade, individual accumulation and gradual land concentration. High Party and State officials and Party cadres, as agents of the state transfers of property to the private sector, contracts, import licenses, land use permits, credits, loans and incentives, enriched themselves and soon became capitalists on their own right. These perquisites were distributed by state officials to the new class of capitalists at a price: corruption was the link between the liberal collectivist apparatus and the capitalists, often blurring the line between public and private ownership especially as a high percentage of new class capitalist were progeny or kin of state officials.

"State Capitalism" became the transitional regime between socialism and neo-liberal capitalism. This transitional regime's most important role was to create the optimal framework for the rapid accumulation of private capital and wealth. This involved the imposition of a harsh regimen of labor control and repression of workers demands and unregulated exploitation by capital over labor. Total labor control allowed the regime to privatize and close numerous enterprises, engage in massive pillage of resources and the creation of a new class of rich millionaires within a decade. Economic liberalization encouraged the growth of two sets of oppositions: A pro-Western/imperialist liberal democratic student opposition bent on taking the "Russian road" and a worker-based opposition which demanded democracy in the name of defending the heritage of full employment, trade union rights, the iron pot' and other welfare measures being undermined by the state capitalists with liberal leanings. The 'Tiananmen Square (1989) uprising was dominated by the student-liberals; in Shanghai and elsewhere the worker-socialist opposition predominated.

Both oppositions were defeated, strengthening the state apparatus and the advance of liberalization in the 1990's until the early 2000. The 'state capitalist' regime attempted to ride two horses, a continued strong state sector, nourishing a privileged and corrupt official elite and a market opening for commercial, agricultural and private business and investors to 'complement' the state sector. The statist sector, initially the dominant group insisted that public banks continue to favor loans to state enterprises, while the liberal factions and other state officials pushed for greater public loans for private firms and wider areas for private investment.

By the end of 1980's and into the 1990's, the internal relation of forces, shifted inexorable toward the 'liberalizing' sectors of the state ruling elite, as the private sector gained momentum and increasing concessions from the state.

In other words 'state capitalism' became the breeding ground for private capitalism.

State capitalism as a "transitional regime" to liberal capitalism combines the outer forms of socialism (the predominance of state enterprises and state planning) while the inner dynamics moved toward capitalist relations (land leasing, export strategy, openings to foreign investments, and privatizations). Most important a new "ideology" encouraging individual enrichment served as a justification and stimulus for the emerging new class of capitalists. The accelerated, if lopsided and income concentrating, growth during the 1980s was underwritten by the basic foundations for development constructed during the preceding Communist period. The newly emerging capitalist regime benefited from healthy, trained and skilled urban industrial working class, basic industries (steel, coal, heavy machines) and light industries (textiles, shoes and related activities) which served as the take-off points for the export strategy. Basic infrastructure (railroads, ports, airports and shipping) and an orderly, stable and unified state capable of defending national sovereignty built under the Communist regime were essential conditions for the capitalist take-off.

The key element within the state capitalist formation that facilitated the movement away from communism and toward the transformation of China into a liberal capitalist state was the re-socialization of the entire policy-making and advisory elite: namely the unquestioning adoption of capitalist criteria, methods, motivations and organizational structures. During the 1980s, a whole generation of children of the state capitalist elite was educated by Western liberal economists both in China and abroad. They were taught market economic models, the equation of "modernization' with capitalist liberalization, the positive role of the multi-national corporations and foreign investment. They were induced to believe that efficiency was identical with profitability and privatization, that inequality with was a result of 'merit' (or lack of it). The entire litany of capitalist virtues was almost universally and unquestionably accepted by the educated elite – and put into practice – because it provided a justification and incentive for their own class ambitions.

The progeny of the state-capitalist elite became the political and economic agency for the transformation of state capitalism to its liberal variant. The emerging new class of liberalizing capitalists benefited educationally and in terms of economic opportunities from the privileged position of their families in the state apparatus. They also benefitted from their political links to state sector officials in terms of the rigged privatization of state property, largely based on corruption, illegal transfers, swindles, under-pricing and other political mechanisms.

The transition to from state to liberal capitalism was based on a kind of 'primitive accumulation' or pillage of public resources, as the motor force of expanded capitalist reproduction in the subsequent liberal capitalist phase. The state capitalist elite justified the opening to liberalization as a means of "developing the forces of production as a prelude to socialism". The emergence of a powerful, influential billionaire capitalist class diminished the credibility of this slogan.

The principal groundwork for the liberal transition performed by the state capitalist was the abolition of all restraints on the most savage forms of capitalist exploitation of labor and the cheapening of labor costs by creating a mass of 400 to 500 million displaced rural and urban workers available for employment in low-paid factors, construction and domestic services. By 2005 China had the worst inequalities of any Asian country – a far cry form the early 1970's when it was one of the most egalitarian countries.

Transition from State Capitalism to Liberal Capitalism

The growing presence of Chinese capitalists throughout all sectors of the economy, their high concentration in the dynamic growth sectors was cause and consequence of their greater political presence directly and indirectly in the top spheres of the political system. The result was the deepening of liberalization: the accelerated dismantling of trade barriers, of protective labor laws, the savaging of the countryside, the massification the reserve army of unemployed and the near unquestioning orientation toward the export market strategy. This led to the emergence of a class of billionaires – 'super-rich' – comparable to the richest of the rich in the imperial countries and the world's greatest inequalities between the top 1 per cent and the bottom 50 per cent of the class structure.

The 'victims of the Cultural Revolution' became the executioners of one of the harshest capitalist restorations in modern history (perhaps exceeded by the Russian and some of the Eastern European and ex-Soviet Republics) if we measure the social losses and the extraordinary mass of profit, rents and land seizures which take place under the ascendant liberal elite.

The predominant group, at least in the early to middle years of the liberal regime, were Chinese national capitalists, though early on a substantial stake was taken on by overseas Chinese from Hong Kong, Taiwan and elsewhere. The advance of national private capitalism took two routes: either through the takeover of privatized state factories or via investments in new enterprises or services. In nearly all cases corruption of state officials played a major role in "lubricating" the process over and above the "entrepreneurial talents", market savvy and innovative behavior of the new class. Privatization beneficiaries – the new owners – were in part former Party-State officials who simply turned elite control into capitalist ownership and aspiring private business people with close ties to the local, provincial or state authorities. Likewise the new private enterprise bourgeoisie benefited enormously from state contracts, land grants, tax exonerations, state-controlled cheap labor and (especially at the beginning) nearly oligopolic markets. In both cases liberalization was as much state-driven as it was market-oriented. The interventionist state remained a key factor but its role changed dramatically from a direct investor to a promoter of private investment.

Rules limiting market activities were superseded by new regulations (or at least practices), which gave capitalists land sites, investment incentives and protection of property rights. Throughout the 1990's and into the new millennium, the one constant was the growing proportion of production, exports, investments of profits controlled by private capitalists. What began in the early 1980s, as a 'market opening', turned into torrents in the following two decades. By the middle of the first decade of the 21st century, private capital accounted for 75 per cent of non-agricultural production. In large part, the growth of private capitalism was the result of the closing of state factories or their sell-offs and the vast infusion of private capital both local and foreign.

The rapid reproduction of private capital at the national level resulted from the expansion of consumer goods production both durables and non-durables, based on the pent-up demand and initially little competition; the property, real estate and construction boom turned well-connected "entrepreneurs" into multi-millionaires. The buyouts of state enterprises also led to the rise of a new industrial bourgeoisie. By hook or crook, swindles, captive markets and above all else an unregulated market to plunder cheap labor, the emerging capitalists catapulted in less than a decade from small-scale businessmen into tycoons with multiple mansions, million-dollar condos, Mercedes, mistresses and overseas bank accounts.

Given the initial high levels of exploitation of labor, the hundreds of millions of unemployed workers and peasants and the high concentration of wealth in the upper tenth percentile, domestic demand was relatively constricted. The regime and the new capitalist ruling class looked toward the export market as a mechanism to retain class privileges and find a profitable outlet for growing production.

Given that the locus of markets was overseas, it was logical and profitable to develop the coastal regions of China, closest to the ports and force labor to move from the interior to production sites. The export markets determined production sites and the latter determined the direction of mass internal migration. The coastal production sites, ports, commercial and banking center became the hotbed for neo-liberal ideology spawned by the academic and research centers. The coastal cities also were the centers for the biggest economic transactions between state officials and the new big bourgeoisie, and between the latter and the foreign investors seeking "strategic partners" and entry into the Chinese market. All the major urban coastal centers became the centers for the most rancid forms of real estate speculation and corrupt land deals, which accompanied the construction of luxury apartments, upscale shopping malls, boutiques, five-star hotels and high rent skyscraper office buildings – to provide work space and cater to the whims and conspicuous consumption of the new bourgeois multi-millionaires and the first billionaires.

Millions of construction workers, miners, domestic servants and assembly-line workers labored under the most abominable conditions: the longest hours, the worst safety conditions, lowest pay and least sanitary and regulated work conditions in Asia produced the huge profit margins, private domestic services and the physical facilities within which the new rich got richer and conspicuous consumption became a daily ritual. Never in Chinese history or for that matter in the history of capitalism was so much private wealth accumulated, in such a short time, exploiting so much labor with so few rights and benefits. Juxtaposed upon the geographical concentration of production and distribution was the class concentration of wealth, consumption and political power. The notion of "Two Chinas" took on an altogether new meaning (no longer referring to the US distinction between China and Taiwan): it referred to the China of the coastal regions dominated by the new big bourgeoisie and the China of the interior made up of hundreds of millions of unemployed former peasants supplying cheap labour, foodstuffs, raw materials and finished goods to the coastal areas for processing, finishing, exporting and...profiting.

Foreign Capital: The First Beachheads

Parallel to the growth of an elite Chinese bourgeoisie, big foreign investors established manufacturing beachheads, and enclaves in key sectors, such as transport and other growth sectors. Major MNCs subcontracted with local Chinese manufacturers in all the major export sectors (clothes, shoes and toys) or directly invested in these sectors.

The turning point came with China's entry into the World Trade Organization: large-scale, long-term policy of state factory closings followed and were accompanied by privatizations and the transfer of ownership to private national or foreign capitalists. Entry into the WTO decisively shifted the balance between private and state capital, and the ideological predominance of the former.

Private capital surpassed state capital in the value of output, exports and employment offerings. Big private firms began to receive an increasing percentage of loans from state banks where in the past they were excluded or restricted. Under the cover and protection of equal treatment for foreign and national capital, Japanese, US, Hong Kong, Taiwanese and European Union MNCs accelerated their entry, spreading to most sectors of the economy from face creams to golf courses, from factories to high tech enterprises. Practically nothing was 'off limits'.

The "bureaucratic statists" engaged in rear-guard actions meant to slow the pace of privatization via regulatory delays and non-implementation of political decisions. Some of these objections were based on political beliefs, others as a means of extracting pay-offs. In the end, however, the statists were clearly in retreat.

High growth meant the expansion of conglomerates under the ownership of billionaires and pervasive family-based capitalist intertwined with overseas Chinese billionaires and Western investment houses.

The state capitalist model based on a triple alliance of state capital – national private capital – foreign investment was replaced by a new dual coalition of national and foreign capital. By the middle of the first decade of the 21st century, the national bourgeoisie had reached the apex of power – surpassing state capital and not yet challenged for dominance by the ascending foreign multi-nationals. Labor unrest was spreading at a geometrical rate, but so were the systems of repressions and special police and paramilitary forces. Cheap labour pools were declining but the inflow from the countryside compensated for high labor turnover. Competition was intensifying but overseas financing was growing and opportunities for strategic alliances were increasing. Opposition for foreign capital penetration was as yet limited to bureaucratic sectors. Most Chinese capitalists preferred to subcontract and form partnerships with foreign capital. Most university graduates were looking to careers in the private national monopolies and foreign MNCs. A state-anchored career was a lesser preference. Bankruptcies among small and middle size firms proliferated as competition intensified and profit margins declined, but new and bigger monopolies took their place.

China was not only a Chinese capitalist's 'paradise' – it was a magnet for capitalists and investors world wide: everyone wanted to get into the act of unrestricted exploitation of labor and the market of 200 million middle class consumers, 10 million millionaires and thousands of super-rich billionaires.

The Future: The Transition from Liberalism to Neo-Liberalism – Eclipse of the National Bourgeoisie?

The present tendencies - the middle of the first decade of the 21st century - mark out a clear trajectory toward a deepening of capitalist, especially foreign capitalist, expansion (barring a major crisis in the global trading system, a social revolution in China, a serious recession in the US or a Sino-US military confrontation).

Foreign investment and overseas MNCs are growing at a rapid rate, moving beyond their initial beachheads as minority shareholders in select firms. From the present to the next decade, MNCs and foreign investment banks will buy into and extend their reach into production, distribution, transport, telecommunications, real estate and the service sectors throughout the lucrative coastal economies. This process proceeds via three routes: via direct investments in new enterprises; the most common approach is to engage in joint ventures with a strategic partner; the third route is to buy shares in existing enterprises. In all cases there is an unmistakable tendency for the MNCs to extend their influence and investments over time, eventually taking control over the strategic management positions. This process is not uniform, particularly where there are conflicts with Chinese management, political interference and sustained economic losses, in which case the MNCs withdraw.

As labor, rent and 'start-up' costs rise in the principle cities and as a relatively prosperous bourgeoisie and petit bourgeoisie emerge in the 'hinterland', the MNC will extend their operations toward the Chinese 'heartland'. Despite the lower living standards among the great mass of workers, peasants and unemployed, there is an internal market of 100-200 million active consumers in the heartland. The historic shift of FI and MNCs is toward capturing a substantial and eventually majority share of the domestic market even as China continues to serve as an assembly and export platform for foreign-owned firms.

The MNCs have launched a multi-pronged economic offensive to:

1. capture control of the banking and financial system.
2. dominate the high and middle sectors of the domestic consumer goods market.
3. penetrate into the telecommunications sector, and
4. gain shares in the cultural, entertainment, publicity and commercial markets.

Through the banking system, foreign capital will gain access to huge sums of internal savings, control credit to large, medium and small firms and more important, will be able to finance MNC investments with Chinese savings. China's leading banks are already selling shares to foreign investors and several major multi-national banks have purchased local banks. Bu the end of 2006, when restrictions on foreign ownership are lifted, the foreign takeover of the banking sector should accelerate. By the beginning of the second decade of this century, foreign banks will likely be in control of the financial levers of the Chinese economy. From there, the strategic leverage of loans, credit, refinancing and investment, foreign capital will be in a position to penetrate the peak industries of the country.

Foreign investors are oriented to capturing the existing consumer market – not in creating a mass market, which would entail increasing income, and/or redistributing income toward the hundreds of millions with extremely limited consumer power. The tendency is to target the higher end of the market - the new bourgeoisie and the more affluent, upwardly mobile petit bourgeoisie. Cosmetics, brand name fashions, transport and electronics are already penetrating the market. It is likely cheaper versions of the same goods will follow, gaining mass-market shares among employed workers and salaried people in the interior and coastal regions.

On the horizon, foreign investors can be expected to use the new world trade agreements to penetrate Chinese communications and service sectors, especially the mass media, entertainment, advertising and marketing outlets, especially the major retail outlets.

The step-by-step gradualist takeover strategy of the 1990s and the first five years of the new century will gain momentum in the following decade. The two step approach of buying into national firms and accumulating shares and influence over time will be replaced by outright buyouts and direct investments in new monopoly firms.

Chinese firms will still predominate in the highly competitive labor intensive sectors. However they will be subject to a greater profit squeeze by the MNC subcontractors and subject to high rates of bankruptcy, opening the way toward greater concentration of ownership.

A "division of labor" between foreign and Chinese capitalists is already beginning to emerge. The MNCs will control marketing, financing, design, technology, R and D, production targets and overseas sales. Their Chinese partners will be in charge of government relations (leveraging contacts, paying "commissions" or bribes, etc), labor relations, hiring of workers (but not necessarily hiring or firing middle and high level personnel, promotions and bonuses), public relations and engineering.

At some point, most likely in the second decade of this century, the cumulative power resulting from the dynamic growth of MNC power in finance, production, political influence and exports will result in a 'Great Leap Forward'. In the fourth great transformation, China will the leap from liberalism to neo-liberalism. The "Chinese" economy will lose its "national identity" and become a territorial outpost for foreign controlled and operated banks and multinational corporations. Quantitative penetration will lead to qualitative change in the commanding heights of the economy and in the elite spheres of the governing class. China's bid to become a "world power" will be subverted. Instead China will become a gigantic proxy for imperial powers, who will increasingly compete for dominance, using different sectors of the political elite, military, students and so on.

The point at which China will be transformed from a burgeoning world power into a proxy for the imperial states depends on when the MNCs capture the key means of production, finance and trade and when this economic power is expressed within the Chinese state. There is a symbiotic relation between the growing presence of MNCs and the conversion of the Chinese state into a promoter of "free market" policies, each reinforcing the other. China's Great Leap into an industrial outpost of empire will be consummated when the share of profits shift from the national bourgeois to foreign capital, a process which accelerated in the first decade of the 21st century.

China's bourgeoisies' lead role in the capitalist transformation is based on two factors: bureaucratic regulation and residual anti-imperialism of political officials. Some public officials undermine, delay and add costs to MNC entry. Another impediment are the investment miscalculations which foreign investors make in terms of corrupt or incompetent "strategic partners". The Chinese bourgeoisie is strongest in the most labor-intensive industries drawing on the mass reserve army of rural unemployed. As this "reserve" is exhausted and urbanized workers demand higher salaries, the comparative advantages of national bourgeoisie over foreign capital will decline. While the national bourgeoisie most certainly will press for greater repression of labor unrest, they will be caught between heightened workers pressures and greater MNC competition. The prospects for 'advance' of the national bourgeoisie will reside in concentration (monopolization), going 'overseas' in search for new cheap sites of exploitation or upgrading their technology and internal organization. The likelihood is that large-scale global Chinese capitalists will seek to find a modus vivendi with the ascending multi-nationals, sacrificing global power for a relatively declining share of the Chinese market and a handful of overseas operations in the poorer African, Asian and Latin American markets and resource enclaves.

The history and logic of large-scale, long-term developments bears out the idea that each preceding social regimes contains the transformative agents of the forthcoming regime. Just as "elite collectivists" (the "capitalist roaders") transformed China from a socialist into a state capitalist economy ("market socialism") so did the political official and the emerging bourgeois lay the groundwork for the rise of liberal capitalism. Finally foreign capital has grown into a dynamic force within the liberal framework, deepening its control within enterprises and banks and expanding across all sectors of the economy. Accompanying this non-violent transformation of China from a liberal to a neo-liberal capitalist state, is the increasingly mass resistance to the harshest exploitative conditions in the world, the most arbitrary usurpation seizure of land, the most dangerous working condition anywhere, the greatest inequalities between the top 1 per cent and the bottom 50 per cent. Added to the Chinese bourgeoisie's brutal exploitation is their laissez faire agricultural import policies which are ruining millions of peasants and driving them to desperation. By the middle of the first decade of the 21st century massive importation of heavily subsidized US cotton, rice and other grains has devastated sectors of the countryside. Increased competition by both national and foreign private capital has set in motion close to 100,000 mass demonstrations involving millions of workers and peasants protesting arbitrary firings, plant shutdowns, stolen pensions, arbitrary seizure of property without compensation.

The Deepening Social Crisis: The Return of Class Struggle

Between 2001 and 2004, major social protests rose from 4,000 to 72,000 a year, and in 2005 they increased to 91,000. Despite the formation of special military police units throughout the country, the rising tide of social protest, especially in the countryside was threatening to destabilize the regime. China's leadership responded by announcing a series of new programs. In March 2006, at the annual session of the National Peoples' Congress, Prime Minister Wen Jiabao promised to build a "new socialist countryside", describing it as a "major historic task". Wen promised that the government would spend an extra $5.2 billion dollars on rural schools, hospitals, crop subsidies and other programs – a 15 per cent increase over the past year. A World Health Organization survey measuring the equality of medical treatment placed China 187th out of 191 countries. The regime's neo-liberal policies were reaping the whirlwind of mass rural protest against arbitrary land seizures by rapacious developers and corrupt officials. To head off the protests Du Ying, Deputy Minister of China's powerful National Development and Reform Commission proposed 'reforms' based on "market mechanisms" to provide "just compensations" for land seized for commercial use. Over 133,000 hectares of Chinese farmland is converted to non-agricultural use every year leaving about 1 million farmers without land to farm. The leadership's "new socialist countryside" proposal included lower taxes and an end to extortionate payment demands by corrupt local officials. To fund these social reforms the leadership announced a slow down in the growth rate to 8 per cent and a plan to reallocate spending to encourage the growth of the domestic consumer market.

These measures, however, are too little and too late. In the first place the groups which would be adversely affected by these reforms are the same people who would be asked to implement the changes – a very dubious proposition. Secondly the additional spending of a few billion dollars will have a minimum effect on 800 million rural poor. The extension of the free market policies in the countryside, especially in the context of the so-called leasehold system, will continue to concentrate landownership and increase the number of rural unemployed. The rich farmers, transport owners, commercial middlemen and informal money lenders, in alliance with urban land speculators, have a stranglehold on political power and will certainly ensure that few if any of the new rural funding reaches the most needy multitudes. The regime's policy to promote domestic consumption requires a sharp increase in the minimum wage and regulation of highly skewed salary-profit ratios, which is not part of the neo-liberal agenda. Since most manufacturers are geared to the export market, the entire production structure would have to be adjusted to potential local market demand – again a costly process not currently on the screen for the new capitalist class. A substantial increase in the domestic consumer market means higher wages and products at affordable prices, both of which impinge on the profits of the new capitalists with the closest links to the leadership. The dilemma of power is that in order to contain rising social discontent by progressive structural adjustments the regime would need to be transformed, a new social power configuration would have to come to power and restrictions in the 'open-door' policy to foreign investors would have to take place.

There are clear signs that the rapid national and foreign private takeover of strategic sectors of the economy has engendered sharp opposition even within the Party. A sharp ideological dispute over a new property law protecting private property in the National Peoples Congress (March 2006) has taken place. Two sets of criticism arose in the debate: some argued that the property protections would shield the billionaires and millionaires who stole public assets or officials who took bribes; others claimed that the property law would obliterate the balance between state and private property in favour of the latter. While the debate is important in highlighting how China's foreign takeovers and rapid privatization has provoked vocal intellectual and public opposition, it is unlikely to have serious implications. The entire leadership of the regime is linked to the powerful expanding private sector elites who have become the essential motor force of growth. The social, familial and economic overlap between the political leadership and the private economic elites and the dominant neo-liberal model precludes any serious reforms. The class struggle will probably deepen.

The old paternalistic communist and state capitalist bonds between directors and workers, cadre collective farm leaders and peasants have been shattered. The spontaneous decentralized protests resulting from the first wave of liberal exploitation of mostly peasant workers is likely to be replaced by the new urbanized workers, angered by the grotesque class contrasts between a ruling class life style of conspicuous consumption and arbitrary power and a growing army of impoverished unemployed urban workers, displaced peasants and exploited workers. The centralization of capital in large factories in concentrated urban settings facilitates organization, exchange of ideas, sharing of experience, recollection of safer more secure guaranteed employment without great class distinctions.

Past recollections, the permeation of workers ideology converging with massified urbanized and concentrated of highly exploited workers is likely to generate a new type of cultural revolution, one with a distinctly class and anti-imperialist content. There is an inverse relation between the rise and relative decline of the national bourgeoisie and the decline and rise of the new working class as the focus shifts from a 'consumerist ethic' to a fight for class dignity and freedom from the thousands of trials and tribulations imposed by the ruling class. The future ruling foreign bourgeoisie will lack the national bourgeoisie's cultural ties, the 'national guise', the messianic discourse of a 'world power' to mystify the workers; Worker-capital relations will revolve totally around the cash nexus. Social relations based on foreign pillage will reawaken both class and national bonds and spread outward toward intellectuals, students, shopkeepers, peasants threatened by the dynamic accumulation of foreign capital – setting in motion new revolutionary struggle in the coming decades.

PART-II: IMPERIALISM

10
Imperial State, Imperialism and Empire

Introduction

Imperialism, the political-economic domination and exploitation of countries via economic penetration and/or military conquest or intervention is the driving force of contemporary history. Whole regions of Eastern Europe, the former USSR, Africa, South-Central Asia and Latin Americas have been converted into neo-colonies, colonies or spheres of influence of the US, the European Union and Japan. Newly emerging capitalist countries, like China, are challenging the established imperial powers for markets, raw materials and energy sources. Imperial wars, colonial occupations, military intervention and military coups to expand the empire are euphemistically referred to as "regime change" and "democratization". In order to understand the nature, structure and dynamics of the imperial system it becomes necessary to identify and explain the key political concepts and their place in the construction of the contemporary world empire.

Three inter-related concepts are central to understanding the contemporary world: imperial state, imperialism and empire. The dynamics of accumulation on a world scale, the need for great concentrations of capital located in large economic units to expand throughout the world is premised on the notion that they can move overseas and can find safe, secure and profitable territories and labor forces which to exploit. The relocation of capital (via multi-national corporations), its ability to exploit raw materials, secure energy sources, lend capital and enforce debt collection, dominate captive markets and mount low wage manufacturing subsidiaries is totally dependent on political relations which facilitate these conditions.

The essential political institutions facilitating the overseas expansion of capital is the imperial state and the emergence within the targeted regions of regimes and ruling classes oriented toward imperial-centered models of capital accumulation.

The organization and activity of the imperial state are crucial in creating the political conditions for imperialism – the economic expansion of capital. Empire is the joint product of the combined activity of the imperial state and the process of imperialist economic expansion. Much has been written about the economic dimensions of imperialism: the growth and role of multinational corporations, the importance of energy resources and the petroleum industry, the take-over and buyout of privatized firms, the economic conditions and structural adjustment policies imposed by the international financial institutions (IFI) like the International Monetary Fund (IMF) and the World Bank (WB). Some studies have linked these imperialist economic forces with imperialist policies and their favorable results for the MNC's and their negative social economic consequences for the targeted country. The common or unstated assumption is that the imperial state is simply a passive reflection, an empty vessel of imperialist capital; the assumption that the imperial state can be reduced to a simple instrument of the collective interests and forces of imperial capital. This confuses an analysis of the political structures of imperialism with the economic processes of imperialism (the expansion of capital). The assumption is that there is such a powerful identity of purpose between 'structure' and 'process' that one needs only to look at the process (capital accumulation) to deduce the nature and internal dynamics of the imperial state.

This simplistic economic deductive approach has several egregious weaknesses in understanding the formation of empire. In the first place the imperial state formulates strategies and tactics, which go far beyond the immediate demands and interests of all or most of the capitals, which are engaged in overseas expansion. Secondly this reductionist approach fails to take account of conflicts of interests between politico-military decision makers and ideologues in the imperial state and the strategists of the MNC's. The reductionists merely assume that whatever the imperial policy-makers decide is automatically in the interests of the imperial economic corporations. There is a presumed unity of policy, strategy and ideology where in fact that should be merely a working hypothesis to be tested by observable historical or empirical facts.

Imperial State: Myth and Reality

The relation of the imperial state to the dominant imperial economic interests is complex and changing, even as they appear to share and/or work toward a common goal of creating a world empire.

The imperial state represents, but is not identical, with the dominant economic interests. This distinction is fundamental because it encompasses two concepts. On the one hand, when we refer to the notion of "representation", we mean that the Imperial State (IS) is, in all cases, organized to expand and defend the dominant economic interests of the ruling class, by pursuing and creating economic opportunities for investment, sales, profits, rents and interest payments on a world scale. Equally important the IS operates to create an optimal political environment for securing economic advantage over and against national and international adversaries and competitors.

On the other hand, when we say that the IS is not identical with the ruling class, we mean to highlight the fact that the key decision-makers and agencies of the IS decide how, when and where to defend and represent imperial interests. Between the ruling class economic interests and imperial policies there are the ideologies, bureaucratic interests, particularistic allegiances and strategic conceptions of the imperial state agencies and decision-makers who assign priorities, devise strategies and tactics and allocate IS resources – namely military troops, CIA operatives, payments to military conspirators and so on. The imperial economic interests of the MNC are filtered through this web of interests and ideologies of the IS policymakers.

While some writers refer to this distinction between representation and non-identity as the "relative autonomy of the state", the term raises multiple questions: relative to what? Where? When? Under what circumstances and time frame? Further related questions are raised by the term "autonomy" – From what? To do what? Sometimes, most of the time or all the time?

The use and abuse of the term "relative autonomy of the state" has led some writers to move on to consider the state as independent of the class-economic matrix in which it is embedded. The "state-centered" analysis is mechanically counterpoised to a "society-centered" (class determined) approach. Both these approaches lack any dialectical understanding of the inter-relations between state-class, reducing state policy to the political conceptions of decision-makers or a direct reflection of ruling class economic interests.

The "state-centered" approach short circuits the analysis by eliminating the structures of economic power, the socialization and selective process that defines the recruitment of state decision-makers and the cumulative historical influences which define the purposes and imperatives of the state apparatus. As a result the state-centric approach cannot explain the long-term, large-scale economic direction and capitalist imperatives which guides state action. What the state-centric approach does provide us with is a description and in some cases an analysis of idiosyncratic and political variation among state decision-makers and the plurality of policies pursued within the larger structural-historical framework.

In a similar fashion the so-called "society centered" analysis (class analysis) describes the ruling class, some of the links, social origins and career patterns of specific state decision-makers and proceeds to attribute specific IS policies to ruling class interests. This approach assumes that all IS policy-makers are direct transmission belts of ruling class interests, emptying them of their ideological and political loyalties and bureaucratic power. This approach fails to explain or simply ignores IS policies which prejudice ruling class interests, prioritize non-economic interests (military-expenditure/wars of conquest) which might threaten the economic stability of the imperial ruling class. Equally significant this approach assumes a monolithic imperial state which always acts in consonance, failing to understand the internal conflicts and their reflection of different power centers outside of the state.

The most egregious examples of this fallacy of misplaced concreteness is found with regard to IS policy in the Middle East. Many leftwing analysts link the US invasion of Iraq with oil interests based on a simplistic syllogism: The US needs oil, the Middle East has oil, therefore the US goes to war to secure oil. This "analysis" is deficient on several counts. First it assumes that the only influence acting on policy-makers are the "oil interests" or a "strategy of war for oil". This totally excludes the powerful role of the pro-Israel "lobbies" and the Zionists and pro-Zionists in making US Middle East policy. Secondly and equally important it overlooks the political, diplomatic and economic agreements (all non-military) which have facilitated US access to oil via political clients in the region. Thirdly it fails to account for the lack of major effort by the Petroleum Industry to secure oil via war (before or during the war) in contrast to the civilian militarists and Zionists. Finally it fails to discuss the prejudicial effects which the war has had on the oil industry in terms of the access, security and stability which existed prior to war or to the difficulties in securing new oil contracts during the war.

By ignoring the specificities of the imperial state (divisions between pro/anti-Zionists), by imputing causal determination on one set of economic interests (petroleum), by reducing policy to one option (war instead of pacts with clients), what appears like a "class analysis" becomes a vulgar caricature of reality, which obscures the complex nature of the imperial state and its internal contradictions.

The Imperial State: Complementarity, Convergence, Competition and Conflict

There are several problems with studies of imperialism. In the first instance they fail to adequately analyze the imperial state. In most cases these analyses focus exclusively on the economic dimensions of imperialism – overlooking the central role of the IS in creating conditions for the advance and security of the multinational corporations. Secondly what passes as a discussion of the politics of imperialism is either anecdotal (CIA intervention to overthrow a regime), single dimensional (role of the Pentagon, of the military) or very general ("Washington"). There are few if any writers who analyze the multiple agencies of the imperial state in a systematic way. Thirdly many writers who do mention the political dimension of the IS fall into two erroneous conceptions. Some consider the IS a homogeneous bloc which always acts exclusively at the behest of a particular set of economic interests. Others, usually US political scientists, who ignore the imperialist content of the state, focus on the internal conflicts and fragmentation within the bureaucratic apparatus of the state. The first group of writers provides no knowledge of the multiple inter-related agencies and activities of the IS and how these converge and conflict over policies in different sets of circumstances. The second school, focusing on internal rivalries, fails to account for the long-term, large-scale convergence of interests and policies among the agencies of the IS, particularly with regard to major adversaries, and in defense of markets, MNCs and strategic materials.

Among leftist and Marxist writers there is little serious discussion of the imperial state as opposed to the debates over the capitalist state. The categories used are very general referring to the "coercive", "ideological" and "regulatory" apparatuses, each in turn associated with a limited number of agencies of the state (State Department, Pentagon, CIA). Once again the writers make sweeping generalizations, attributing to the "military" the aggressive bellicose positions and the civilian administrators the 'soft' diplomatic, political approach. In reality almost all of the major agencies of "the state" are predominantly involved in the spread of empire, over and above their domestic activity. Agriculture, Treasury, Commerce and many other cabinet and specific agencies are engaged in, and allocate the bulk of their personnel and budget to promoting the economic interests of MNCs in competition and conquest of foreign markets and investment opportunities. In the age of imperialism, especially in a conjuncture when the majority of profits of the biggest MNCs comes from overseas activities and the Government has defined a state of world-wide, permanent conflict, the center of activity of the imperial state focuses on world empire-building and its defense.

The predominant role of the IS is evident in the vast resources and personnel channeled toward promoting overseas investment and lending on the one hand, and on the other, the enormous sum devoted to colonial wars, covert operations, military bases and offensive weaponry. In contrast the "capitalist state" focused on the domestic economy has run up huge budget deficits and current account deficits and allowed domestic industrial and agricultural producers to become uncompetitive and dependent on massive government subsidies and protective legislation. In the age of empire building the IS is the central unit for understanding the direction and flow of "domestic politics" – budgetary politics and trade - as well as questions of war and peace. "Domestic politics" are subordinated to the welfare of the empire and the priorities of the IS set the parameters for domestic political debate.

The imperial state has different 'components', agencies with specialized but overlapping functions or activities. These agencies include all the economic, intelligence, military and regulatory departments. Underneath each is a vast hierarchical structure which in turn have detailed specialized units organized to deal with specific policy areas, territorial units and operation. At the top these agencies of the IS complement each other in pursuit of imperial goals, converge as well as compete and conflict for jurisdiction, resources and privileged positions in the imperial decision-making structure.

Within the parameters of the transcendent goal of empire building, and the imperatives of permanent expansion and conquest, the different agencies struggle for pre-eminence, giving the appearance of a 'fragmented', 'plural' structure of power. In reality the very solid, vertical control and homogeneity of imperial interests of all the agencies and their convergence with the larger imperial goals, define the boundaries for the intra-bureaucratic rivalries. In fact the main points of dispute between the State Department, the CIA and the Pentagon is over which agency's policies and personnel are best suited at a particular time and place to implement the commonly agreed imperialist policy. In almost all cases on questions of economic penetration, war, markets, destabilizations of nationalist regimes, the activities of the agencies of the IS converge and complement each other.

There are three broad components of the IS – each with its specific set of activities and extensions in "civil society" overseas.

The first component of the IS focuses on the political, ideological, diplomatic and cultural activity, usually associated with the State Department, but with overlap in the Pentagon and the CIA. Essentially this component is directed toward consolidating allies or clients, winning over "center" or "center-left" political regimes or leaders and isolating anti-imperialists.

The second component of the IS is the economic agencies like the Treasury Department, Commerce, Federal Reserve and Agriculture which are directed to promote US MNCs, conquer markets, smash trade and investment barriers, secure strategic energy and primary materials, finance exports, create financial circuits and undermine competitors. Once again these 'economic components' of the imperial state work in tandem with the political and military components in pursuit of their goals. Diplomatic pressure, ideological warfare and CIA covert operations create malleable interlocutors in target countries amenable to signing trade and investment treaties favorable to US MNCs.

The third component of the IS is the military and intelligence apparatus which usually but not always work in tandem with the political and economic components. There are at least 10 distinct intelligence agencies involved in assassinations, information collection and processing, destabilization campaigns and other covert and overt activities involving civilian state operatives, NGO's, military officials and private sector elites including especially the mass media. The military empire extends to over 180 bases in over 125 countries, ranging from direct colonial occupations, to the deep penetration of Defense Ministries, to the direct influence over operational counter-insurgency efforts and in advising and financing mercenary clients against state adversaries. The military-intelligence apparatus engages in sequential wars, multiple wars, threats of war (psychological war), proxy wars, separatist wars, as well as assassinations, kidnappings and torture of adversaries. The military-intelligence component of the imperial state operates on the imperial principle that the laws, edicts and interests of the empire are paramount and have precedence over international law, Geneva Accords and US constitutional principles. The empire recognizes no frontiers, rejects national sovereignty except as it fits with its own interests, declares its laws supreme and the right to the pursuit of adversaries anywhere, any time – the imperial principle of 'extraterritoriality'. A corollary of this imperial principle is the doctrine of permanent offensive wars (euphemistically called "preventive wars"), an approach designed specifically to secure unquestioned world domination. Given the sweeping 'world historical' tasks embraced by the imperial state and its limited formal capacity, a key element in the operation of the IS is to contract and secure mercenary forces, client regimes and civic groups to act as 'extensions of the IS'. This refers to organizations which are not formally linked to or legally attached to the IS but which are deeply penetrated, funded and directed by key operatives or representatives of the imperial state. Each of the components of the IS has its special links with these 'civil society' organizations and institutions which play a highly significant and successful role in the empire building process. In large part their success in empire building is based on the ideological cover, the appearance of being unaffiliated to empire, of being 'international' rather than imperial, of being 'non-governmental' instead of imperial transmission belts, of being of 'society rather than by and for the IS. As such they deflect hostile attention from the role of the IS to 'international institutions', convert international aggrandizement to an 'internal struggle' between local antagonists, and provide an ideological cover of 'expanding democracy' to justify imperial hegemony or domination.

The civil extensions of the economic components of the imperial state include: (1) the international financial institutions (IFI) including the International Monetary Fund, the World Bank and regional banks. The US members of the IFI are selected and instructed by the US Treasury and their loan decisions are exclusively based on the political and economic interests of the IS and US MNCs. (2) The MNC operate both as economic units and as political instruments; they provide intelligence, operative positions for agents of the IS, they disinvest or invest, provide services and finished goods or parts or withdraw them, according to IS policies. (3) Civic-private foundations and universities are key instruments in recruiting politicians, journalists, intellectuals, artists and other 'opinion-makers' via scholarships, grants, academic appointments and honorific awards. The academic world frequently provides specialized intelligence following "field work" via de-briefing sessions to top IS operatives. The role of 'private' philanthropies, like the Ford Foundation, the Soros Foundation and scores of others fund, subsidize and indoctrinate entire strata of future pro-imperial ideologues and technocrats in the ex-Communist countries. Their role cannot be over-estimated. (4) In this regard a special importance should be assigned to the self-styled "non-governmental organizations", a misnomer if there ever was one. The NGO's are government-funded (mostly by imperial states), work with governments and create or engage collaborator NGO's in targeted countries in implementing political and economic tasks beneficial to the empire. In the socio-economic sphere they compete with and confront socio-political movements, fragmenting poor communities, co-opting leaders, depoliticizing struggles, localizing "solutions" in micro-projects and diverting attention from the pillage and exploitation by neo-liberal elites. In the political realm, the NGO's receive millions to propagandize and mobilize mass support to destabilize anti-imperialist regimes, promote pro-empire electoral clients and provide cadre and leaders for the subsequent client regimes. The NGO's perform overtly the exact same tasks that the CIA used to pursue covertly. The NGO's market-oriented economic agenda at the mass level complements the IFI agenda at the national level.

Several more recent "international" organizations have emerged, such as the World Trade Organization (WTO), which are under the joint control of the European and US imperial states and provide a legal enforcement framework for facilitating the expansion and conquest of markets and investment penetration throughout the world, which benefit the powerful MNCs in the imperial countries and the agro-mineral export elites in the client states.

The political components of the MNC operate out of some of the same 'civil' organizational weapons as the economic. The private foundations provide funds for ideological indoctrination, training economists, social scientists and other professionals into capitalist cadres ("entrepreneurs") and provide them with a doctrine legitimizing the pillage of the economy ("privatization"), denationalization of ownership ("free-markets"), and the promotion of inequality ("individual social mobility"). The foundation recruits serve as "go-betweens" or "intermediaries" between the imperial state and the client state, between the MNCs and local lucrative resources.

Civic organizations and NGO's heavily funded by IS conduits also play a major role in expanding the political reach of empire. Locally sponsored political parties, civic groups and NGO's, some pre-existing others recently created, are provided with funds, training schools, scores of IS advisers from imperial trade unions, political parties and consulting agencies on strategies and tactics, biased polling and electoral "watch" committees. The IS deep penetration of "civil society" via local transmission belts highlights the growing importance of "civil organizations" to empire building and the projection of imperial policies into new territories.

The optimal result of the IS civil strategy is the creation of "viable legitimate client states" which provide a façade of democracy for subservience to the economic, military and political interests of the empire.

The military component of the imperial state works with local paramilitary groups, retired military officer organizations as well as through bilateral treaties and military "alliances" which are largely staffed and directed by imperial officials. Through the local military elite and in consonance with the political clients of the imperial state, the imperial military recruits mercenary armies to serve in the colonial wars and occupations. Through the indoctrination, training and arming of client military officers, the imperial military can extend its war-making and intervention capacity beyond its domestic capability. The client states proximity to new regions of potential conquest facilitates penetration while lowering the logistical costs. Military bases provide joint security for the local client state and the IS: the client regime can count on imperial protection from a popular revolution; the dependence of the client regime assures continuation of the imperial military outposts.

In evaluating the strength or weakness of empire, a serious analyst must go beyond a cost-benefit analysis of the domestic returns and expenditures of the empire to take account of the multiple effects which overseas extensions can have in perpetuating and expanding the empire. The successful multiplication of political, economic and military "extensions" relieves the economic and personnel costs of empire maintenance. Moreover the framework for measuring the cost and benefits of empire in examining its sustainability has to take into account the heavy up-front costs to the state (until conquest is achieved and exploitation started) and the downstream benefits that accrue to the private sector (once implanted in the economy).

Moreover the entire calculation of costs and benefits has to be based on a fundamental distinction between the larger public (taxpayers, soldiers) and the elite classes (which benefit). What some writers cite as the "heavy cost of empire" to an ill-defined "nation" (the US) is in reality a redistribution of income from the wage and salaried classes to the wealthy via the IS.

In so far as a particular IS strategy toward empire building does not jeopardize the profits, investment opportunities and partnerships of the economic elites, the 'costs' of empire to passive citizens are irrelevant. However when IS policymakers adopt strategies which both prejudice the economic interest of the MNCs and provoke popular unrest, elite divisions appear in the Imperial State, between components and within components of the IS.

Complementarity Components of the Imperial State

The everyday reality of the operations of the IS agencies is the complementarity of their activities. At the pinnacle of power - 'the White House' and the 'National Security Council'- a common position is usually hammered out. Policies however are dictated by the imperatives of empire building inherent in the perpetual expansion and accumulation of capital – the essential necessity to expand or decay. The accumulation and overseas expansion means increasing imperial political power, securing markets, imposing client regimes and establishing spheres of influence in which favorable macro-economic policies favoring the MNCs are in place. It means expanding military influence via bases or local officials, displacing competitors, undermining anti-imperialists (nationalists, socialists, Islamists), overthrowing regimes, promoting pro-imperialist parties and civic organizations. Each component of the IS operates, largely within its specialty area: The State Department funds political groups, pressures politicians, recruits intellectuals; the Pentagon activates the military; the Treasury via the IFI intervenes in the formulation of economic policy; and the CIA infiltrates groups, engages in violent direct action via clandestine operations. The "extension groups" in civil society are activated to denounce, propagandize and demonstrate for elections or against elected officials, to provide a legitimate cover for coups or to destabilize regimes.

The key theoretical point is that above and beyond the usual bureaucratic rivalries, the components of the IS converge in mobilizing resources, human and material, especially in time of crisis, war, revolution, coup-making and counter-revolution to secure the empire. At the level of serving the imperatives of empire building, there are usually no major divisions between the State Department, the Pentagon and the CIA. There are no "invisible" governments operating "behind" the apparatus of the IS. That is not to say that the activities and operations organized and directed by the agencies of the IS are open to public perusal or accountability. What it does mean is that the clandestine, violent actions or acts of political subversion are organized by identifiable official agencies of the IS, and are designed to implement specified imperial policies.

Conflicts within the IS

Having stated the general rule of the complementarity of activities within the IS, there are however two types and moments of internal conflict between components of the IS. The most commonplace occurrence is the competition between agencies for resources, jurisdiction, personnel and budgets, what can be called bureaucratic enhancement. This may effect the degree to which one or another of the agencies of the IS may increase its role in pursuing the empire building agenda. These "intra-bureaucratic conflicts" are common subjects of conventional political scientists, who describe these conflicts as the major determinants of foreign policy, blissfully ignoring the larger convergences and complementarities. In most cases these conflicts may reveal tactical differences and emphases in imperial policymaking.

The second and very infrequent type of conflict within the IS, and yet the far more serious one, is over ideology, strategy, priorities and political loyalties. The major conflicts within the IS usually occur at a time of a major turn in foreign policy, emphasizing an escalation of aggression, the launching of a war, a shift in alliances. For example there was debate and conflict within the IS over the launching of the Cold War against Russia, with a few officials arguing for the maintenance of co-operative politics as a way of gradually undermining communist power against the bellicose majority. The debate was brief and ended in a total political rout – the Cold Warriors not only dictated policy but also purged their opponents from the State Department. Likewise toward the climax of the US losing war in Vietnam, a debate within the IS emerged between those who called for cutting losses and ending the war in order to defend other strategic regions of the empire and to end internal political turmoil and those officials who sought to continue or escalate the war with a disintegrating colonial army. A compromise, between the two groups was reached: The Vietnamization of the war involving the withdrawal of the bulk of the US troops and the reliance on US advisers and Vietnamese troops. What is clear in these divisions in the IS is that they all take place within the framework of the best approach to empire building. None of the participants question the empire itself – only the best combination of military force, diplomacy, political priorities and economic interests. Nevertheless these differences do have substantial consequences in the short and medium run for the people affected and the future of empire.

At then end of the 20th Century and into the new millennium a major new division has opened within the IS over strategy, ideology and political loyalties, between Zionist-extremists (Z-E) and traditional conservative empire builders. The Z-E occupy key positions in several components of the IS, including the Pentagon, the State Department and have established their own intelligence networks. They have the unconditional backing of the major Jewish organizations and their civic networks, influencing the Democratic and Republican Parties, Congress and the mass media. The Z-E in the IS have made the expansion and enhancement of Israeli power in the Middle East the central priority in shaping the IS foreign policy. The Z-E have been the strategic architects of the Iraq war, the cost of which runs to over $250 billion dollars in its first two years, with several tens of thousands of US casualties. The Z-E in the IS, more than any other past influential group have an active, powerful set of organized and influential backers in civil society, a well-organized group of extremist ideological "think tanks" linked to the mass media vigorously propagandizing the educated classes and a powerful set of Jewish organizations censoring and intimidating critics of the Israel Firsters in the IS. This powerful civil apparatus is politically connected to the legislature, parties and executive and provides protection for an otherwise extremely controversial group within the IS – one which has loyalties to a foreign state (Israel) over their commitments to US empire building. More accurately, the Z-E have shaped US empire building around the needs of Israeli regional hegemony. Moreover when there is a conflict of interest between empire building and Israeli interests they have prejudiced the former to serve the latter. The persistence and expansion of Zionist power in the IS, despite the major problems (political isolation, exposed lies and universal hostility) it has created for empire building, not to speak of the horrendous casualties for the victimized peoples of the Middle East, can only be explained by the high level of influence or hegemony which the Jewish pro-Israel apparatus wields over US society and especially political institutions.

Given the array of forces in opposition to the Z-E in the IS, only its powerful supporting cast outside of the IS can account for its continued dominance in US foreign policy, especially in the Middle East. The opposition to the Z-E has been forced to operate in a semi-clandestine way – and has at best been a critical force which has lost more often than won the policy-debates within the IS.

The Middle East war policy designed, propagandized, promoted and implemented by Z-E in the IS provoked opposition within the professional military, the CIA and State Department as well as from a multitude of former officials. It provoked concern among major oil companies, diplomats and the energy markets. The post-invasion occupation strategy of the Z-E, in line with Israeli interests, favored the destruction of the Iraqi state and the disarticulation of society, hindering reconstruction but destroying a major adversary of Israeli conquest and annexation of Palestine. The fragmentation of Iraq into ethno-religious sub-regions, the use of Israeli urban warfare techniques and torture were encouraged by the Z-E. The policies of war, the occupation and the dismemberment of Iraq were executed by the civilian militarists in the Pentagon, namely the Z-E in opposition to many professional officers. The entire fabrication of the pretexts for war – the weapons of mass destruction, the links to Al Queda, etc. – were propagated by the Z-E to justify their sometimes explicit, sometimes implicit real agenda of promoting Greater Israel. The political lies served their higher purpose.

The exposing of their lies and their disloyal collaboration with a foreign state however did not lead to any hearings, any firings or forced resignations, as normally would be the case in a situation where a war has turned into a costly debacle. The reason is the unconditional unanimous backing the Z-E received from organized Jewish civil society and its hegemony over the political institutions. On the other hand, the critics in the IS, legislatures, the media and academia, who have challenged or criticized the Zionists in the IS have been castigated (as Anti-Semites), marginalized and in some cases driven from office. As a consequence the Z-E retain their posts or have advanced to even more influential positions, e.g., Elliot Abrams, neo-fascist, convicted felon, is now in charge of Middle East policy in the State Department.

The Z-E policy of sequential wars against Israel's adversaries is at the top of the IS agenda: announced targets include Iran and Syria. New divisions have appeared over the 'next' war, between a minority who argue for a negotiated settlement and the strident Israel-First crowd which demands immediate military attacks. The larger issues of oil access and oil prices, long-term, large-scale warfare and instability in the Middle East, raised by the powerful petroleum companies, international bankers and consultancies have taken a distant second place to the Zionist agenda of destroying Iran, Israel's defiant neighbour.

This raises several larger theoretical issues: Under what conditions is there a breech between IS policymakers and the interests of the MNCs and empire building? How well does the IS represent major sectors of the ruling class today?

Only the ignorant can assume that because the US has major oil interests in the Middle East, that US foreign policy follows or pursues those interests to the exclusion of others, or that it is the determining factor in that policy. The latter position has been put forth by a number of well-meaning progressives who are short in analysis or who by omission or commission do not which to offend their Jewish colleagues – even in the face of contrary evidence.

Imperial State: Does it Always Represent the Ruling Class?

Under most circumstances (but not all, as we previously discussed) policymakers in the imperial state represent the interests of the ruling class, the major banks and corporations. However the question arises as to how well the imperial state – its various components – represents those interests?

An evaluation of the effectiveness of the IS is central in analyzing its role in empire building. To answer that question one needs to ask another: Do the personnel, policies and strategies expand opportunities and enhance security of the MNCs, increase access to or control of strategic resources, expand markets and facilitate lucrative partnership with local elites? Do imperial policymakers pursue military policies which are compatible with economic interests?

These are complex questions because one of the defenses put up by policy makers faced with apparently "failed policies" is that the 'positive results' would appear in the 'long run'. Whatever the complexities of measuring the success or failures of imperial policies over time and place, in most instances, an objective determination can be made. For example, the decisions to go to war in Korea and Vietnam, to invade Cuba, to intervene in Somalia were clearly failed policies from the perspective of the costs to the imperial economy and the negative outcomes in terms of opening new economic opportunities and expanding territorial control. In other cases imperial policies of intervention in smaller, defenseless countries like the Dominican Republic, Guatemala, Nicaragua, Panama, Grenada and El Salvador were successful in destroying progressive regimes or movements and foisting client regimes, but provided few substantive economic opportunities for MNCs as the economies stagnated, consumer power contracted, few natural resources were exploited and labor out-migration lessened the reserves of cheap labor. In the case of imperial policies toward more lucrative resource-rich countries, like Iran, Chile, Argentina, Brazil, Bolivia and the Congo (Zaire), the outcomes are mixed. The short-term gains in overthrowing the nationalist regime of Mossadegh in Iran and installing the Shah provided great opportunities for US MNCs and a staunch politico-military client in the Gulf region for 26 years; however the dictatorial neo-colony was overthrown by a coalition of nationalist Islamic and secular forces in 1979 and became a strategic adversary for the next 26 years and perhaps beyond. In contrast, the US intervention in Chile, Argentina, Bolivia and Brazil in the 1960's and the subsequent client military regimes elaborated a political-economic framework for long-term, large-scale US economic penetration. Even more important the transitions to civilian electoral regimes and their subsequent policies were conditioned by the 'lessons' dictated by imperial politics. While the imperial state and MNCs have reaped the benefits of 30-40 years of pro-imperial regimes, it has not been without violent massive challenges as has been the case of popular rebellions and the overthrow of client regimes in Argentina and Bolivia and continued instability in Peru and Ecuador.

The US war in Iraq was clearly a blunder from the perspective of empire building: it has led to tactical defeats, prolonged unwinnable street warfare, decline in military enlistments, demoralized National Guard and Reserve troops, ballooning budget deficits, isolation from EU allies and abandonment by coalition clients. Moreover the military debacle provides a demonstration that the US empire is not invincible. Clearly the key architects of this war have inadvertently dealt a severe blow to the military component of the empire. From the perspective of economic interests of the US, the costs of the war far outweigh any benefits from oil ownership or extraction, now or in the medium future. The gross massive violations of human rights and civilian killing have generated universal hostility throughout the Middle East (except Israel) making investment and market activities by the MNC very insecure and problematical. Were the IS architects of war so obtuse, so ignorant of the opposition, cost and consequences of the war? Clearly there was every historical reason to anticipate severe resistance and casualties. Even granted the mediocrity of the key decision-makers there is no basis for thinking that the persistence of the war and the policy of following the Iraq debacle with a new catastrophe in Iran is simply ignorance. The Iraq war was a success in the eyes of its makers, because their criteria was: *Does it benefit the Jewish State?*, which it did, and not how does it affect US Empire building. The fact that the Z-E are strenuously pushing for a new war with Iran, which will wreak havoc on the empire and its client regimes and generalize conflict throughout the Middle East, is further indication that policy effectiveness is measured by whether it furthers Israel's power in the region, diminishes its enemies, and not how it effects US empire building.

In terms of the "quality" and competence of imperial policy-making, it is clear that Z-E performed superbly in pursuit of Israeli State interests – maximizing benefits at virtually no cost – and miserably in term of furthering US empire building. The difference in performance is not a result of lack of political skills but a result of different priorities, motivations and strategic goals.

The ascendancy of civilian-militarists, including but not exclusively the Z-E, has largely relegated economic interests of the MNC to a secondary position in IS empire building. While military spending increases, the foreign debt grows exponentially, the budget deficit and interest payments weaken the economic foundations of empire and dependence on foreign financing grows. Increasingly most of US MNCs produce abroad and export to the US increasing the trade deficit of the domestic economy. Equally important the civilian-militarists do not have a strategy in which high immediate military expenditures and intervention will lead to future economic gains for the MNCs, as took place after World War II and during the Cold War. Since most of the military expenditures have been directed toward the destruction of the Iraqi civilian-productive infrastructure, they have put in jeopardy the principle sources of profits and driven out or killed most of the key professional/scientific community. The politics of colonial occupation, destruction and pillage by colonial satraps has severely restricted imperial 'gain via pain'. The civilian-militarist politics of total war, permanent occupation, and regime imposition undermines the possibility of long-term stability and security necessary for large-scale productive investors, at best it encourages speculative capitalists, smugglers and mafia oligarchs interested in short-term, high-profit ventures.

Conditions for Conflict: Imperial State - MNC

We can now specify some of the conditions under which components and agencies of the IS conflict with MNC over alliances, priorities, policies, regional and global strategies and tactics.

The first point of conflict between IS and MNC is over ideology: the IS, especially under civilian-militarist influence, focuses on military alliances with ideological cousins, while the MNC look toward lucrative investments, trade agreements and economic partners based on notions of free markets and free trade – as mechanisms for eventual penetration and domination. Several contemporary cases come to mind involving the US relations with the Middle East, China and Cuba. In each region the civilian-militarist ideologues pursue policies designed to further military confrontation to the detriment of lucrative MNC investment and trade agreements. In the Middle East the civilian-militarists line up with Israel against Saudi Arabia, Iran, Syria and the rest of the Arab Islamic world, while the MNC engage in investments and trade with the Arab and Islamic countries. With regard to China, the civilian militarists pursue a policy of military encirclement, back Taiwan independence and engage in shrill rhetorical demonization of Chinese defense policy, while the Fortune 500 firms have invested over $300 billion dollars in China and Peking finances the US trade deficit, much to the relief of US bankers. A similar conflict is evident with regard to Cuba. The civilian militarists – led by progeny of Cuban exiles — pursue policies ranging from sponsoring exile terrorists to an aggressive economic boycott, while major US MNC engage in a billion dollar trade in food and pharmaceuticals with Cuba. Similar conflicts are evident with regard to Venezuela where the civilian militarists have organized coups and funded extremist civic organizations to install a pro-imperialist regime, while major US oil companies like Chevron-Exon have signed multi-billion dollar investment agreements with the social-liberal nationalist regime. There are other regions and issues of IS-MNC conflict with regard to Western Europe and Russia.

What is clear however is that imperial policy reflects the strengths and weaknesses of the civilian militarists and MNCs in specific areas. In the Middle East, the power of the civilian militarists, backed by the major Jewish organizations and their power over Congress and the mass media, is more than a match for the petroleum MNCs, the professional diplomats and sectors of the professional military. In contrast, in China the vast array of MNCs and the sheer size of US investment and trade clearly has greater influence over policy than the civilian militarists, who lack the equivalent of an influential domestic power base comparable to organized Jewry. With Cuba and Venezuela, there is a 'trade off', where the US MNC work around trade restrictions and engage in trade and investment in the case of Venezuela while the civilian militarists work to overthrow the regimes without opposition from the MNCs.

The Mind of the Civilian Militarists

While it is clear what motivates and drives the CEOs of the MNC (profits, markets, resources, and low operating costs) there has been less understanding of the mind-set of the civilian-militarists and the Zionist subset. In telegraphic fashion we can specify eight characteristic, some of which apply only to the subset of Zionists:

1. Military priorities over economic. Most of the militarists have had no direct and deep involvement in big business or direct military combat. The live and work in a rarefied world of ideologues, ingrown ideological institutes and interact with like-minded extremist politicians. They have little knowledge or interest in the human or economic consequences of imperialist wars, which are seen as good in themselves, as 'liberating' experiences.

2. They obsessively see the world exclusively as an area for seizing power at any cost. They pursue policies of mass killings without a second thought and are totally dismissive of charges of genocide and war crimes. They have an absolute belief in the righteousness of mass killings in enhancing political power for their own empire and for their adopted 'mother country'.

3. Many are driven by a religious or quasi-religious vision that ignores all economic constraints. The virulent arrogance of their righteous style is as revelatory as is the proto-fascist substance of their politics. One hundred thousand Iraqi deaths are nothing; the mind of a professional assassin acting on behalf of a 'holy cause' writ large. The

> Zionists never admit any failing or any crime. They use their influence to shift responsibility to others – torture at Abu Ghraib and Guantanamo are attributed to the military officials or to the White House Attorney. Not a single top Zionist appears on the list of those responsible for the abuses although they were organizationally complicit. The sources of the Zionist mind-set reflect their intimate embrace of Israeli methods of rule over the Palestinians: massive displacement and destruction of the means of livelihood and institutions, collective punishment, torture, long-term imprisonment without trial, indiscriminant military attacks on population centers and slaughter with impunity.

It is absurd to search in the writing of obscure, mediocre political theorists dabbling in astrology (Leo Strauss) for the roots of the totalitarian imperialist practices of the Zionist policy-makers, when their whole formative active political life was deeply involved with the terrorist policies of the Israeli State from which they took their ideological cue and political lessons.

The convergence of Christian fundamentalism, Zionist extremism and imperialist power has driven the totalitarian doctrine of permanent offensive warfare, total war, without distinction of civilian or military objectives and undisputed world domination. What sustains these extremist elites in power and the reason why they retain power, despite disastrous policies, is that they have formidable constituencies in civil society who have substantial influence over key political institutions like the US Congress and the mass media.

The extremist civilian militarists have not been severely tested by the MNC for several reasons. In the first place the MNC have received enormous benefits from the imperial regime in the form of very substantial tax reductions and subsidies, low interest rates, aggressive policies opening markets, promoting privatizations and enforcing debt payments overseas. In addition, the White House has defended US MNC against competitors weakened labor and environmental legislation and in cases of uncompetitive enterprises, provided protective legislation.

These benefits have outweighed the conflicts between the MNC and the civilian-militarists in the IS. The conflict between the MNC-IS plays out in competing pressures over specific policy areas, with the civilian militarists most influential over Mid-East policy and 'global strategic' pronouncements and the MNCs carving out favorable policies on China and to a lesser degree Cuba and Venezuela.

Structural Basis of Ideological Conflicts in the IS

The political differences between the civilian militarists and the MNC are in part based on conflicting ideological perspective. In the case of the civilian militarists (CM) their conceptions are explicit while for the MNC, they are less clearly articulated.

Voluntarism Versus Global Integration

The CM operate under the assumption that "political will" can overcome all obstacles, that 'projecting power' can 'create facts' that other countries (former allies or adversaries) have to live with - hence the notion of unilateral action and multiple wars. Voluntarism presumes unlimited capacity for military action, limitless capacity for material 'sacrifices' all sanctified by ideological platitudes ("democratic crusades") and intangible rewards. Voluntarism assumes a high degree of elite autonomy and mass submissiveness, based on the visionary mission of the former and the ignorance, reflex loyalty or fear of the latter.

The voluntarist philosophy is profoundly authoritarian; leaders are (self) chosen to lead, and the followers are to follow. The formulae to justify wars in pursuit of world domination vary according to circumstance from outright blatant lies, demonization, deceit and fabrications to magnifying minor incidents into world threats. Voters are a mass to be deceived, cajoled, flattered and manipulated via the mass media and critics threatened by punitive authoritarian edicts and legislation. Congress is to be disciplined and mobilized behind leaders via imminent threats of war and terrorism.

In contrast the implicit and explicit assumptions of the MNC is that the world economy has become an integrated structure, in which rival imperial enterprises coalesce and compete; the MNC recognize a multi-polar economic world which requires support from the IS as well as accommodation with the rules of other IS (European Union and Japan). MNC do not eschew limited wars and military subversive activities as long as it doesn't substantially disrupt the ongoing circuits of trade, investment or access to strategic materials. The most competitive and powerful of the MNCs as well as the powerful financial institutions promote multi-lateral trade and investment agreements, and see the military-political activities of the IS as securing or negotiating international support for these agreements among clients and allies. The less competitive MNC are more 'unilateral', protectionist and state centered – dependent on protection of domestic markets and subsidies to compete in foreign markets. There is a closer political identity between the less competitive MNC and the civilian-militarists in terms of 'unilateral action' but often conflicts in terms of overseas trading partners.

The CM belief in "extra-territoriality", the supremacy of US laws and enforcement authority over national sovereignty and its logical extension and colonial occupation. This position is in conflict with MNC demands for a recognized international legal order to defend and promote capitalist relations and adjudicate disputes. However this conflict is muted by some of the special privileges that accrue to MNCs under US colonial control, such as special access to lucrative privatized enterprises, reconstruction contracts and military related purchases. On the other hand the CM embargo policies hinder overseas subsidiaries of MNC from engaging in trade or restricts the commodities to be sold. The conflict between the military centered CM policies and the 'free market' policies of MNC however does not prevent co-operation in destabilizing vulnerable regimes. US oil refineries refused to process Cuban oil imports in the early 1960's in line with US efforts to overthrow the revolution. During the early 1970's under the socialist government of Allende US copper companies pursued judicial suits to prevent Chilean copper exports in tandem with the CIA efforts to overthrow the regime. US aeronautics industry co-operated with the IS in pressuring the Chavez government by refusing to repair and upgrade its fighter planes.

The theoretical point is that within the empire-building project there are "special interests" and the "general interests" of the ruling class. There is no such thing as an "imperialist logic" that provides a coherent homogeneous set of policies anywhere and anytime. The 'inconsistencies' occur for both domestic political reasons, as well as because of the influence of different ideological groups within the IS. For example though "free trade" is the general doctrine of the MNC, the exceptions include protection of uncompetitive but politically influential agricultural interests. The Cuban American lobby backing a trade embargo against Cuba, the Israeli State and economy heavily subsidized by the US for over a half century are clear examples contrary to the "free market" doctrines of the MNCs. When "special interests" like the Zionist/Jewish power configuration impose policies favourable to Israel but which prejudice major oil MNC interests, undermine alliances with EU and Arab countries and in the course of pursuing their agenda marginalize traditional components of the IS, a major "subterranean" but vicious conflict emerges over personnel, jurisdiction and strategic policy.

The second Bush presidency represents further consolidation and expansion of power of the civilian militarists in strategic positions. The Zionists remain in control of the Pentagon, while expanding their reach within the National Security Council and Middle East policy with the ascendancy of Elliott Abrams. Meanwhile Homeland Security is to be run by another member of the Zionist network, Michael Chertoff, who demonstrated his zeal by arbitrarily rounding up and jailing hundreds of US Arabs and Muslims simply because of their ethnicity or religion. The key to the growing ascendancy of the CM is the strategic appointment of Porter Goss to head the CIA. Goss is an ardent proponent of the military confrontationist doctrine toward China and certainly reflects a weakening of the MNCs "free trade" policy-makers.

There is a negative interdependence between economic expansion and war, particularly in the Middle East and Asia. Greater military threats and tighter encirclement of China emanating from the dominant CM can have extremely destabilizing effects on China's continuing financing of US enormous trade deficit and prejudice US investors in China – leading to a weakening of the dollar and the profitability of the top 500 MNC. A new series of US-Israeli military attacks of Syria and Iran can lead to a general military conflagration throughout the Middle East, precipitating an oil crisis, skyrocketing prices and further instability of US clients, leading to a crisis in the US economy and a greater series of wars, further bleeding the country. Israel, of course would be the only beneficiary in a region which becomes a Middle East wasteland (a 'howling wilderness' of Biblical proportions) and in which the US will be exhausted by wars, an over-extended military and economic crises. What is more likely is that the imperial policies of the CM will result in losses for all parties: the US will go into crisis and the anti-imperialist countries will suffer massive destruction. The long-term effects on empire building will depend on the political consequences of failed imperial policies – the way the failures are analyzed, the policies and policymakers involved and the political alternatives which emerge.

The diagnosis of the reasons for imperial failures is crucial because it can lead to either re-building and further strengthening the empire or to a challenge to the policies, personnel, ideologies, institutions and interests which directed the failed policies. The most conservative critics will argue that empire building was the correct approach but the implementation was wrong – the occupation wasn't handled properly, too few troops were utilized and so on. Liberal critics will argue that policies were mistaken, that the war should have been a 'multilateral affair' with the EU, in which the war and the booty would have been shared. The progressive minority will argue that institutions like the Pentagon civilians played too strong a role, instead of the diplomats in the State Department.

Each of these diagnoses and prescriptions are guided by the idea of reversing the negative fall-out from imperial failures and defeats and reconfiguring the IS in order to reconsolidate the forward positions of the empire. At best they lead to some personnel changes, ideological adjustments (the shrill war cries of the CM are toned down), a re-shuffle of agencies (with a recovery by the professional military and diplomats) and efforts to reconcile with international allies. The potentialities for these "changes so that nothing changes" depend on the capacity for the IS to "reform itself" in time of crises. Imperial reform however will not be easy given the entrenched nature of the CM, their backing among the Zionist zealots, Christian fundamentalists and subservient masses.

Only if the new wars result in prolonged conflicts costing thousands of lives, in massive disruption of the economy leading to an international crisis affecting the MNC and the domestic economy can we envision a significant opposition arising among an otherwise cowed and fragmented populace lacking an authentic anti-imperialist political organization. The emergence of mass discontent will require a clear understanding of the responsibility of the civilian militarists and the Zionist "Israel Firsters", the principle architects of the war policy. It will need to bring to bear an analysis of the geopolitics of war, the role of the MNC and the necessity of sacrificing the empire to rebuild the 'republic'. This requires a class war against the costs of empire and for the transformation of the US economy, property ownership and direction.

Empire building by its nature is violent and disruptive to others; resistance and defeat, especially involving strategic sectors of the imperial state always have violent repercussions within the empire. Its weakest link, the workers and taxpayers, exploited and sacrificed to sustain the empire, will only react when forced by external circumstances. Only "outside" shocks will detonate internal reaction in a population imbued with imperial beliefs and righteous submission.

The IS, contrary to the CM and their zealous Zionist counterparts, is not invincible; Iraq has demonstrates the same lessons taught earlier in Korea and Vietnam. The US economy cannot sustain the CM agenda of new, multiple wars and prolonged mass resistance in multiple sites. The CM can ignore the loss of allies, the abandonment of clients from the war coalition, the vulnerability of new points of conflicts in the Empire... The CM can substitute like-minded ideologues to run the CIA, the Pentagon, the White House and the State Department who will echo each other doctrines, but their collective will cannot change fundamental structural constraints on power – budgets, debts, draft resistance, armed resistance, vulnerable armies, diplomatic isolation, the lack of mercenaries... The will to power can do many things destructive, but as Hitler realized (or proved) it can also destroy itself.

11 The Ascendancy of Finance Capital: Record Profits and Rising Authoritarianism

James Petras
March 28, 2006

Introduction

No sector of the US economy, in recent years, can match the rate and size of profit which have accrued to the biggest financial institutions. For the first quarter of February 2006, Goldman Sachs (GS) broke Wall Street records by reporting new profits of $2.48 billion dollars (annualized at over $10 billion dollars). Earnings were up 64% over the same period last year (which was also a very lucrative year). Return on equity rose to 38.8 per cent, topping the record for a top investment house. Total revenues rose $10.3 billion dollars. GS has had record earnings in five of the past nine quarters (Financial Times (FT) 3/15/2006, p. 1). Morgan Stanley reported a 17 per cent increase in net income to $1.64 billion dollars for its first quarter in February 2006. Revenues rose by 24 per cent compared to 19.7 per cent last year. Lehman Brothers reported a 24 per cent increase in profits in the first quarter to Feb. 2006 to a record $1.1 billion dollars. Revenues increased 17 per cent to $4.5 billion dollars. Bear Stearns (BS) joined the dance of the billions of Wall Street, reporting first quarter profits of $514 million dollars; earnings were up 34 per cent from the year earlier. BS new revenues grew 19 per cent to $2.3 billion, while return on stockholders equity rose 20.1 per cent in the first quarter of 2006. The combined profits of these 4 banks total $5.73 billion dollars for the quarter November 2005 – February 2006, or $22.9 billion annually – and that does not include the profits for three of the top 5 banks (Citigroup, JP Morgan and Merrill Lynch) whose quarter runs January to March 2006, which are expected to have equally high returns, doubling the new profits to over $12 billion dollars for the first quarter and increasing profits to nearly $50 billion for 2006.

No other sector of the economy can boast such high rates of return, nor can any top seven enterprises even approach the record profits. The banks draw their biggest profits in facilitating the concentration and centralization of capital (dubbed "mergers and acquisitions"), charging lucrative fees for "advising" and underwriting bonds to fund the mergers and acquisitions. The second source of profits is speculating, including debt trading, betting on global equity markets – especially in energy where Goldman and Morgan "have been making a fortune in recent quarters".

While US consumers, demagogic politicians and anti-war activists have blamed the oil producing countries, they have entirely overlooked the big speculative banks in pushing up the price of oil.

The key political point is that the driving force of the most important economic sector – services – in the US is the financial sector, the one least engaged in productive activity, meaning production of goods and services for the population. Moreover its high profits, the astronomical bonuses and income of its leading elites, and its role in promoting the concentration of capital play a major role in increasing income inequalities. The costs they impose on enterprises for their "services" contribute to indebtedness which in turn leads to massive layoffs, reduction in health and pension benefits, as part of the "advisory" messages of the implicated banks.

In addition to their speculative activity, the banks have become significant equity holders in non-banking sectors. They play a major role in cutting labor costs as a route for maximizing short-term profits as the expense of long-term investments in research and technology. Finally the most lucrative and dynamic source of speculative profits is in overseas expansion, particularly in Europe and especially in Asia. For example, Lehman Brothers announced in mid-March 2006 an "aggressive expansion in Asia". While overall revenues were up 17 per cent, overseas revenues rose 30 per cent, while Asian revenues rose by 67 per cent. David Goldfarb, Chief Administrative Officer stated that Asian expansion was Lehman's "number one priority". All the major banks have or are in the process of securing beachheads in the banking sectors of China and India. Financial imperialism is becoming a major vehicle for market-driven empire building in the 21st Century.

Finance Capital: Political Power and Economic Policy

Financial capital wields enormous power over government economic policy through its direct representation in the controlling body of US monetary policy via the President and Executive Board of the

Federal Reserve. The key explicit criteria for the appointment of the President of the Federal Reserve is the "confidence", close ties and solid relations which the candidate has with Wall Street. The same criteria are applied to all the key economic appointees, including Treasury, Commerce, World Bank and International Monetary Fund. Long time Federal Reserve President Greenspan was highly respected and lauded not for his abysmal economic performance but for his favourable policies to Wall Street Bankers. Under Greenspan's Presidency, the US economy de-industrialized, accumulated huge trade and budget deficits and went through two speculative bubbles (information technology and savings and loans). He presided over an economy which reached unprecedented levels of public debt – doubling in five years. Greenspan's backing of Bush's tax cuts for the rich (income, capital gains, etc.) contributed to the huge budget deficit and widening inequalities. His policy of low interest rates fueled the speculative bubbles at the expense of productive investments. His backing for unregulated capital (dubbed "globalization") led to the re-location of US multi-nationals abroad (many of whom export to the US) and led to huge trade and balance of payment deficits. Yet all these policies which led to the disastrous state of the national economy, created extraordinarily favourable conditions for the domestic and international expansion of finance capital, as well as the concentration and centralization of banks into ten controlling units.

Wall Street's impact on the economy and social structure can be best illustrated by examining New York City – its center of operation. The distribution of assets in New York City is among the most unequal in the world. Slightly over 1 per cent of the population control over 80 per cent of the assets – comparable to land inequalities in Guatemala and Brazil. Secondly, Wall Street is closely tied to real estate capital in New York, and both were instrumental in raising property values and rents, leading to the destruction of over 500,000 manufacturing jobs over the past three decades. Most of the former industrial properties were "redeveloped" to provide office space for finance related activities and high end housing for wealthy financiers. New York Senator Schumer, a notorious backer of Wall Street, leads the US in scapegoating China for the loss of manufacturing jobs, ignoring the essential role of finance – real estate in deliberately destroying the manufacturing sector in New York City. Of course, the demise of manufacturers in New York city was not only due to finance capital; the local garment capitalists and the trade unions were also partly responsible. The former relied on low-wage labor to compete – a losing proposition against China – instead of upgrading its technology, computerizing design and production and specializing in high-end products. The trade unions (International Ladies Garment Workers Union – ILGWU, later re-named UNITE) reinforced the failed cheap labor strategy of garment bosses, by discretely allowing de facto wages to fall below the minimum wage and what was stipulated in collective bargaining contracts. No doubt the ethnic-class differences between the six-figure salaried Jewish labor bosses and the low-paid Asian and Latino workers and the common class-ethnic positions of the labour bosses and the manufacturers facilitated these failed policies: loss of manufacturing competitiveness and loss of jobs for workers.

Finance Capital and the War in the Middle East

Finance capital was until recently predominantly made up of white Protestants and Jews. In the most recent period, Wall Street's ethnic and religious base has broadened as corporate capital has taken over from family-owned banks. Nevertheless among the new generation of upwardly mobile speculators, there is a pronounced disproportion of individuals of Jewish origin, who are not necessarily religious or involved in Jewish or Israeli communal activities, fund raising or politics. Nevertheless a significant affluent minority of prominent Jewish banking and real estate millionaires are active in financing and promoting Israeli policy either directly or through the key pro-Israel lobbies like AIPAC and the President of the Major Jewish Organizations. These lobbies have been in the forefront of promoting the Iraq War, a boycott or military attack on Iran and the ethnic cleansing of Palestinians. The political muscle of this minority of Israel-First wealthy Jewish financiers is not countered by any countervailing organization by other Jewish financial bankers or for that matter by Gentile, Muslim or Hindu financial tycoons. Through the political use of their wealth, strategic location and high status, this minority of politically active financiers is in a position to establish the parameters and policies of Middle East policies vie their dominant role in funding political parties (especially the Democratic Party), candidates and congressional representative.

The Jewish and Gentile critics of the war deliberately exclude the role of the minority of wealthy Jews and their political lobbies in shaping US policy in the Middle East by focusing on the US and overseas oil companies ("No blood for oil!"). There is an abundance of evidence for the past 15 years that:

1. The oil companies did not promote a war policy.
2. The wars have prejudiced their interests,

operations and agreements with prominent Arab and Islamic regimes in the region.

3. The interests of the oil companies have been sacrificed to the state interests of Israel.

4. The power of financial capital via the pro-Israel lobbies exceeds that of the oil companies in shaping US Middle East policy.

A thorough search through the publications and lobbying activities of the oil industry and the pro-Israel lobbies over the past decade reveals an overwhelming amount of documentation demonstrating that the Jewish lobbies were far more pro-war than the oil industry. Moreover the public records of the oil industry demonstrate a high level of economic co-operation with all the Arab states and increasing market integration. In contrast the public pronouncements, publications and activities of the most economically powerful and influential pro-Israel Jewish lobbies were directed toward increasing US government hostility to the Arab countries, including maximum pressure in favour of the war in Iraq, a boycott or military attack on Iran and US backing for Israeli assassination and ethnic cleansing of Palestinians.

The most striking illustration of Jewish power in shaping US policy in the Middle East against the interest of Big Oil is demonstrated in US-Iran policy. As the Financial Times notes: "International oil companies are putting multi-billion dollar projects in Iran on hold, concerned about the diplomatic standoff (sic – US economic-military threats) over the country's nuclear programme" (FT March 18/19, 2006 p.1). Despite the fact that billions of dollars in oil, gas and petro-chemical contracts are in play, the pro-Israel lobby has influenced

Congress to bar all major US oil companies from investing in Iran. Through its all out campaign in the US Congress and Administration, the US-Jewish-Israeli lobby has created a war-like climate which now goes counter to the interests of all the world's major oil companies including BP, the UK-based gas company, SASOL (South Africa, Royal Dutch Shell, Total of France and others.

The myth of "war for oil" is circulated by almost all the major progressive Jewish intellectuals and parroted by their Gentile followers, who are in word and deed prohibited from mentioning the AIPAC word in any public meetings or manifestos. The power of the minority of politically active Jewish financiers in the pro-Israel lobby is spreading far beyond the area of US foreign policy into the cultural, academic and economic life of the US. Three major events immediately come to mind.

In New York City, a major theater production of the life of Rachael Corrie, an American humanitarian volunteer murdered in the Occupied Territories by an Israeli Defense Force soldier driving a bulldozer, was cancelled because of Jewish pressure and financial threats. The theater admitted that the cancellation had to do with the "sensitivities" (and pocket book) of the issue to Israel-Firsters. The pro-Israel lobby's defense and support of a minority opinion in favor of Middle East aggression is now extending its authoritarian reach into undermining the basic freedoms of American to free and open expression.

The second example of the growing tyranny of the pro-Israel minority over our civil liberties is the virulent campaign waged by all the major Jewish publications and pro-Israel organizations against a well-documented essay written by Professor Walt of Harvard University and Professor Mearsheimer of University of Chicago critical of the lobby's influence on US Middle East policy. From the ultra-rightwing Orthodox Jewish Press (which claims to be the largest "independent" Jewish newspaper in the US), to the formerly Social Democratic Forward, to the Jewish Weekly, all have launched together with all the major Jewish organizations, a propaganda campaign of defamation ("the new Protocols of Zion", "anti-Semitic", "sources from Neo-Nazi websites...") and pressure for their purge from academia. The Jewish authoritartians have already partially succeeded. Their press releases have been published by the mass media without allowing for rebuttal by the academics under attack. Harvard University has demanded the identification of the Harvard Kennedy School be removed from the paper. The financier of the professorial chair (in his name) which Professor Walt, as academic dean, occupies at the Harvard Kennedy School, is no longer mentioned it in his publication. Ultra-Zionist Professor Dershowitz and his fellow Harvard zealots call into question their moral and academic qualification to teach. Both in the United States and France, legislation is being prepared to equate anti-Zionism with anti-Semitism and to criminalize as a 'hate crime' the free expression of outrage over Israeli atrocities and any criticism of the Lobby's control of US Middle East policy. In the US, the proposed legislation would take the form of withdrawing federal funding from any academic institution where the policies of Israel are criticized. As yet there is no organized opposition in the US by Jewish or Gentile academics or journalists to this erosion of free expression or a defense of the integrity of the two critics of the Lobby. There is no group of Jewish investors or financiers willing to fund a civil rights campaign in defense of free speech, academic and artistic freedom, to counter the minority Zionist financial elite. It is business as usual.

Some Myths and a Few Insights: Capitalism and War

In addition to the myth of the "war for oil" there are several facile misconceptions:

Myth 1 the dominance of financial capital leads to war: There is no evidence that financial capital performs better under war time conditions than in peace. In fact recent history demonstrates that 'crisis' provokes market volatility and sudden disruption which prejudices important financial 'bets' even as other benefits. Most of financial profits accrue from mergers and acquisitions with tend to increase due to competitive market conditions – not wars. The financiers who support war do so for their own personal-ideological reasons, ethnic identification and usually do so via ethnic-affiliated organizations not through financial associations. Thus the big contributions by a minority of Jewish financiers to the pro-war Zionist lobbies have less to do with their class affiliation and more to do with their identification with Israel First organizations.

Myth 2 While financiers are a major funding source for the bellicose pro-Israel lobbies and their congressional spokespeople, they are a minority among Jewish investment bankers, whose prime concern is maximizing the earnings of their banks and hence their incomes, and engaging in many non-Jewish social cultural and professional activities. Over half do not even marry within the Jewish community.

Myth 3 Many writers cite polls which suggest that most Jews, like other Americans now oppose the Iraq war. The fact remains however that they are not willing to criticize the pro-war Jewish lobby or to mention Israel's involvement in precipitating the war through its occupation of Palestine.

Myth 4 The pro-Israel lobby is just like many other lobbies. The Jewish pro-Israel lobby is uniquely powerful because it commands a vast network of grass roots organizations,150 full-time functionaries in Washington operating under discipline and commitment to a foreign power, Israel. Moreover the lobby is financed by wealthy individuals in highly lucrative growth sectors (such as in the banking sector). Thirdly its long established reputation of threats and rewards to recalcitrant and to loyal Congress people, executives and opinion makers makes it an extraordinary and dangerous lobby.

Conclusion

The ascendancy of finance capital and its influence over US economic policy has had major, largely negative, consequences for the US economy, especially our living standards, external accounts and budget. The deregulated financial markets have led to record profits for Wall Street but it has also led to a series of speculative bubbles, which have bankrupted millions of retail investors.

The loss of US industrial competitiveness is largely the result of the transfer of capital from productive innovations which increase competitiveness to speculative activity several times removed from the actual production of goods and services. "Derivative" and "Hedge funds" now equal the size of the US economy at $12 trillion dollars...a financial collapse waiting to happen. Financial capital in its most advanced stage of derivatives is based on bets on bets on bets...which has vastly increased the likelihood of economic collapse even as it widens the chasm between bankers and wage earners.

The political power of finance capital has been exercised in the realm of economic policy and executive appointments; it has not been directly involved in formulating or benefiting from the war policies. However it has been compatible, supportive and benefited from its close ties and relations with the militarist policy elite in Congress and the Executive. The relation is mutually supportive. The Executive deregulates financial markets, lowers taxes, cuts social spending, appoints Wall Street friendly Federal Reserve Presidents, and in exchange Wall Street supports the imperial war ministers in the Cabinet and in Congress.

Investment banks have been deeply involved in recycling Arab petroleum funds and engaging in large-scale mergers and acquisitions in the Middle East, while a minority but deeply engaged Jewish financiers have funded the pro-Israel lobbies pushing for a more bellicose US policy toward the Arab and Islamic world.

Wall Street's position on the erosion of democratic freedoms has ranged from ambiguous to authoritarian. While backing the Administration's Patriot Act, they opposed the blocking of Dubai's purchase of US port terminal management. While an active minority backed the banning of the Rachael Corrie theater production and funds pro-Israel organizations attempting to purge academics critical of Israel, the majority look on with indifference.

Rising authoritarianism and lucrative financial profiteering are compatible with the ascendancy of finance capital.

12
Foreign Investment: Prejudicial Incentives

James Petras – May 25, 2005
Corrected June 28, 2005

Foreign investment by MNCs is highly prejudicial to most Third World countries, because of the non-market incentives that it demands. Much of what passes as favorable "market conditions" are in large part political decisions which maximize benefits to the MNC at the cost of the local economy, its tax payers, consumers and workers. The meaning is clear – investments are not merely market transactions, in which MNCs justify their profits on the basis of the risks they run, the innovations they introduce, the capital they invest. Abundant evidence is available to demonstrate that most foreign investment is subsidized and risk-free, and relies on securing monopoly profits based on the appropriation of existing national (state) enterprises and control of strategic markets.

Privatized Lucrative Public Enterprises

A great deal of foreign investment adds little to new productive or distributive systems since it is directed at purchasing existing privatized public enterprises directly or via the take-over of the same from original private national capitalists. The transfer of ownership from state to private/foreign capital increases the outflow of profits, which previously accrued to the national treasury or were reinvested in the local economy. Privatization is part of the structural adjustment policies imposed by the IMF and World Bank as conditions for refinancing debt payments. The sale of national assets more often than not is hardly transparent and the sales take place far below market value, let alone their value to the indigenous population. In other words, privatization has served to create a class of capitalists or 'oligarchs' who perform none of the 'tasks' associated with capitalist enterprises: they neither invested in training labor, invested capital in infrastructure, innovated nor located new markets. Privatization in the context of the ex-communist and nationalist countries most closely resembles pillage rather than investment. The process of privatization follows one of two paths: either direct buyouts by foreign capital or the theft in public properties by former state managers and/or their oligarchic-gangsters, the emerging 'national bourgeoisie'. During a second phase many of the national oligarchs sell part or all their shares to foreign capitalists/MNCs. These political "incentives" for foreign capital and oligarchic groups are justified by "free-market" ideological dogma of the governing elite.

The infamous author of Russia's disastrous privatization (Anatoli Chubais), which led to the massive disarticulation of the economy and the impoverishment of the Russian people, justified his "shock" policy by citing the need to make capitalism irreversible, to undermine any effort to sustain a mixed social economy. In other words, privatization was an ideological decision. Corruption, vast concentrations of wealth, and a vertical fall in living standards, including an unprecedented decline in life expectancy, were the accepted costs to establishing capitalism at any price.

De-Nationalization of Natural Monopolies

One of the key justification used by ideologues of FI is that is encourages "competition" with local monopolies, increases productivity, lowers costs and prices and increases employment. Most of the available data would argue otherwise.

One of the favorite targets of foreign investors and one of the prime incentives offered by neo-liberal regimes are public utilities (electricity, power, energy, gas, communications) which are 'natural monopolies'. The real effect is to transfer public monopolies to foreign-owned private monopolies leading to an increase in charges for services, decline in services to less profitable regions or low income consumers, an end to subsidies to emerging industries and the impoverished urban and rural poor.

One of the most powerful 'incentives' which FI demand and pliable regimes offer is the privatization of energy sources. Once held up as strategic national assets, FI have successfully secured control over the most lucrative oil and gas fields from compliant rulers.

The obvious result has been a huge transfer of wealth from the national economy to the MNCs under the assumption that new investments and foreign 'know-how' will provide compensatory benefits. The problem is that energy corporations are notorious in not fulfilling their investment obligations, charge international prices for local consumers, pricing endogenous producers out of international markets and impoverishing low-income local energy users. While the privatization of energy and utilities attracts foreign investors (indeed it is one of the most favored incentives for FI), it has several strategic drawbacks: Higher charges make local competitive firms less competitive; it deprives the capital-starved state of a source of public revenues; and it heightens inequalities between the foreign rich and their local associates and the rest of the population.

Three other economic areas are targeted by FI: telecommunications (especially cell phones), transport and high demand raw materials (such as iron and cobalt) and agricultural products, like soya and forest products. Telecom contracts with FI has frequently led to the demise of local hi-tech enterprises and virtual monopolies, rather than heightened competition, leading eventually to monopoly profits. FI have also targeted all the transport sectors: railroads, airlines, ports, and highways. Once again FI gain monopoly markets and increase rates. Preceding privatization, FIs demand that the state pay the costs of the 'transition' period - firing workers, paying pensions or severance pay - and promise higher rates. To create the political climate for privatization the state usually dis-invests in public enterprises and runs deficits via high tax rate policies, thus worsening public services, in order to provoke popular discontent with the public sector. Given the government induced debts and deficits, the public transport systems are sold at low prices to FI, who are enticed by promises of rate increases, tax concessions, reduced staff and cuts in less profitable routes. Most important no independent regulatory system is put in place to check the inevitable abuses of the FI. The result is the disarticulation of the transport system, as only major routes to large metropolitan centers are kept operating while the outlying regions suffer severe reductions in transport, undermining local economies.

Privatization and de-nationalization of airlines has led to the stripping of assets, decline of services and ultimately the bankruptcy of the firm. A case study of Iberia's purchase of Argentine Airlines, stripping assets and running the airlines into bankruptcy, illustrates this pattern.

Foreign investors have never shown any interest in maintaining and upgrading any railroad lines and port facilities, which fail to generate the profit ratios, which their influential shareholders demand. Where regulators are in place they either lack authority to enforce contract obligations on FI, are co-opted, or subject to political pressure to overlook FI failures to comply with investment agreements.

When foreign investment in infrastructure, for example highway construction and toll roads, fails to provide the necessary profits or their high rates force users to secondary roads, they frequently demand compensation or the re-purchase by the state at inflated prices.

The most highly publicized and disastrous privatization in which FI has been involved was in water distribution in Bolivia (Cochabamba and El Alto) and in Peru, where mass popular uprisings protested the high rates and the failure to connect the majority of working poor with water lines.

While FI has been deeply involved in most of the disastrous privatization activities in the Third World, and the ex-Communist countries, many similar experience have taken place in the imperialist countries. The privatization of the power and electricity sector in California led to major blackouts and exorbitant price hikes due to corporate malfeasance. The privatization of the passenger rail services in Great Britain led to safety hazards, exorbitant rates and unprecedented delays due to ancient equipment. The privatization of water in England led to health problems forcing public investigations and a move to re-nationalize.

In summary, by offering choice profitable economic sectors as incentives to FI, Third World regimes have fostered private monopolies, not competition, and a high-cost infrastructure, which fails to integrate regions because of narrow corporate calculations of cost-benefits. Incentives to MNCs have prejudiced long-term, large-scale industrial diversification by offering raw materials, energy and natural resources as incentives to attract FI.

Using privatization as an incentive for attracting FI has had an extremely harmful impact on the deep structures of the economy, polarizing society by privileging elite enclaves and local oligarchs and influential public figures.

Subsidies, Tax Exemptions and Export Processing Zones

Many foreign investors demand and obtain, from pliable TW regimes, direct and indirect subsidies in the form of lengthy tax exemptions or reduced tax rates for periods between 10 to 40 years on imports, exports, corporate earnings and foreign executives salaries. In addition, regimes provide land for enterprise construction free of cost or at minimum price, subsidize utility and energy prices, state-financed infrastructure, labor training and policing. The net result is that poor TW countries pay to be exploited. Frequently the only 'benefit' to the country is a minimum tax, and low wages to highly regimented workers confined to export processing zones. By not paying taxes, the FI deny TW states revenue for public investment in education, health and skill upgrading. States lacking tax revenues frequently resort to borrowing, setting in motion new concessions to FI, as a condition for receiving loans from the IFI.

Export Processing Zones

The most striking development in the TW has been the massive growth of export processing zones (EPZ). By 2005 there were 5000 EPZ employing 40 million workers, under the most arduous repressive work conditions and the lowest pay in absolute (living standards) and relative terms (output/productivity to wages). The EPZ are not the first step toward higher skill, higher wage, technically advanced industrialization – that takes place outside of or parallel to the EPZ. The EPZ are attractive to FI because owners and managers have absolute control over labor and the environment, free of environmental, health and safety regulations. Many regimes which conceived of EPZ as the first stage of a process of 'deeper industrialization' have been disappointed: EPZ are simply 'pieces' in the MNC production strategies – a locus for cheap labor in the labor intensive 'assembly stage' of manufacturing.

Tax Privileges

The tax incentives for the MNC means a higher tax burden on local workers, peasants, professionals, public employees, and small and medium sized business, if their children are to receive an adequate education and health care. The people pay to produce healthy, literate workers to be exploited at low wages by tax exempt MNC who then transfer their untaxed profits to millionaire (billionaire) CEOs, stockholders and speculators. The list of tax "incentives" or privileges is lengthy and extremely costly to the countries, and working population because what the MNC and foreign investors don't pay, is shouldered by the local taxpayers or else public services suffer dire consequences.

Tax revenues finance on-going basic social services and pay for the maintenance of the state and infrastructure as well as potential public investment for long-term growth. Tax privileges for foreign investors lower state revenues and hence expenditures on upgrading (or even maintaining) basic services as well as undercutting national investments to diversity the economy and move beyond a FI 'enclave' economy.

The better known and most common tax privileges extended to foreign investors include exemptions on imports of parts and other inputs as well as exports, low or non-existent property taxes, minimal profit and revenue taxes, generous depreciation allowances, tax holidays of between five and twenty years. In addition, expatriate managers and CEOs receive their salaries, bonuses and stock options tax-free. If we add the cumulative sum of tax losses which the state does not receive to the vast expenditure of state resources invested in infrastructure, severance pay, and 'restructuring' costs to attract FI, it is clear that the total cost of attracting FI far exceeds the benefits in employment and future taxes which might accrue over the foreseeable future.

If we add the loss of tax revenue from displaced local business-driven to bankruptcy – we face even fewer benefits resulting from FI. Finally it is common practice of foreign investors to relocate their enterprises when their tax holidays expire, or when workers salaries begin to increase. The idea propounded by FI apologists that 'present sacrifices and for future gainsis an illusion – an ideological ploy to secure current privileges.

Market Liberalization

Under conditions of total liberalization, the strategy advocated by the IFIs and followed by many Latin American and ex-communist rulers, all barriers to foreign investors entering the local economy have been lifted. Studies have demonstrated that where local establishments go head to head with large MNC, they almost always lose out, either going bankrupt, being bought out by the bigger firm or becoming a satellite supplier. Since most employment in the Third World takes place in small and medium size enterprises, the result of the entry of FI leads to an increase of unemployment as millions of firms providing jobs go bankrupt.

FI relies heavily on suppliers, experts and consultants from their home base to externalize costs (and maximize profits) and to maintain control, thus savaging existing local suppliers who were linked to local small and medium size producers. Only a small number of local firms survive the large-scale entry of foreign-owned MNCs. This is not surprising given the tax incentives, credit access, economies of scale and 'monopoly tactics' which they employ to capture markets (initially lower prices to drive out competition and then price increases once monopoly is established). The emergence of a minority of locally owned competitive firms is commonly publicized by neo-liberal ideologues as part of their success story, excluding the much bigger story of failed enterprises and the foreign takeovers of majority shares of the local market.

The invasion by foreign investors of local economies seriously compromises efforts to construct 'regional integration'. This occurs because the principal beneficiaries of broader markets are precisely the large foreign-owned enterprises, not the national firms. This is particularly evident in MERCOSUR (the association of Brazil, Argentina, Uruguay and Paraguay). By locating in the country with the lowest labor and tax costs, the MNCs can dominate regional markets, undermine protected industries in neighboring countries and generate severe and destabilizing trade imbalances between different members of the regional integration pact.

Contrary to most 'progressive' opinion, regional integration, far from being a nationalist or regionalist alternative to imperial domination becomes a FI launching pad for entry into broader markets. What gives a particular reactionary cast to "regional integration" proposals is that they skip over the more obvious problems of the lack of national integration within the participating countries: the decline of the domestic rural market because of inequalities of land tenure, the concentration of wealth in the urban central city and the vast impoverishment of sprawling suburban slums, the growth of dynamic enclaves in a sea of low paid, precarious, informal economic activities.

"Regional integration", which is anchored in large-scale foreign and national owned MNC, becomes a strategy to expand sales without changing the national class structure, the unequal distribution of land and income.

Opening the economy to FI is almost always accompanied by the "de-regulation" of the economy, or more accurately, a change in rules which facilitate the movements of capital in and out of the country. In particular the 'liberalization' of financial markets, meaning the decline of public oversight of financial transactions, allows FI to 'launder' unreported revenues and profits and transfer funds overseas.

The net effect of increasing market access for FI is to replace a market attuned to transaction between local producers, to a market constructed in the image of FI – with a heavy import content and deleterious nutritional effects (like soft drinks and fast foods) accompanied by colonial ideological-cultural propaganda.

Cheap Labor: Unskilled, Skilled and Professional

One of the most striking incentives to FI offered by Third World and ex-communist states is state-promoted cheap labor in manufacturing, services and the primary sector. In order to attract FI, states frequently following IFI directions have initiated a whole series of decrees and laws dramatically favoring capital over labor: wages and salaries have been reduced, frozen or kept below the rate of inflation; job protection legislation has been abolished or severely modified to allow investors to hire and fire without any restrictions or due process; severance pay has been eliminated or reduced; the work day and working conditions have been revised, extending and intensifying exploitation; pension and health benefits have been reduced, eliminated and privatized, trade unions have effectively lost the right to strike, have been repressed or incorporated in state-run, investor-dominated 'tri-partite' pacts.

By concentrating power in the hands of capital (euphemistically called "labor flexibility") the neo-liberal regimes compete with each other in bidding for FI. Favorable anti-labor legislation and draconian restrictions on trade unions have lowered labor costs and have favored foreign investors in labor-intensive manufacturing.

Since the 1990's however FI has increasingly looked toward 'outsourcing' skilled jobs to low-wage/salary regions. This requires state promotion of an educated low-paid work force and financing of local business elites to act as recruiters and point men for the FI. Overseas relocation, the reality and the threat, is a common policy to lower wages, pensions, health benefits and job security in the imperial countries. Foreign investors benefit from both ends: exploiting skilled and unskilled labor in both assembly plants and high tech (IT) industries in the Third World and ex-communist countries and reducing labor costs within the imperial countries, playing off one against the other and securing labor incentives from neo-liberal states in both. The net effect is to increase profitability by squeezing out greater productivity per worker at lower costs, expand market shares and create lucrative export platforms to sell back into the "home market".

The same practice and logic which applied to the outsourcing of unskilled labor to low-wage areas has been extended to high end skilled labor in an array of activities from specialized software programming, accounting, engineering, research and development and design. The notion propagated by neo-liberal apologists that the loss of manufacturing jobs would be 'compensated' by the growth of skilled service positions fails to recognize that corporations would follow the same logic with regard to skilled service jobs.

The net result of low-cost labor incentives to attract or retain FI has been to widen the economic gap between labor and capital, deepen the inequalities in political and social power, and dissociate growing productivity and profitability from wage returns. Wages and salaries increasingly lag behind capital gains in productivity, profits and export earnings largely as a result of the vast and profound labor incentives – privileges to FI. Under the rule of labor incentives to FI, growth of GNP has few spread effects to the rest of society, creating highly polarized growth.

One of the primary concerns of FI is securing ironclad legal guarantees against nationalization, expropriation or new regulations, no matter what the circumstances or non-compliance of MNCs. To attract FI, neo-liberal regimes legislate or decree measures, which over-rides constitutional, health, environmental and other laws, in order to provide the absolute security which FI demand. The pursuit of 'low risk' status by many Third World and ex-communist countries in order to attract FI, undermines the countries' sovereignty in several ways. In the first place, it opens the country to international judicial processes, embargoes and heavy fines if and when a future government decides that the non-nationalization and expropriation agreements violated the country's laws, were signed under duress, lacked transparency or simply gave undue privileges to FI. In other words, the pursuit of 'low-risk' status sacrifices future options and raises 'risks' for future governments intent on restructuring or transforming the country or merely altering the balance between public, private and foreign investment. 'Low-risk' agreements for investors may close the book or make it costly or 'high-risk' for future regimes designing new strategies, as the economy outgrows the FI-dependent stage.

In practice, there cannot be any durable investment 'guarantees' against expropriation, new regulatory or tax regimes or even confiscation because the conditions for FI vary with the fortunes of the class struggle, national liberation movements, global economic conditions and the changing priorities and internal dynamics of MNCs. The 'low-risk' agreements between an authoritarian regime and FI will last as long as the regime can silence or co-opt opposition.

Elected regimes which single-mindedly provide generous contracts and opportunities to FI while imposing prejudicial austerity programs on working majorities have caused the greatest damage among more highly developed economies, like Argentina and Russia, with a highly trained labor force, a developed home market, reasonably, sound infrastructure and an advanced social welfare system.

Large-scale privatization and denationalization promoted by regime ideologues, aided and abetted by US free market academics, have provided innumerable incentives for FI buyouts. In both Argentina and the former USSR, privatization and financial deregulation did attract FI but with catastrophic results for the economy and the population. FI bought public enterprises at bargain prices, especially oil and gas fields, communications and other lucrative areas; financial deregulation led to massive bank frauds, and transfers of huge sums out of the country. The economies collapsed and foreign debt payments overwhelmed the countries' capacity to pay. Living standards plunged, with over one third of the workforce unemployed: Over half fell below the poverty line. The ranks of the truly indigent climbed to over 15%. Pension plans, advanced medical systems, educational and scientific facilities crumbled and skilled professionals fled the country in droves. Foreign investors initially prospered with their privileged access to the economy, but uncontrolled plunder led to a general crisis, which eventually engulfed the very speculators who brought it about.

Given the severe drawbacks in providing long-term, large-scale privileges to attract FI, what is the response of FI to a shift in policy, from providing corporate incentives to progressive social reforms, economic regulation, re-nationalizations, prosecution of tax evaders and money launderers and environment protection?

FI: Strategies to Counter Social Reform and Popular Responses

For policymakers intent on constructing an alternative development model to the FI centered approach it is important to anticipate the strategies of opposition, which FI will adopt and be prepared to put in place timely counter-measures.

The most likely first move of FI, to counter policies designed to enhance the national economy and popular living standards, is to threaten or practice disinvestment in local facilities. This involves lowering production, closing facilities, reducing or withdrawing capital to destabilize the economy and force the government to withdraw, rescind or not implement legislation or executive rulings. Disinvestment can be accompanied by the threat of an "exit strategy" – putting in jeopardy the employment of local workers, suppliers and other satellite enterprises.

Knowing this is a real probability, the state can raise the stakes by insisting that disinvestment can lead to the cancellation or re-negotiation of the original investment agreement and/or state intervention into the enterprise, followed by outright state takeover in the public interest to safeguard employment, production, maintenance and shares of export markets. In other words, firm assertion of state purpose makes FI disinvestment a two-edged sword: either abide by the new legislation or lose access to the local market, exploitation of local resources and supply of strategic goods. The state can also affirm that there is 'no return' once an "exit strategy" is adopted.

To back up the counter-strategy and make it more credible, the state should be ready to replace senior corporate personal with local specialists from within the plant, or from other agencies or from the outside. Negotiations with suppliers and purchasers should be in place. Most of all the employees, workers and professionals in the affected economic sector should be mobilized, consulted, organized to respond favorably to the impending confrontation. They and the larger public – the workers, peasants, lower middle class, professionals — should be informed and prepared for a period of transition to the new socio-economic model, in case there are sacrifices and temporary hardships.

A reduction or the elimination of privileged place of FI in the economy will likely lead to a run of liquid assets, which will certainly cause financial disruption. Here decisive and rapid action is essential – including the freezing of assets, generalized capital controls and other restrictive measures on the movement of capital, while maximizing the role of state-sponsored policies to maintain levels of credit and to maintain production even if it means a spike in inflation and monetary emissions, requiring price controls or subsidies on basic items of popular consumption.

Failing to intimidate the progressive regime through economic threats or actions, FI will turn to their imperial state to exert bilateral or multilateral pressures. These can range from threats to cut off loans from IFI, to restrictions on imports and exports, to destabilization efforts and/or threats of military intervention. Several contingencies may influence the effectiveness of these political pressures. In many cases the key competing imperial countries may not be in agreement on these measures, especially if they affect mostly one or another imperial power. Secondly the global economy is neither homogenous nor 'unipolar' in trading or military policy: losses by one imperial power can be gains for another. Thirdly threats to cut off financing by the IFI is a two-edged sword: ending of financing can lead to debt default, the refusal to pay past loans, setting a precedent for other debtor countries, and escalating the conflict to the global level. Once debt payments are suspended, the 'extra revenues' can be used to compensate enterprises prejudiced by IFI cut-offs. The larger the debt, the greater the destabilizing impact of a debt moratorium will have on international financial markets.

Clearly in anticipating this escalation of the conflict with FI, the state must view the problem through political lens in order to best prepare its counter-attack. Imperial threats usually radicalize and mobilize popular movements, isolate elite allies of the imperial power, and polarize the country in a way favourable to the regime, if the latter has clearly defined and demonstrated the socio-economic advantages of pursuing its new development model. If the imperial state pursues a military-political interventionist strategy, the regime in consultation with its mass constituency must rapidly pursue a multi-layered national defense strategy, which can range from anti-terrorist measures, to legislation outlawing imperial funding of political parties, NGO's and media outlets.

Clearly significant changes in one vital sector of the economy imply changes in the totality of the society and state. By regulating or redefining the state-FI relationship, new political actors are drawn in as the conflict spills over to other sectors of the economy and across frontiers, leading to the need for further changes in the economy and state security structure. Looking at the problem of FI conflict in narrow economic terms of a state-investment framework, can lead to unanticipated attacks and likely defeats and retreats.

FI can rely on their associates in the mass media to launch "scare propaganda campaigns", which demonize progressive regimes: labeling them terrorists, rogue states and communists – part of the battle of ideas. The regime must be prepared to counter elite media warfare through its own mass media within the country and via progressive social movements and media throughout the world. Internet sites, community radios, videos and international solidarity organizations can be effectively mobilized to reach the active populations who would respond to the positive changes initiated by the progressive regime. What is essential is to move beyond "critiquing" the power of the adversarial corporate media toward the creation of multiple mass outlets and activities to gain political support.

It needs to be emphasized that 'changes' in relation to FI are interconnected with and activate other structures of the state and economy. The media, ideological and cultural wars are essential to sustaining or undermining efforts to limit or eliminate the dominant privileged role of FI.

A third strategy to undermine progressive legislation, which is almost always adopted by FI, is the corruption of government officials – especially regulators—, trade union officials and the political elite. This involves cash payoffs in foreign accounts, job offers to relatives or promises of managerial positions after serving office, visiting professorships to prestigious universities with lucrative stipends, and a host of other remunerative rewards. Judges appointed by the pliable executives can be expected to rule against state measures to revise FI contracts or to rule in favor of extra-territorial judicial sites (lawsuits in imperial jurisdictions).

While "international" and NGO investigatory agencies have established "transparency" ratings for countries, few if any have examined or established corruption ratings for MNCs and FI, despite their widespread use of bribes and illicit activities and the devastating effects it has in undermining progressive changes. Corruption by FI can be limited by introducing a number of institutional changes: by creating workers, consumers and environmental oversight committees with open access to all accounts, transactions and especially government contracts. Secondly, corruption can be limited by publicizing all stages of negotiations between state and MNC and making it obligatory and subject to scrutiny by the classes and organizations most affected. Auditors and investigators who have no ties to FI interests can serve a technical advisory role in preparing evaluations of contracts and state-FI agreements. The reform of the public administrative structure must include deep ethical and political changes, inculcating members with a commitment to national and class values, from top to bottom. Ultimately technical and ethical/political commitments are the best safeguard for neutralizing the FI corruption designed to undermine the implementation of progressive legislation.

Finally FI may accept regulations and reforms, but resort to increasing prices, and lowering labor costs to maintain profits. State intervention fixing rates is an obvious counter-measure, along with threats to re-nationalize if FI decides to hold back on promised new investments. Enforcement of labor legislation and price constraints monitored by organized consumers can block corporate efforts to "pass the costs" of state reform to the consumer.

Conclusion

Incentives to FI usually come at an unacceptable cost to workers, consumers, taxpayers, local producers and environmentalists – all have to pay for state subsidies which privilege FI in the way of higher taxes, lower social services, scarcer and more expensive credit, and higher prices. Alternatives to incentives and privileges to FI are readily available, feasible and beneficial when a regime is prepared to withstand the inevitable threat, pressures and propaganda, which emanate from the imperial state linked to FI. Taking a broad strategic approach prepares the state – allowing it to develop effective countermeasures to the reprisals taken by the FI or their colleagues in the IFI and the imperial state.

Index

J

K

L

M

T